Race, Rights and Rebels

Global Critical Caribbean Thought

Series editors:
Lewis R. Gordon, Professor of Philosophy and African Studies, University of Connecticut

Nelson Maldonado-Torres, Associate Professor of Latino and Hispanic Caribbean Studies and Program in Comparative Literature, Rutgers University; and Research Fellow in Political Sciences, University of South Africa

Jane Anna Gordon, Associate Professor of Political Science and Africana Studies, University of Connecticut

This series, published in partnership with the Caribbean Philosophical Association, turns the lens on the unfolding nature and potential future shape of the globe by taking concepts and ideas that while originating out of very specific contexts share features that lend them transnational utility. Works in the series engage with figures including Frantz Fanon, CLR James, Paulo Freire, Aimé Césaire, Édouard Glissant and Walter Rodney, and concepts such as coloniality, creolization, decoloniality, double consciousness and *la facultad*.

Titles in the Series

Race, Rights and Rebels by Julia Suárez-Krabbe
The Desiring Modes of Being Black: Literature and Critical Theory by Jean-Paul Rocchi
Decolonizing Democracy: Power in a Solid State by Ricardo Sanin-Restrepo

Race, Rights and Rebels

Alternatives to Human Rights and Development from the Global South

Julia Suárez-Krabbe

ROWMAN & LITTLEFIELD INTERNATIONAL

London • New York

Published by Rowman & Littlefield International Ltd
Unit A, Whitacre Mews, 26-34 Stannary Street, London SE11 4AB
www.rowmaninternational.com

Rowman & Littlefield International Ltd. is an affiliate of Rowman & Littlefield
4501 Forbes Boulevard, Suite 200, Lanham, Maryland 20706, USA
With additional offices in Boulder, New York, Toronto (Canada), and Plymouth (UK)
www.rowman.com

British Library Cataloguing in Publication Data
A catalogue record for this book is available from the British Library

ISBN: HB 978-1-7834-8460-7
    PB 978-1-7834-8461-4

Library of Congress Cataloging-in-Publication Data Available

Cataloging-in-Publication Data

ISBN 978-1-78348-460-7 (cloth : alk. paper)—ISBN 978-1-78348-461-1
(pbk. : alk. paper)—ISBN 978-1-78348-462-1 (electronic)

∞ ™ The paper used in this publication meets the minimum requirements of American
National Standard for Information Sciences—Permanence of Paper for Printed Library
Materials, ANSI/NISO Z39.48-1992.

Printed in the United States of America

Contents

Preface

Instead of concluding that there is a need to progress towards pluriversality, as many texts written by decolonial scholars do, this book seeks to start conducting some pluriversality, and so, it is from the outset necessarily incomplete. Specifically, it addresses the complexities and the global entanglements of histories, identities, struggles, and ideas that entwine human rights and development. This effort displays how human rights and development are the products of race, and function as technologies of implementation of the death project. As the tools of race, or more precisely of white supremacy, human rights and development have been forged to legitimize and maintain coloniality. However, rights have also emerged through rebellion, negotiation, or pressure from those oppressed, and can be used as tools to achieve protection, specific political goals, or access in the dominant society. Rights can contribute to protect the lives and wellbeing of some, but they cannot solve the problems that produce the threats to the lives and wellbeing of vast populations and indeed of all living beings on earth. Because they are framed within a specific dominant ontology, and sustain a particular political horizon, human rights and development limit radical social change.

The search for alternatives to these problems is the main concern in this writing. It is a pursuit that recognizes that knowledge production itself is part of the problem, and that to move beyond the dominant epistemological and ontological frameworks, we need to enter into dialogue with those knowledges, which have been produced as absent. In doing so, however, we cannot fall into the trap of pretending that the dominant frameworks of thinking and the practices that they authorize have been overcome. A careful attentiveness to the conceptual frameworks of *other* knowledges needs to happen in equilibrium with the criticism of coloniality and the death project, and of our own positions within the global articulations of power. This balance is reflected in the way this volume is organized.

The book's material organization also tries to obey the pluriversal character of knowledge, being and time. As such, it attends to different temporalities (part one) and geographies (part two) of reason, including the dominant. It uses theories and concepts that have been produced as absent by hegemonic knowledge production, some more than others. Among these is the knowledge that emerges from the work of the spiritual/political authorities of four indigenous peoples in Sierra Nevada de Santa Marta in the Colombian Caribbean: the Arhuaco, Kogi, Kankuamo, and Wiwa. These are four distinct peoples—yet intimately connected—and their spiritual authorities have a common denomination: Mamos. Their thought is significant to the theoretical and contextual apparatus used in this book, but not the only one. However, because of the fundamental influence they have had on the ideas presented and due to the fact that their thinking has been invisibilized, greater attention is given to their historical, temporal, epistemological, and ontological references than to those of other theoretical sources. As theoretical and contextual sources, and not empirical material, the Mamos' knowledge also displays alternatives to human rights and development.

The ideas presented in this book have been shaped through the encounter with many people and collectives. I refer to many of them throughout the text. Some of them, however, are worth mentioning here. Working with Ramón Grosfoguel gave me important insights on how to walk the path. Of that I am immensely thankful. I cherish Lars Jensen's unconditional support. Lewis Gordon's living thought is the best tool to dismantle the master's house that I know of. I am also grateful to Boaventura de Sousa Santos for his unique, unsuspected lessons. All four have deeply influenced my thinking and activism. My love for Karen, Samuel, and William made Copenhagen meaningful. However, Copenhagen only started to make sense politically in my encounter with three rare and beautiful friends: Nanna Leets Hansen, my intellectually sharp colleague with whom work is politically consequential and fun; Milton Almonacid, the _interepistemic Mapuche_ whose energy shines from Temuco to Copenhagen; and José Arce, who knows how to make the path while walking, and, in this sense, reminds me of Serankwa. My families in Varde, La Calera, Copenhagen, Orlando, and Calgary illustrate how freedom, love, and respect go together. Assisting Gabriel's, and then Isa's, birth turned out to be attending lessons taught by the Mother. My extended family in Atánquez, and in Bogotá my kin organized around the Asociación Nacional de Abogados Litigantes and Revista Jícara, together with my friends from Proyecto Pasos, all engage in rebel dignity. I also thank the following organizations, their leaders, and activists who are involved in diverse offensive struggles: Decoloniality Europe, ALICE, the Popular University of Social Movements, the Parti des Indigènes de la République, the Islamic Human

Rights Commission, the youth from the Sindicato Andaluz de Trabajadores, the African Empowerment Center, the Trampoline House, and Freedom of Movements.

In the course of the last ten years, the period during which this book has been underway, there have been two constant presences. One has been my family; Andrés is my life, my strength, and an unceasing source of power. Luna and Mayté are my being and my future. Without them this would make no sense. The other ceaseless presence has been Mamo Saúl Martínez whose influence reaches way beyond the pages of this book, and who helps me navigate within this larger world-being in which I now, and thanks to him, live. This book, together with the influence of all these persons and groups, I leave to our future generations.

Chapter One

Bad Faith and the Death Project

Coloniality underlies western knowledge production, western-centric political practice and notions of common sense. These ways of knowing, being,
and political practice produce and reproduce racism, patriarchy, capitalism,
and the depredation of nature. They have multiple expressions: in both left
and right political positions, in conservative and critical dominant academic
thinking, and in the minds and hearts of many people. They are the dominant
frameworks of thinking, which have been established as truth through the historical processes of colonialism and coloniality, and as such are rarely questioned. Rather, the main tendency is that these truths are reinforced. The
problems emerging from this can be exemplified through the folktale *The
Emperor's New Clothes*. In Hans Christian Andersen's classic version of the
story, the emperor's vanity and his subjects' complicity with the illusions of
power lead to the emperor being cheated by two tailors who make him a dress
of a supposedly fine fabric, so sublime that only the rich and powerful can
see it. The fable's point is that there is no such fabric—only the claim to
its existence and the privileges that come with affirming its existence. This
nonexistent fabric leads the emperor and his subjects to pretend that the
emperor is indeed wearing exquisite dress, and to praise his attire. The
emperor, however, is naked. The force of colonial discourse lies in how it
succeeds in concealing how it establishes and naturalizes ontological and
epistemological perspectives and political practices that work to protect its
power. Indeed,

> In colonialism, there is a very peculiar function to words, words do not designate,
> but conceal. . . . The words are a fictional record, full of euphemisms to veil reality
> rather than to designate it. Public discourses are ways of not saying. And this uni-
> verse of meanings and un-told notions, of belief in racial hierarchy and the inherent
> inequality of human beings, are incubated in common sense. (Rivera Cusicanqui
> 2010, 19, translated from Spanish)

But discourses do not fashion themselves independently, and neither do ontological truths. The example of *The Emperor's New Clothes* serves to highlight that those verities are not true. Rather, they are presented as true by
global elites, and many defend them as true ignoring the perceptible facts and
social actors that tell them that they are false. Lewis Gordon calls this *bad
faith*. Bad faith implies choosing to believe and defend comfortable lies about
other groups of people and about one's own group. Choosing the lie is, at the
same time, giving up freedom (Gordon 1999, 75). Bad faith is also important
in understanding how the power of colonial discourse operates, and how it
succeeds concealing its own establishing of ontological truths from itself. We
all share responsibility in the defense of these truths—or rather falsehoods—
and in choosing to work against these. When the people in the story of *The
Emperor's New Clothes* pretend that the emperor is wearing a suit, they are
defending the emperor, and reinforce the lies of power. There is another significant aspect in this regard—it is not simply a matter of choosing to reject
the lie to work towards the truth. The problem is that colonial discourse is not
just a story. It is also material, political, social, existential, and powerful.
Among other things, it has the power to offer privileges to those who engage
in defending it. Colonial power is not something outside of our everyday
lives, it is also part of our everyday—and through this, it is complex, but
never abstract. It is key to understanding the problems we face globally.

One of the lies rarely questioned in dominant society concerns the idea of
what defines a human being. The idea of *the human being* seems to refer to
all beings on this planet that descend from monkeys. *But we are all human*
is a well-known adage, that is, it is an utterance that pretends to state an overcoming of racism through a methodological abstraction from the very historical fact from which the deep inequalities that we continue to face today on a
global scale have emerged. This is not to deny that we descend from primates.
It is to highlight, among other things, that the idea that this is the only important defining factor concerning humans is part of *The Emperor's New
Clothes*. The term *human being* as it exists today is a colonial category that
claims to be neutral, but is in fact formulated on the basis of a series of historically constituted hierarchies of race, gender, and living beings. It does not
refer primarily to our ascendance to primates. When discussing notions of the
human being in relation to human rights and development, it is important to
highlight how the colonial category *human* goes hand in hand with that of
nature. As the spiritual authorities of the four indigenous peoples that live in
Sierra Nevada de Santa Marta in the Colombian Caribbean teach, *human* and
nature together are pivotal to understanding how the dominant practices of
human rights and development cannot be understood as separate ideas: while
human rights deals with human beings and their relationships as these are

defined within the colonial ontology, development concerns humans' relationship to nature, and also to the management and exploitation of nature in ways that privilege humans. This relationship is characterized by an important paradox, that is, while human rights negate colonialism and coloniality as intrinsic to it, the ideas of progress and development justify colonialism and coloniality. Both human rights and development are important axes in the defense of the *death project*. As I understand it, the death project is inherent to coloniality and contains a complexity of relationships. When employing the term *coloniality*, I primarily refer to the system of domination that emerged with the European expansion initiated with the Castilian colonial endeavor in the Iberian Peninsula—more specifically the conquest of Al-Andalus, the subsequent conquest of the Americas, the witch hunts in Europe and the Americas, and the establishment of the transatlantic slave trade (Grosfoguel 2013; Mignolo 2000, 2006; Suárez-Krabbe 2014b; Wright 2001). This system of domination is still in play. European colonialism generated a specific coupling between racism, capitalism, patriarchy, and the depredation of nature that became globalized, and whose effects we still have to fight. This modern/colonial interlinking involves modes of production, living, political organization, spatial organization, relationships to other people and living beings, ways of thinking, modes of acting, practices of production and reproduction of life and death, sexuality, aesthetics, spiritualities and knowledge construction. Coloniality emerges as a local (European) colonial project, but becomes globalized in several ways. First, by territorial and economic expansion and political and social control—imperialism. Second, by the spread, mutual influence and institutionalization of these practices of domination among the colonizing powers. Third, it is globalized by racialization, sexual domination, and labor exploitation and, finally, through cultural, spiritual, and epistemic domination.

Significantly, although coloniality is a globalized system of oppression, it does not localize in the same ways. One of its crucial strengths is its capacity for adaptation to and assimilation of local social, political, cultural, and spiritual configurations. Following the lead of the indigenous Nasa people in Colombia, my understanding of the death project refers to the exercise of violence in coloniality, which targets the actual processes of life and the conditions for existence: in short, plurality. The Nasa describe the death project as such: 'The conquerors brought with them their death project to these lands. They came with the urge to steal the wealth and to exploit us in order to accumulate [wealth]. The death project is the disease of egoism that turns into hatred, war, lies, propaganda, confusion, corruption and bad governments.'[1] In my understanding of the term, the death project is, like *necropolitics*, attached to the 'power and the capacity to dictate who may live and who must die' (Mbembe 2003, 11), but is complemented by the *ethics of war* as 'one of the characteristic features of European modernity [naturalized] through colonialism, race, and particular modalities of gender' (Maldonado-Torres 2008a, 4). To highlight the ethics of the death project is to reject the idea that a politics of death, 'consists fundamentally in the exercise of a power outside the law (*ab legibus solutus*)', as Mbembe states it (2003, 23). Indeed, as will become evident in chapters 3 and 4, it is insufficient to conclude that the colonies are ruled in 'absolute lawlessness' (24); quite the contrary, they are and have historically been ruled through thorough elaborations of law—this includes their philosophical basis (Ferreira da Silva 2014; Bogues 2012). The Code Noir from 1685 is an excellent example.[2] While Mbembe notes that colonial warfare is subject to legal and institutional rules (2003, 25), the notion of the death project follows Boaventura de Sousa Santos's lead when emphasizing that legality is used to make people lawfully, as well as politically, inexistent, and is intimately linked to serve the interests of the past and present colonizers (Santos 2007). The notion of the death project refers to the exercise of coloniality; it is (as is Mbembe's necropolitics) concerned with the power and capacity to dispose of life, but implies the death ethics of war, which underlie the legal systems that legitimate it. In this way, the death project is also concerned with the behaviors that accompany these systems, pointing to the international complicity in its continuation. Consequently, the death project involves the set of hegemonic practices, where racism, capitalism, patriarchy, and predatory behaviors against nature are closely linked. It adds a crucial aspect to Maldonado-Torres's and Mbembe's notions as it includes considerations about the negation of the Mother World and of spirituality. As such, the concept of the death project apprehends aspects and interrelations of reality and politics that are essential from within the thinking of the spiritual authorities of four different but interdependent indigenous communities. These four different communities, the Arhuaco, Kankuamo, Kogi, and Wiwa, share common name for their spiritual/political authorities: the men are Mamos, the women Sagas.

My collaboration with the authorities of Sierra Nevada de Santa Marta in the Colombian Caribbean, and especially our discussions on human rights and development, are decisive to the theoretical, epistemological, and ontological stakes in the discussions that follow. My main contact and advisor among the spiritual/political authorities of these four peoples is Mamo Saúl Martínez from the Kankuamo community. The Mamos and Sagas are experts in the Law of Origin. The Law of Origin, or law of Sé, is *written* on the very territory of Sierra Nevada, and contains both the principles of life, and the principles that allow for the continuity of life that are intrinsic to the Mother, that is, to being and becoming. This is why the law is never absolute or abstract; it does not fade, wither, or fail. As will become particularly clear in chapter 6, nor is it law in the western sense of the term. The Mamos and the Sagas are adepts of the world, of life, and its equilibrium. Their elder peers teach them to commune with spirits, with ancestors, with nature, and to mediate between the Law of Origin and people. At the same time, they are their peoples' libraries, political advisors, spiritual leaders, and the guardians of the world. Simplistically put, human rights violations, climate change, illness, wars, earthquakes, and so on happen in terms of the Law of Origin because of the world's disequilibrium. This imbalance affects all spheres of life, from the micro and intimate, to the macro structural and macrocosmic. It stems from a lack of reciprocity—more exactly, from some human beings' unwillingness or inability to recompense the Mother for what She has given, and to attend to Her teachings. This inability to work with the Mother is part of that, which continues to give force to the death project. Indeed, the Mother is not simply translatable to the term *nature*. Rather, the Mother is one who has given life and She allows for the perpetuation of life; She is both a she and a he.

HUMAN RIGHTS AND DEVELOPMENT

Sierra Nevada de Santa Marta is the highest coastal mountain in the world. Its location in the Colombian Caribbean connects this territory and its peoples culturally, socially, geopolitically, and economically both with the Andean region as well as with the Caribbean. The history of the four peoples of Sierra Nevada, of Latin America, and the Caribbean is also part of a history of globalization. The Spanish Hapsburg empire (that rose in the sixteenth century and fell in the eighteenth) paved the way for many of the traits that, by subsequent imperial domains, continue to be considered the exclusive terrain of Enlightenment thought in Europe. One of the first things that Mamo Martínez suggested in our collaborative work was that I critically review the common history of human rights and development. Following his counsel I found that, while the ideas and practices of human rights and development are obverse sides of the same coin, they have, nevertheless, seldom been studied together. While a possible exception to this rule is the relatively recent *rights-based* approaches to development (Mikkelsen 2005; Sano 2000), the general tendency within these approaches is to argue for the integration of human rights practices with development practices in development projects in the so-called Third World. In this manner, human rights and development are regarded as distinct phenomena from the outset. Similarly, historical approaches tend to center either on human rights (Ishay 2004; Douzinas 2007), or on development (Rist 1997; Escobar 1996). It is well known that human rights and development operate in conjunction and often in interventionist endeavors; proof for this abounds, and includes examples in Colombia, Bolivia, and Honduras.[3] Beyond this conjunction, however, human rights and development are united by race as an idea and practice. Contextually, it is important to underline that while it is not possible to speak of *human rights* and *development* as such before they are named, formulated, and institutionalized as such after the Second World War, it is possible to trace the history of the globalization of the localisms that support them to the period around 1492.

Although ideas of rights and development existed before that date such as the Code of Hammurabi (1760 BC, Babylon) and the English Magna Carta (1215)[4] in terms of rights (Ishay 2004, 15–61) and Augustine's philosophy of history in terms of development (Rist 1997, 31–40), the arrival of the Spanish to what came to be known as *America* had a momentous impact in this regard. As we know, Columbus's initial travels were aimed at finding an alternative access for Spain to the Asian commercial circuits and markets. With Amerigo Vespucci's realization that the lands to which Columbus had arrived were not on the Asian continent but a different one in 1502, the formation of the Atlantic commercial circuit was initiated. The Atlantic commercial circuit connected the existing commercial circuits in the 'Americas', Anahuac (now Central America), and Tawantinsuyu (large parts of today's South America) with the commercial circuits existing in Europe, Africa, and Asia. An additional circuit was established in 1571, which connected the Americas, especially from the Pacific coast of Mexico, with the Philippines and China. In this manner, Spanish colonialism had decisive effects in the integration of the world system, understood in a literal sense as encompassing all areas of the globe (Mignolo 2000; Bjork 1998). These two new commercial circuits, the Atlantic and the Pacific, connected the major channels of commerce in the world for the first time (Mignolo 2000). Of special significance for the history of human rights and development as globalized institutional practices of execution of the death project is the transatlantic connection; it played a crucial role in the embryonic stages of coloniality and the globalization of its rationality. As such, investigating the Hispanophone domain permits an expansion of modernity via the distinction between the first and second modernity (Dussel 1995). Such an investigation, however, cannot stay exclusively within the Hispanophone domain, inasmuch as this would amount to ignoring crucial developments that occurred in the Caribbean, which had a profound impact on modernity/coloniality. The Spanish imperial framework, and events in the Caribbean, are also part of a history of globalization, and prepare the way for changes in the second modernity, which are often thought to be the exclusive domain of Enlightenment thought in Europe. Many scholars have illustrated in detail some of the different dimensions of the impact that the arrival of the Spanish conquistadors in America had in the hegemonic thought, and in the excluding practices that have characterized global history since then.[5] The conquest meant that the European elites of the time had to rethink their established truths, for example, with regards to the nature of the different populations they encountered, in order to be able to make sense of the existence of what, to them until that time, had not even been a possibility—America. The subjugation of the Americas implied deep ontological change. As Sylvia Wynter (2003) has shown, before 1492 *humanness* was primarily determined through the idea of spiritual perfection among the Spanish Christian elites. This meant that being born Christian was regarded as the most *human* condition. Below the Christians were the converts who to some extent could be included into the category of *human*. Then there were those *untrue others* who, having had the chance to convert to Christianity, nevertheless, did not. America challenged this religion-based ordering of the world because the people whom the Spaniards met in the so-called new world had never had the possibility to convert to Christianity in the first place. These processes revolved around the idea of race and were pivotal to the emergence of human rights and development. As globalized institutions for the implementation of the death project, human rights and development are also continuous processes of ontological construction of the human. By separating the human and the natural and the spiritual from the secular, they also justify the destruction of the Mother World. Additionally, the dominant practices of human rights and development are linked to the Eurocentric secular rationality. Thus, to criticize human rights and development, as I do in this book, is labeled irrational by the same dominant logic and the likelihood of *other* futures is discredited precisely because of that likelihood's supposed irrationality. Due to these problems, considering the critical thinking that comes from the global south is vital in working towards the formulation of strong proposals that operate against coloniality and the death project. As we will discuss later, however, it is not enough to include the thinking of the global south in writing if we thereby absolve ourselves from participation and complicity in the continued processes of colonization.

The politics of the death project advocate for a global order in which the life and wealth of the few is defended at the expense of the lives and good living of the vast majority of the world's population, and at the expense of the Mother. When the possibility of existence of my people, the *Mestizo* populations in the Americas, became apparent over five hundred years ago, this political project simultaneously emerged and became globalized. The death project uses segregation as a tool to manage and neutralize its opposition. It is an essential part of coloniality (Quijano 2000b). In many ways, human rights and development function as institutionalized practices of implementation of the death project, and therefore it is necessary to understand their modus operandi well. This implies addressing the racial character of the social, economic, and epistemological divide that segregates the north from the south.[6]

OFFENSIVE AND DEFENSIVE STRUGGLES

Like human rights and development, the university—particularly, in the social sciences and the humanities—is an institution linked to the defense and the practices of implementation of the death project. However, there are theories, practices, and perspectives that fissure the socially constructed walls generated through the exercise of coloniality. Transformative dialogue and change occur, and so part of our endeavor as intellectuals committed to decolonization must include pinpointing places where these divisions are reinforced, and also sites where they are being demolished. While the practices and ideas that reconstruct these social, economic, and epistemological barriers work as *defenses* of the death project, the practices and ideas that demolish these obstacles are *offensive* struggles.[7] The offensive struggles oppose European modernity at least in aspects that link it to capitalism, racism, patriarchy, and the depredations against nature. In general, the offensive struggles succeed in diminishing the sites in the (non-)*other*, the negated, counterhegemonic side that is deemed nonexistent through hegemonic thought and practice (Fanon 1967). Although diverse, these offensive struggles share key elements in nature and scope, which determine the nodes where they contribute to the transformation of human rights and development. The offensive struggles are based upon the awareness that there is a correlative interdependence between exploitation of labor and the primitive accumulation of capital, that is paid labor, is inseparable from violent exploitation—including slavery, patriarchy, knowledge appropriation, and the patenting of life. The international division of labor and the different labor forms that work to sustain this global system are also racialized, that is, while forms of exploitation such as slavery and serfdom are naturalized as colonized groups' modes of work, other forms of production of goods, such as paid labor, are reserved to middle- to lower-class groups (Quijano 2000b). Another central element in the context of these struggles regards colonialism's intense impact on epistemic, spiritual, social, material, and political relations worldwide. Indeed, the struggles against colonialism's impact also concern the very ways in which the colonial dominant logic produces reality within a framework that defends the death project at the same time pretending that there are no *realistic* alternatives to it. The offensive struggles oppose these hegemonic structures, but they also use hegemonic tools in counterhegemonic ways. In this sense, any possibility of accessing the system is seized to the extent that it can serve to be used against that very system. As such, the offensive struggles also employ treason as a counterhegemonic tool. For example, they can appropriate human rights to such an extent that these contribute to their struggles through step-by-step victories that can open up spaces from which the system sustained by rights' thinking itself is betrayed. In academia, the offensive struggles operate diversely destabilizing the death project in at least two interrelated ways: by theorizing struggle and change, and by shifting the geography and temporality of reason. I draw decidedly on some of these contributions in tandem with those of the Mamos. However, and this is a major difficulty, many of the ideas of which the offensive struggles speak are still underrepresented in academia, effectively weakening the offensive struggles within what remains a globalized institution of legitimation for the death project. This places the offensive struggles in a vulnerable position and increases the risk of their being appropriated and neutralized by the defensive struggles.

THE GEOGRAPHY AND TEMPORALITY OF REASON

To shift the geography of reason and address the political economy of knowledge are fundamental steps to working effectively against the death project. The contributions of epistemologies from the south (Santos 2014) regarding local and global processes of change discuss fundamental themes pertaining to knowledge, being, exclusion, and transformation. The transformations that precede the contributions of epistemologies from the south involve the ontological and philosophical frameworks we employ to understand social reality and global processes of change, and they necessitate different understandings of concepts such as knowledge, rights, development, freedom, culture, and identity. They also require addressing 'the economic strategies and material mechanisms that operate behind discourses', and knowledge construction

(Rivera Cusicanqui 2012, 102). Shifting the *geography of reason* necessitates, in this context, thinking from and approaching Latin America and the Caribbean as places from where theory and philosophy emerge. In addition to using scholarly sources predominantly written by people who think and work from Latin America and the Caribbean, I also work *with* the Mamos, who are experts with whom theoretical and philosophical discussions are relevant within their own localized realities and in relation to themes and questions that involve all of humanity, such as the ideas and practices of human rights and development. The crux of our cooperation is that I have worked with the Mamos, but not in order to study them.

Although many southern scholars have recognized shifting the geography of reason as a vital necessity, it continues being a difficult task in academia as a whole. We still need to work on several areas such as methodologies, ontology, bad faith, and strategies in order to respond to these impediments. How do we open up spaces in dominant academia to carry out cooperation with *othered* peoples? In the case of Mestizos, how do we position ourselves when we shift the geography of reason, and to what extent is this positioning informed by bad faith? Additionally, the problem is not whether the subaltern can speak but, rather, how do we open up spaces where the academic world can hear the subaltern and change accordingly? This problem relates to openness versus closure in dialogue, and to how to engage in discussion within a context where we do not have a common humanity but instead are differently positioned in the global hierarchies of power. As such, discussion can never be equitable and, at the very least, it requires a prior recognition of the various levels and dimensions of power, violence, and complicity with power, which also involve academic practice. To pose this critical problem differently: sincerely engaging with the critical thinking that comes from the global south is vital in order to effectively operate against coloniality and the death project. It is, however, not enough to include the thinking of the global south in our writing if we thereby absolve ourselves from participation in the continued processes of colonization. The problem pertains to different dimensions connected to how the *who* we are cannot be disassociated from *what* we are. That is, identity cannot be detached ontology and sociogenesis.

An important aspect that informs my elaborations in this book relates to my working at a university in the far north, a place in which whiteness, coloniality, and Eurocentrism remain uncontested, and thus, largely the norm, as well as the logic by which quality in research and teaching are defined. Decolonization of these spaces is simultaneously of utmost political urgency and an extremely difficult task. This will be evident throughout the book. For now, it is important to emphasize that the difficulties of decolonizing the universities in the north relate to two interrelated discrepancies; first, the mismatch between the understanding, if any, shared by most academics in the north, of colonization as something of peripheral importance that happened in a more or less remote past on the one hand, and the ways in which colonization actually functions in the present and is being analyzed and conceptualized by anticolonial thinkers throughout the world, on the other. This gap manifests as the negation of coloniality and by extension of the colonized subject and his and her analyses.

The second mismatch is evident between the understanding about how contemporary problems are imbued in colonialism and coloniality and, in contrast, the idea that we can overcome these problems by theoretically resolving some or the other element that is mistakenly taken as being central to these legacies. Through this mismatch, the conclusions reached are either that coloniality has been resolved—implying that anticolonial scholars are behind in relation to the analyses of reality—or that the criticism of Eurocentrism may be obsolete. Let me exemplify. In a talk given at the University of Witwatersrand on the decolonization of the university,[8] Achille Mbembe noted that there are contributions coming from European scholars that challenge at least some of the constitutive pillars of Eurocentric thinking (human-nature, mind-spirit, reason-emotion, tradition-modernity, etc.). His point—one I agree with—is that European is not the same as Eurocentric. However, the problem that interests me is that in many of the contributions to which Mbembe refers, coloniality remains unsolved. According to the definition of coloniality presented earlier, those separations or dualisms cannot be properly understood nor effectively contested without taking their core determinant and organizing principle into account—coloniality. The contributions that seem to overcome the classic separations often pretend that the dualisms in and by themselves are central. In doing so, these contributions continue ignoring that the condition of possibility of these dualisms is the colonial/racial ontology and politics: that which makes the separation between human and nature, mind and body, spiritual and secular, modernity and tradition, and so on problematic, violent, and epistemicidal is their entwinement with coloniality and the death project.

Coloniality—the nexus of racism, capitalism, patriarchy, and the depredations of nature—is the pillar of Eurocentrism, and so the scholarship that in some way or the other declares itself able to overcome one or several of the separations mentioned has not overcome coloniality. Instead, it mistakes dualisms with the core problem. As such, breaking with one or two of these separations does not equal to breaking with Eurocentrism, not to mention coloniality. It is possible to produce a well-written book that breaks with the idea that Europeans are modern (Latour 1993), while leaving concerns with coloniality largely unexamined. In doing so, one is basically continuing the colonial tradition of making invisible the problems of the *other*—and retaining the privilege of deciding what is a legitimate scientific or social problem. A person can contribute to breaking the spiritual-secular and human-nature divides by engaging seriously in the thinking of indigenous peoples (Ingold 2006, 2007), leaving untouched and unchallenged the problems of coloniality/racism, among them epistemic *extractivism*. My point is that it is important to be wary of whether self-acclaimed challenges to Eurocentric thinking leave its pillar, coloniality, untouched. Leaving coloniality untouched and unchallenged means that the concerns with colonialism and its legacies are whitewashed and thereby neutralized. The whitewashing of the criticisms from the global south happens, among other reasons, through the selective and dehistoricized challenges to separations that together articulate the ontological groundings of coloniality. Separating these dualisms from one another is to make invisible and negate coloniality; it is to engage in the practice of the death project.

These two discrepancies force us to ask some crucial questions: Is knowledge decolonized when it follows many or some of the ideas presented by the scholarship born out of struggles for decolonization while failing to acknowledge that these ideas emerge from struggles for decolonization precisely because decolonization has not yet been achieved? Is knowledge decolonized when it follows many (or some) of the ideas presented by the scholarship arising out of struggles for decolonization while sanctioning the sociohistorical and economic-political location of the writer, the sociohistorical and economic-political location of the sources she has been inspired by, as well as the sociohistorical and economic-political relationship between the two? Is knowledge decolonized when it follows many or some of the ideas presented by the scholarship born out of struggles for decolonization while depoliticizing these contributions? Is knowledge decolonized when it follows many or some of the ideas presented by the scholarship born out of struggles for decolonization while deleting or trivializing racism and coloniality? My answer to all these questions is *no*. As Gordon has stated, decolonization is taking responsibility for thought and ideas and it is articulating the conditions that make us *what* and *who* we are.[9] Shifting the geography of reason is, consequently, fundamental to decolonization. To shift the geography of reason implies working at a different pace, within a temporal logic that differs from the one sustained in the death project.

Time is not an abstract phenomenon that can be detached from actual events, or from knowledge production and the specific existential, political, material, and geographic places from which knowledge emerges. Different forms of knowledge also produce time in different ways that can diminish the future, or bring it to the present moment, in which we might exist forever and so plan our actions and the ways we want to contribute to the lives of next generations, together with the activities we do in the next half hour. To the spiritual authorities of the four peoples of Sierra Nevada de Santa Marta, the Mamos, the construction of the future is not just a matter of human beings, as for instance stones, seeds, the weather, and the trees are also active agents in this endeavor; that is, they are an active part of the political field. By contrast, the dominant temporality, the temporality that sustains the death project, captivates those futures that are not coherent with its own conception of time. In dominant knowledge construction, radical social and political change is not possible because it itself delimits the horizon of possibilities—a horizon that dismisses as impossible, unrealistic, and even superstitious the political projects of liberation against the death project. The notion of an irreversible future embedded in the death project produces practical and political inertia, thus effectively colonizing the political field and the imaginary of possibilities that might just bring about radical social change.

The rationality that follows and sustains such a temporality must therefore be understood as lazy (Santos 2014): even if its present might seem to be heading forward at high speed (and so many people in urban, modern societies live at a fast pace and suffer from severe stress-related problems), that same momentary quick pace requires that these same populations think of the future as something far away, onto which we have no possibility of real impact beyond specific individualized preoccupations with pension plans and old-age care. Other, bigger concerns and events might become history, but inasmuch only the big people make history, this way of thinking the future disregards, *a priori*, the active political engagement and participation of the majority of the world's population. The vision of history associated with the death project is modern/colonial, where the arrow of humanity's unrestrained progress and innovation is stuck due to its attachment to the crises of the movements of capital within the circuit of globalization.[10] This inertia, the ways in which the death project incarcerates the future, also sustains the persistence of planet-wide injustice and inequality. In contrast, *other* reasons regard the present in ways that include the past and the future actively, for example, by way of the ancestors' participation in the realities and concerns of the living and that of those who are yet to become. Such is the case of the Mamos' temporality.

MESTIZAJE

The ideas presented in this book are informed by the sociohistorical and economic-political experience of my being a Colombian-Danish Mestiza placed in the bright-skinned spectrum of *mestizaje*. The Latin American idea of mestizaje (mixture) is an ideology and institution of domination that was heralded by Latin Americans of European descent during the independence struggles. While mestizaje was used by the elites of the time to legitimize their belonging to and ownership of the territories in Latin America, it also emerged as a counternarrative and counteridentity to the ideas of purity of blood by which the Spanish colonial powers organized the social, political, and economic hierarchies of the empire. It was also a continuation of the colonial logic at play in the Spanish imperial endeavor: in practice, the whiter the mix, the better. The whitened idea and identity of mestizaje has, to this day, remained largely naturalized.[11] Mestizaje is also a militant identity that challenges racial thinking and engages powerfully in the offensive struggles, most notably perhaps in its Chicana expression. My being a Colombian-Danish Mestiza, scholar, and activist cannot be disconnected from my being so within an ontological, social, political, and economic order that privileges whiteness, including skin color. While in Latin America, I enjoy the privileges of dominant mestizaje, in Europe I am able to pass as white. More precisely, I am often decoded as white. Passing as white is only a possibility in a world where the governing logic reduces people to their appearance in accord with racial stereotypes that invisibilize our sociohistorical and economic-political complexities. In chapter 4, I describe some of the general contours of these complexities. Focus is on the relationship between structure and identity, paying attention to the ways in which mestizaje has obeyed coloniality.

In his discussion regarding the pitfalls of national consciousness, Frantz Fanon warned of the dangers that emerge in the wake of the decolonization of administrations, where new hierarchies begin to settle between those who led the struggles for decolonization and the rest of the population. According to Fanon, those who have taken the lead in processes of decolonization may have been fit for those purposes, but unfit to undertake the next task—that of nation building (1963). First, by winning the struggle of decolonization, the leaders of the struggle enter to believe that the rest of the population is indebted to them. Gordon labels this the Moses syndrome.[12] Second, a leader whose position is legitimated by his struggle against colonialism will continue depending on an enemy that justifies a continued anticolonial endeavor. By indicating this, Fanon was not denying the resilient nature of colonialism. He was, rather, pointing to the decadence and stagnation of decolonization when persons who lead take for their own purposes the power to define what colonialism is, and how it is to be fought. They additionally demand the continued loyalty of people not because they continue deserving such a loyalty, but because they translate their part in the decolonization process as an absolute defining factor of who they are, and their inherent, self-perceived *goodness*. This is a replication of the colonial attitude of former colonizers by the national bourgeoisies (Fanon 1963).

There is now a similar mechanism at play among some of the intellectual, and predominantly male, Mestizo populations from Latin America that herald the decolonial perspective.[13] While in some ways contributing decisively to decolonization, at the same time they seem to oscillate in an infertile, and sometimes corrosive, in-betweenness. I am aware that colonial scholarship may take advantage of this criticism and misuse it to dismiss the contributions of the decolonial perspective. This is indeed how coloniality works. However, if we are to avoid stagnation in our discussions, this is one of the risks we must take in the process of strengthening our struggles. Being a Mestizo entails embodying a trickster figure that is similar to that of the Scandinavian mythical figure Loki. Loki is neither god nor frost giant, but he is considered both. He is a shape shifter, who sometimes assists the gods and sometimes causes problems for them. At times he even betrays them to the frost giants. As Loki, being Mestizo has the power of the trickster: a form of power that comes from his mixed status and being in-between worlds (politics, ontologies, epistemologies, temporalities) and projects. If the trickster, however, gives no direction to her in-betweenness (in time-space and politics of being), she will remain an infertile figure at best, a defender of the colonial death project and the maximum expression of assimilation of coloniality at worst.

The figure of Loki is useful to make manifest another element of mestizaje: that many Mestizos tend to think of ourselves more as individuals, and less as products of history, and as part of a collective. In other words, unlike Loki, mestizaje is a colonial social category just as much as the category *indigenous*. At the same time, however, mestizaje is markedly different from indigeneity because it was created as a category whose central interest was to access white privilege—as against to change the system that upheld those privileges. As such, mestizaje is both a colonial social category and a social, political, and economic institution. Another facet of this challenge of being Mestiza is to acknowledge us as part of a larger imagined community (Rivera Cusicanqui 2012), as well as heirs of colonial—and not only decolonial— legacies in Latin America. Giving direction to the in-betweenness is, among other things, to work against the historical structures of power that have made us who we are, and in which we continue to play a role: albeit in differing ways, for instance, the Mestizos continue enjoying (white) privilege in Latin America. And we enjoy those privileges because our people themselves created the social, economic, political, and educational structures that secure those benefits. By contrast, giving direction to in-betweenness entails the destruction of racial dominance, both individually and socially.

The big questions that Mestizos engaged in the decolonial turn in Latin America generally continue to avoid are connected with this privileged stance, and to the fact that this privileged stance requires that we reconnect to our ancestors—both those who colonized and those who were subject to colonization; that we analyze the ways in which their legacies have shaped our present, and relink in the world learning from them—both from their violence, and from resisting violence. This historical understanding I term *decolonial historical realism*. Indeed, many of the otherwise rich discussions taking place within the vast scholarship emerging in the wake of Aníbal Quijano's crucial coloniality of power essay underline the importance of the *locus of enunciation* while at the same time ignoring decisive elements to this locus of enunciation. Unsurprisingly, critical engagements with mestizaje are more common among decolonial feminists than among the male, nationally and/or internationally recognized Mestizo thinkers.

Deep analyses concerning settler colonialism and how it has impacted their places of enunciation, for instance, are saliently absent from the elaborations of central thinkers as Quijano, Mignolo, and Dussel. However, through settler colonialism, we Mestizos granted ourselves rights over lands that were and are not ours to take. Latin America was named by our people to forward colonial and white interests, and this was part of the process of naturalizing settler colonialism: in the process of naming Latin America, we became the continent and its history, and indigenous and African-descendent populations became our colonial subjects. They were part of our legacy only to the extent to which this claim could improve our position in the hierarchies of power. As intellectual Mestizos living in colonial empires such as northern Europe and the United States, we are not relegated to the zone of nonbeing. We are, rather, as Loki, in-between the zone of being and the zone of nonbeing. Although we are far from always welcome, we have the possibility to enter the zone of being, and we are often offered privileges in exchange for our collaboration with it.

The rewarding part of reconnecting with our ancestors is the part that connects to our indigenous and African heritage. In this context, we tend to leave out considerations about the sexual violations that often were part of that, which produced our mixed status. Of course we prefer the affirming part; the violent part hurts. However, in a similar way to which Malcolm X defended anger, I argue that the aspect that hurts is the element from which the power to destroy our colonial identities and institutions lies. The part that hurts is also the part that forces us to take responsibility for thinking and action, and as such it is not only a destructive but also a productive force. One of the hurtful elements of reconnecting with ancestry as Mestizos regards the material dimensions. Indeed, our parents or grandparents may have been poor—nonetheless, many had private property. To take my case as an example: on the part of my father, my grandfather had private property that produced potatoes, milk, maize, and wool. His complexion informed us that he was most probably descendent of the German explorers that were contracted by the Spanish Crown to colonize what is now Boyacá, in Colombia. My grandmother is clearly more indigenous, both in terms of knowledge and in terms of how she looks. She was an orphan. The day my grandfather bought a truck, the economic situation of the family improved, and his transportation business allowed his sons and daughters to move to the capital, Bogotá, and study at the university. My father accessed a scholarship to study in Switzerland, where he met my mother, with whom he returned to Colombia after they finished their studies. I was born into this lineage, by which it is clear that my condition also rests on the privileges—and violences—of settler colonialism and coloniality, and not only in the resistance of my Colombian grandmother to marriage and procreation, and her and my grandfather's indigenous and peasant knowledges. On the part of my mother, my grandparents were Danish peasants from what until recent times was a particularly marginalized area in Denmark: Thy. They, however, owned their land. Their children also acquired private property, and access to school and to higher education. And as is known, Danish welfare is closely tied to its own engagement in colonialism and slave trade (Jensen 2012). So, I have inherited indigenous and peasant knowledges and forms of resistance, but also their ways of assimilating in order to access privilege. I have also inherited the violence that made my existence possible, starting with the material conditions that enable education, a full belly, and good living conditions. This inheritance has direct lines to settler colonialism and slave trade.

Many of my colleagues heralding the decolonial perspective occupy similar loci of enunciation and, as Loki, an in-between, or rather as both: a European colonial power and a colonized subject. Despite this, many often continue to position themselves on the side of dispossessed colonized subjects without considering how this very act may be replicating, or readapting, colonialism. While the decolonial perspective pays attention to historicity, most of its adherents largely avoid placing themselves sincerely and existentially as part of this history. Instead, they seem to employ racial privilege to choose which aspects of our history and legacies they take on as constitutive of their places of enunciation, and which aspects they simply deny or downplay. Thereby, they tend to act in bad faith (Gordon 1995), positioning themselves as being for decolonization, at the same time largely defining the terms of decolonization, its priorities, and in some notable cases even who valid *decolonials* are, how they are to act, and what they look like. As Milton Almonacid (in a personal communication) points out, we also avoid confronting the material consequences that such a theoretical exploration of our loci of enunciation would have over our ways of living. It is, indeed, in terms of materiality that the consequences of coloniality are spelled out; it is here that the intersections between race, class, and gender are most obvious. For instance, they are noticeable because it is predominantly the male Mestizo's voicing of decolonization that regionally, as well as internationally, is considered the instrument of contemporary critical thinking in the Americas—in spite of the large and complex traditions of thinking in this direction represented in Latin America among indigenous and Afro-Latin American and Caribbean men and women. These unaddressed issues and unanswered questions suggest that we still have a considerable distance to traverse in relation to decolonization.

DECOLONIAL HISTORICAL REALISM

In considering the different sociohistorical and economic-political experiences and the intellectual contributions coming from the global south, I adhere to the call of many southern intellectuals (More 2002; Eze 1998; Mudimbe 1988; Ndlovu-Gatsheni 2013; Mignolo 2000, 2005; Quijano 2000b) of historicizing the coloniality of power, without falling into the trap of presupposing that coloniality only operated in one or the other part of the globe, but also neither presuming that it operated in the same way everywhere. Understanding how coloniality impacted different peoples in different ways is pivotal both to thinking through *what* and *who* we are, and to understanding the conditions of possibility of pluriversality. As decolonial historical realism, this demands examining how the different continents and peoples emerged historically, not as the dominant Eurocentric colonial history teaches us, but considering that dominant versions of history were shaped by the interests of colonial domination and are reproduced by them.

The decolonial realism I advocate rejects the relativism embedded in the idea that history will always be partial as it will always be related by the dominant powers. While it is true that history entails a large portion of issues whose political and broader meaning and significance depends on interpreters who often use it to legitimate power or resist it, it is also valid that there are historical facts of such crucial importance that we, as scholars struggling for decolonization, must insist that these facts are not trivialized through discussions of interpretation. The transatlantic slave trade being one of them, but I also refer to the fact of coloniality and the death project.

Although increasingly accepted in some activist and academic circles worldwide, coloniality and racism continue to be trivialized and negated in dominant knowledge construction—not to mention media representations of, for example, military interventions, drowning individuals in the Mediterranean, or transnational extractivist practices backed up by most (trans)national political elites in the world. A decolonial realist approach defends that one cannot deal with these problems without taking into account the historically constituted system within which they continue being produced. McCullagh (1980, 423) explains historical realism as follows:

> The basic reason for believing in the reality of historical events is the same as the reason for believing in the reality of unobservable physical events, namely that they best explain features of the world already known to us. [. . .] If an historical narrative accounts for certain facts believed to be true of the world, and does so better than any other explanation of them we can devise, that is a reason, if not always a very strong reason, for believing that the narrative correctly describes what actually happened to bring about the facts which it is designed to explain. The true explanation might always be other than the one the historian has thought of. But if the best one he can devise accords well with much that we believe about the world, there is at least some reason for believing it to be true.

The decolonial historical realism entails the above, but is understood through a shift in the geography and temporality of reason. As such, it starts off from the recognition of coloniality, and how 'that, which is believed to be true of the world' is at this point in history part of the overdetermination and overrepresentation of whiteness; therefore, the need to decolonize it.

Additionally, decolonial historical realism requires constant dialogue with our ancestors, so that we can learn from the conditions that made them who and what they are, but also learn from their struggles, their violence, their mistakes, and their achievements. For instance, a necessary step to understanding what Africa, Latin America, and Europe are is to take into account how coloniality shaped them in different but relational ways. To illustrate this crucial point, let us follow Mudimbe's logic in *The Invention of Africa*—here presented by Ndlovu-Gatsheni: 'The making of Africa and its people involved the work of explorers, cartographers, missionaries, travellers, colonial anthropologists, colonialists, African kings and chiefs, ordinary Africans as makers of history, historians, imperialists, pan-Africanists and African nationalists, and others too numerous to mention' (Ndlovu-Gatsheni 2013, 100). Indeed, the making of Latin America similarly involved the work of explorers, cartographers, missionaries, travellers, colonial anthropologists, slave masters, enslaved Africans, colonialists, indigenous leaders, ordinary people, historians, imperialists, communists, socialists, Catholics, and so on.

In addition, the making of Europe also correspondingly involved the work of the above. What I want to illustrate with this is the following: it is important to recognize that a vast diversity of actors shaped Africa, Latin America, and Europe, as it is crucial to acknowledge that that diversity involves overlapping actors who have produced the continents differently: the colonial historians and ethnographers did not participate in the making of Europe in the same way that they participated in the making of Africa or Latin America. Moreover, these processes of making implied processes of unmaking, deletion and violent impositions, so that in reality these processes of making also happened at the expense of something and someone(s). Taking into account this diversity in the shaping of Africa, Latin America, and Europe is important, but not sufficient. It is as imperative not to lose sight of the certainty that, however diverse, all have happened within a single globalized mode of domination, that is, within coloniality. Coloniality also consequently connects these histories. Taking coloniality into account does not mean deleting plurality, it simply implies recognizing that plurality came to be shaped as part of, in opposition to, in complicity or subversive complicity, assimilation, revolt, rejection, negotiation, or welcoming of the imposition of racism, capitalism, patriarchy, and the depredations against nature, and that this all happened in different ways—in short, coloniality localized and adapted.

POWER AND GLOBALIZATION

Taking the above into account, it is obvious that in order to understand the relationship between the global and the local we need to move away from dominant globalization theories. These obey the logic and temporality of the death project, and so prove insufficient to processes of liberation and transformation. It is important to exemplify some key concerns with the prevalent approaches to support my critique and alternative reading, and to elucidate the ways in which academic scholarship participates in the global mechanisms of power.[14] Many of the theories used in the social sciences and humanities to analyze globalization convey relevant descriptions of how globalization is experienced in the zone of being, addressing, for example, the changes in notions of space, place, and time. Frequently, these theories apply a technological determinism, according to which these changes are predominantly an outcome of digital and high-speed technologies. Additionally, these theories often closely associate globalization and modernity. In the view of Anthony Giddens, for example, globalization is constitutive of modernity, this last described as:

At its simplest, modernity is a shorthand term for modern society, or *industrial civilization*. Portrayed in more detail, it is associated with (1) a certain set of *attitudes* towards the world, the idea of the world as open to transformation, by human intervention; (2) a complex of *economic institutions*, especially industrial production and a *market economy*; (3) a certain range of *political institutions*, including the nation-state and mass democracy. Largely as a result of these characteristics, modernity is vastly more dynamic than *any previous type of social order*. It is a society—more technically, a complex of institutions—which, *unlike any preceding culture, lives in the future, rather than the past.* (Giddens and Pierson 1998, 94, emphases added)

This definition refers to some aspects of hegemonic processes attached to modernity. Significantly, this denotation obscures the death project and the coloniality that made modernity possible. This clouding occurs as the starting point of dominant theories of globalization in an implicit (or explicit) paean to technological achievements of Europe, in praise of some of the social and political processes that take place in Europe connected to the Industrial Revolution, in a European geo-temporal logic that conflates Europe with the beginning and end of history and of a philosophical tradition predominantly associated with Germany, the United Kingdom, and France. Largely, these theories attach globalization to the dissemination of these processes and ideas to the rest of the world. This is a spread that involves not only an increased access of the supposedly global—but actually the predominantly elite—populations to some technological, social, cultural, and economic assets, which are themselves supposed to be the fruit of European modernity. This is exemplified in Giddens's assertion that 'globalization . . . is *no longer* primarily a matter of the expansion of the west across the rest of the world' (Giddens and Pierson 1998, 186, emphasis added).

The overall horizon of these theories consists of Europe, primarily, in what I, with Enrique Dussel, call the *second modernity*—the part of modernity whose central axis is the Industrial Revolution (Dussel 2007). To some extent, current dominant theories have broadened their Eurocentered horizons to conceptualize the emergence of new global economic powers—Brazil, China, India, Russia. This 'late modern age' or 'reflexive modernity' (Giddens 1991) not only implies increasing risks, but also the possibility of conceiving a global order within which human rights and new conceptions of citizenship—often referred to as *cosmopolitanism*—would play an important role (Beck 2000). Based on the contemplation of the new emerging economies, these theories tend to oppose the idea of a hegemonic economic or political power. Useful as they may be in understanding some limited aspects of hegemonic globalization, these theories are (as any theory is) inherently political—implying of course that they are also pivotal to specific projects (Kumar 2003). In this sense, the main problem with such theories is that they fall short when it comes to conceptualizing the role of *other* actors in global processes, and that they, at best, represent the experience of globalization of a segment of the population in the west. They tend to be instrumental to the death project. Many theorists of globalization—such as Ulrich Beck and Giddens—are inclined to describe hegemonic globalization from the vantage point of the elites, thus invisibilizing *other* processes of globalization. By describing aspects of hegemonic globalization, they are reproducing the dominant temporality as well, contributing to narrowing the space of the present so that it is a fleeting moment, and they are putting the future out of our reach. This temporality is depoliticizing, and the theories of globalization that reproduce it do not allow us to shift the temporality of reason. To shift the temporality of reason, we need to investigate what there is in globalization that escapes the logic of hegemonic globalization, as Santos could put it. Indeed, global mechanisms of power connect to specific temporalities and values (Santos 2002a; Gordon 2006b), which are hegemonic. However, antihegemonic projects are not consequently powerless. This insight is central to understanding that while the struggles that defend the death project are hegemonic, terming them defensive means acknowledging that their hegemony is being challenged. Thereby, I am also acknowledging the power of the offensive struggles. Power must be understood in a way that takes into account these dynamics:

> Everyone has a sphere of influence over his or her body and what he or she can immediately hold. That sphere is 'force'. Other people, however, have a sphere of influence that goes well beyond their immediate spatial-temporal coordinates. Thus, they could be at one point of the world while influencing the activities of people at another point. They could have died many years ago, while conditioning many people in the present and the future. [They] could even be inside one's head. This is power. (Gordon 2006a, 46)

To refer to a sphere of influence allows avoiding denying agency to individuals and groups without forgetting that the impact of different groups is simply not the same for each group, and the effect they have does not necessarily occur in the zone of being.

As Antonio Gramsci showed, hegemonic power also includes social and cultural consent—a majority's 'adoption' of dominant ideology—as well as wealth accumulation through exploitation (Crehan 2002, 99–105). It is however important to understand that consent involves both imposition and bad faith. Consent requires that there be a choice to believe what one does not really believe (Gordon 1999). It requires one to defend that the Emperor is garbed, when the Emperor is actually naked. Bad faith varies from the belief that things are indeed as hegemonic power presents them, to the acquiescence in that one cannot do anything to change a given situation or the status quo: indolence, indifference and powerlessness. To include these existential facets is important because they stress freedom to choose (which is, however, not the same for everyone) and the renunciation of freedom that bad faith implies. In my characterization of struggles, I underscore not the relative power of hegemony versus subaltern, but the projects that these adhere to. Hence, my understanding of the offensive struggles as participating in an offensive against the death project. This intention is to work against the rendering invisible of the force (understood in Gordon's sense) of these struggles, and to underscore the ways in which they transcend their own spheres of influence to reach other similar struggles—including those that happen within the academy.

Observing the global manifestations of power requires keeping a careful balance that implies awareness that they are also linked to the local. An appreciation of this balance assists in distinguishing the different forms constituting the global. Consequently, we can consider that not everything we can call global is part of hegemonic power. For example, the Zapatista struggle in Mexico has become global and achieved some degree of power by transgressing, reaching over spatial and temporal frames. The Zapatista struggle is a struggle against the death project and it has influenced other struggles and theories. It is not, however, part of hegemonic globalization. A problem with many contemporary approaches to globalization and localization is that they prove insufficient to account for the different forms that globalization takes, its particularities, while simultaneously attending to the truth that, precisely because the colonial structures of hierarchization and power continue to dominate, neither globalities nor particularities can be universalized. Furthermore, the complexity increases when we consider that there are indeed general things that we can say about the dominant structures of coloniality, and the ways in which these are lived, defended, and legitimized, precisely because of structure and theme. It is helpful in this context to distinguish between that which is globalized through colonial logics and in defense of the death project, and that which is globalized by means of resistance to and struggle against the death project. What is different in these processes of globalization is, thus, the way in which globalization is achieved (imposition, violence, coloniality versus resistance, defense of life, community) and the political projects that are sustained in them (defense of the death project— offensive to the death project). Thus, when referring to dominant globalization, I sometimes use the term 'colonization'. Because all that is globalized emerges in specific localities and is localized within specific contexts, Santos's distinction between globalized localisms and localized globalisms is useful (Santos 2002a, 25–26). I will be using this distinction to refer to the different levels and unequal scopes needed in order to account for globalization. When referring to globalized localism, I refer to the *global* in the localism: for example, human rights, development, and Zapatismo can be studied as globalized localisms: they all emerge from specific localities, yet represent very different political projects that have globalized. Significantly, although their reach in time and space differs, they can nevertheless be named as globalized. To examine globalized localism implies paying attention to how they have become globalized, and to account for, that we cannot speak of globalization in the abstract nor solely as a description of elite processes, access and possibilities (as do Giddens and Beck). We can speak of something as being globalized by paying attention to commonalities across time and space; thematic and grammatical continuities, and power. From these, we can also generalize. When referring to localized globalism, I will in turn be discussing the *local* level—and so focus will be more particularly on the form that is globalized, takes in specific time-spaces. This involves looking into continuities across time as they take shape in space/place and person/community, and thematic and grammatical variations-in-commonalities (dialects)—how both the dominant and antihegemonic global is *trans-lated* into the local. One of the most overseen localized globalisms that work in the defense of the death project is whiteness.

There is a strong anthropological current in academic scholarship on human rights, which emphasizes the importance not of examining what human rights are or should be, but rather how they are used by people around the world (Wilson 1997, 14–17). Their attention lies on the ways in which human rights can be used as a counterhegemonic tool. In keeping this focus, however, they tend to leave epistemological and ontological concerns aside and, as such, to ignore the ways in which rights frame the horizons of possibility of transformation. To avoid this, it is important to scrutinize the realities and ways of knowing that rights and development authorize, as well as the realities and ways of knowing that they do not warrant. Many of the critiques against human rights and development from the global south are based on such reflections. These critiques relate to the understanding that many movements share that it is impossible to separate human rights from the rights of nature, and from economic, social, political and juridical organization.[15] To be relevant to these movements, and respectful of their social, political, and juridical organization and projects, human rights must, at the very least, be transformed. In effect, the fact that globalized practices around human rights and development authorize some realities and ways of knowing while rendering others irrelevant or impossible is highly significant in political terms: what we will see in the following is that *other* political projects are precisely *other* because they exceed politics and reality as dominant society and dominant knowledge production know them.

NOTES

1. The *death project* is used in a communiqué written by the Nasa indigenous people in Colombia, where they present their political action-plan, 'the plan of life of the peoples'. It is worth reading the communiqué in its entirety. It can be found at http://www .nasaacin.org/propuesta-politica-de-los-pueblos. Last accessed in August 2015.

2. The Code Noir was established by colonial France, and 'became the slave laws that governed master-slave relationships in the colony. . . . The code was a mixture of political control and explicit disciplinary measures for slave control. Precise and concrete, these measures shaped the everyday lives of slaves. For example, the code stated how much food a slave was to get and how many suits of clothes per year s/he was allowed. Although in the code's early years its so-called protective aspects were emphasized . . . these aspects were increasingly forgotten as the objective of the control of the slave population came to the fore. . . . Thus its overriding framework was to confirm the inferior status of the slave and to maintain public security under the control of the planter colonial class' (Bogues 2012, 219–20).

3. Notable examples of the ways in which human rights and development operate in conjunction in interventionist endeavors are the activities of the US Southern Command—SOUTHCOM—and those of the United States Agency for International Development—USAID. See, for example, http://www.southcom.mil/AppsSC/pages/humanRights.php and http://www.usaid.gov/locations/latin_america_caribbean/. See also http://centrodeal erta.org/documentos_desclasificados/libro_completo_la_agresion_.pdf and http://www .voltairenet.org/article121344.html, Avilés 2005, Suárez Salazar 2007.

4. Together with the Code of Hammurabi (1760 BC, Babylon), the English Magna Carta (1215) is one of the often-cited expressions of human rights. However, as Wright notes, 'the Magna Carta was a purely political arrangement dividing power between the Crown and the nobility' (2001, 44).

5. For investigations into America's significance to the global workings of power, see, for example, Lander (2000, 2004, 2008), Mignolo (2000), Quijano (2000a, b), Dussel (1995, 2004, 2007, 2008), Wynter (2003) and Conwell Cox (1959).

6. For discussions of global segregation and its connection to racism and capitalism, see Davis (2012), Césaire (2006), Gilmore (2007), Robinson (2000) [1983]; as global apartheid see Kohler (1995), Dalby (1998), and Harrison (2002).

7. At the conference, '*Refundación del estado en América Latina. Perspectivas desde una epistemología del Sur*', Boaventura de Sousa Santos used offensive and defensive struggles as a means to illustrate the major differences in terms of the social struggles that are currently taking place in Latin America. The conference was held at the University of Los Andes, Bogotá, on 1 September 2010, and transmitted live on the Internet through http://www.expresa.la, where it was available as of December 2010. I have adopted and adapted this conceptualization to refer to the dynamics in play in relation to the death project.

8. Achille Mbembe's public lecture 'Decolonizing the University: Five New Directions' was presented at WiSER on 22 April 2015. Accessed in May 2015 through the following link: http://wiser.wits.ac.za/content/podcast-achille-mbembes-public-lecture-de colonizing-university-12046.

9. Lewis Gordon lecture organized by the *Pan-African Baraza* and *ThoughtWorks* to mark the ninetieth anniversary of the birth of Frantz Fanon. Held in Nairobi on 8 January 2015. Available at https://www.youtube.com/watch?v = ixNrKiW19mU.

10. I thank Oscar Guardiola-Rivera for his clarity in a comment on a very early draft of this book—he will recognize some of his words in this section of the text.

11. *Mestizaje* is widely discussed in Latin American critical thinking, and these discussions show how mestizaje is both a notion of whiteness and domination, an identity used strategically by racialized populations on the continent, and a category that in some cases is redefined 'from below'. Contributions on these issues can be found in de la Cadena (1996), Cusicanqui (2012), Gómez (2011), Rivera, Hale (1996), Sanjinés (2002), Segato (2010).

12. Talk in Nairobi, cf. footnote 9.

13. I thank Milton Almonacid for all the conversations through which we have elaborated on the problems I present here concerning mestizaje, and also thank Herson Huinca-Piutrín who joined the discussions at a later point. All the reflections pertaining mestizaje, whiteness, and the decolonial perspective are as much theirs as they are mine. I hope we can continue elaborating on these issues together.

14. For a critical discussion of the main characteristics of scholarship on globalization, the reader can consult Santos's paper, 'The Processes of Globalization' (2002a).

15. For examples of how different indigenous, ethnic, and social movements in Latin America defend the argument that it is impossible to separate human rights from the rights of nature, and from economic, social, political, and juridical organization, see Comunidad de Paz San José de Apartadó—CDP-2004, Cuatro Etnias 1999, Grueso 2000, Grueso, Rosero and Escobar 1998, Organización Indígena Kankuama—OIK-2006.

Part One

TEMPORALITIES OF REASON

One of the processes through which dominance forms occurs as an effect of the violent imposition of some entities (institutions) and realities (ontologies) that thereby come to be globalized, while in the same process other entities and realities become local. Although this may be referred to as the process of globalization, it is actually the process of colonization, which has the death project as its core. Due to this process, the global and the local are intimately linked and the one cannot be understood without the other. Yet, all realities and entities, globalized and localized, connect to specific locations: geographic, social, economic, epistemic, in power relations, and so on. What is globalized as dominant necessarily involves normativity, and provides the framework within which every other position is valorized, categorized, made absent, neutralized, or exploited. Pluriversalization means, among other things, taking seriously these last different but entangled histories that emerge from distinct power positions in the processes of colonization. In other words, to counter the logic of dominant globalization in terms of history, and to take some initial steps towards shifting the temporality of reason, it is necessary to read the history of colonization in ways that privilege those entities and realities that became localized, or invisibilized, in the processes of domination, and to consider that not all entities and realities became localized and colonized in the same way, nor to the same extent. Indeed, while some entities and realities became localized—as the Mestizo populations—others became invisibilized —as indigenous and African or diasporic African populations. It is equally important to interrogate the ontological and epistemological frameworks within which the various global processes function, and to examine the realities that these processes authorize, and those that they exclude. This part of the book explores the links that entwine human rights and development through race, focusing of globalization and localization processes pertaining to the four peoples of Sierra Nevada de Santa Marta, my own people—the Mestizos in the Americas and especially Colombia—and in relation to the global elites.

Chapter Two

Teyuna and Columbus

Employing the decolonial historical realism to shift the temporality of reason, I take the territory of Sierra Nevada as the point of inception to understand how conditions were shaped for the four peoples to whom the Mamos and the Sagas belong: the Arhuaco, Kankuamo, Kogi, and Wiwa. From Sierra Nevada, I also consider regional, national, and international events when necessary to grasp the locality. To avoid reinforcing the logic of dominant globalization, we also need to take into account the resistance to the localized globalisms. The struggles of the four peoples of Sierra Nevada are among those that oppose the rationality and ethics of the death project, and they take a multiplicity of forms. The interrelations between my people and the peoples of Sierra Nevada happen at many different levels, and are traversed by my people's dominance over them. Indeed, to center on the localized globalisms of human rights and development in the Sierra, and so consider the resistances of the four peoples throughout history, proves complex. To begin, there are three main problems in this undertaking: the first connects to the nature of resistance. The second is that with the different scholarly Mestizo and/or Eurocentric representations of the history of the four peoples regarding central elements, sometimes the accounts are contradictory. The third problem relates to the second, and involves questions of how we can understand cultural interaction and identity in nonessentialist terms without, at the same time, neglecting the difference of the other and the nature of domination. This last often includes the scholarly approaches that otherwise intend to be counterhegemonic.

The first problem is related to the innumerable ways in which resistance has occurred in Sierra Nevada. Some of the most tangible efforts of opposition include withdrawals Sierra-inward, armed struggle in the early colonial times, and in more recent times, isolation, secrecy, education, and organization. Generally, despite defiance occurring in a variety of ways, it is erroneous to presuppose that 'completely autonomous subjects' exist (Gledhill 2000, 68). In other words, to presuppose that there are actors outside the field(s) of power relationships that determine oppression and resistance is to be mistaken. In these fields of power relationships, the outcomes of struggle are difficult to establish, and indeed one form of resistance—such as the Mestizo peoples' struggles for decolonization in the eighteenth century—can also be another form of oppression. Additionally, it is also important to consider that structures of oppression are neither fixed nor unchangeable; not structurally, not temporally, nor epistemologically. This is why resistance makes sense.

The second problem is concerned with there being no consensus among scholars that the peoples of the Sierra are *who* and *what* they claim to be; namely, descendants of those whom the colonizers called *Tayrona.*[1] Contemporary studies often show an explicit rejection of essentialist understandings of identity. The rejection functions as a device to create distance from the often racist terms upon which indigenous groups have been studied earlier in Colombia. The tendency is to suggest that before the Spanish arrival, the Sierra was inhabited by diverse groups that were not necessarily united (Sánchez Mojica 2008, Uribe 2000). This idea contradicts what the peoples themselves state; that is, it suggests that the peoples of the Sierra were not Kankuamos, Kogis, Arhuacos, and Wiwas before colonization. It also implies that their own claims to being different—but united by the task laid upon them by Serankwa/the Mother—are an outcome of recent cultural and political strategies.

In this context, it is noteworthy that features in these studies display interesting contradictions and illustrate the Loki-like position of Mestizos. Dairo Andrés Sánchez's considerations reflect these dilemmas:

> before the first ethnocide there were various groups that inhabited the Sierra and were not unified. The name Tayrona was imposed by the Spanish who fought these heterogeneous groups for almost one hundred years until they achieved their dismemberment and subsequent retreat to the highest peaks of the mountain, simultaneously breaking the cultural and commercial flows that joined the Sierra to the interior of the continent and Central America. The Tayrona civilization is, paradoxically, the unit that seeks to essentialize from the locus of enunciation of the white conqueror the multiplicity of political, cultural and economic experiences that existed in the mountains in order to control them: to name in order to manage and dominate. (Sánchez Mojica 2008, 79, translated from Spanish)

Sánchez's words specifically address the ways in which Ciudad Perdida (*Lost City*), a sacred site and old city found by archaeologists in the 1970s in Sierra Nevada, was named and classified—signified—by the government, scholars, and indigenous peoples, respectively. He emphasizes that anthropology reinforces patterns of domination when finding evidence that confirms the Tayrona homogeneity and essence. This observation is relevant because it is concerned with anthropology *in* the world, but also because it speaks to the practices carried out by the Mestizo populations and the global elites. Yet, I want to point to the contradictions stated earlier because they convey the problems that Mestizo scholars critical of the coloniality of power encounter in the process of criticism. In his study, Sánchez acknowledges what the Lost City means to the peoples of the Sierra, but as mentioned, also seems to imply that they, too, founded their 'cultural-political strategies' upon colonially imposed, and ultimately false, narratives (Sánchez Mojica 2008, 88–90). The emergent contradictions need some attention. What happens to forms of domination, naming, and controlling—in short, the problems of ethnographic authority—when scholars, criticizing their peers for being essentialist, however, exercise the power of characterizing indigenous peoples even in nonessentialist terms? This concerns an understanding of the socially constructed identity as false if it is not coherent or verifiable according to a disciplinary canon, or if it is the result of the histories of oppression lived by colonized peoples. These postures relegate colonized peoples to the zone of nonbeing, as a positivistic reading of their realities might do. A decolonial historical realism runs counter to these tendencies.

If social scientists expect colonized peoples to be other than what they are, then they expect colonized peoples to live in bad faith and renounce freedom. If we expect ourselves, as Mestizos, to be individuals detached from past and present colonial projects, we also risk incurring bad faith. Contemporary approaches seem to imply that history is one thing, and identity another thing, thus negating their interrelatedness. In these approaches, the real indigene is the one who has been untainted by colonial history—that is, the indigene that has remained in the past imagined by dominant Eurocentric elites and must, in addition, live up to disciplinary standards concerning who she should be, and how she should understand herself and the world. This assumption leads to the conclusion that indigenous peoples, as *indigenous*, have been destroyed by colonialism: for instance, an indigene's using a mobile phone would be proof of this.

Although the effects of colonialism towards the indigenous peoples cannot be understated, the problem I address concerns how to consider the genocidal and epistemicidal effects of colonialism without presupposing that this destruction means that the indigenes no longer exist or that, in order to be real indigenes, they must be untouched by modernity and the genocidal and epistemicidal effects of colonialism. In any of these options, the indigenous peoples cannot be thought of as modern, even less are they seen as capable of articulating the conditions that make them who and what they are. However, as the Mamos argue, in the same way that colonialism is not static, they and their peoples cannot be understood as being the same as scholars believe they were five hundred or more years ago, or want them to be now. The Mamos must, however, be taken seriously and literally when they state that they are essentially the same as they have always been.

This brings us to the third contradiction, that is, understanding cultural interaction and identity in nonessentialist terms, without concurrently neglecting the difference of the *other*. Enrique Dussel (1995) has accounted how the *other* historically was *covered over*[2] by Eurocentric thinking. We will delve into depth with the historical aspects of covering over in chapter 3. In this chapter, it is important to note that covering over indicates that the standard is sameness; sameness implies an *us*, in this case an *us* constructed through 'the transformation of hegemonic interests into true knowledge' (Santos 2004, 161). It also suggests that *we* define who or what a person is in relation to how similar *we* think he is to *us*, rather than on his own terms. Only at this point, when *we* have already defined whom and what the other is, do *we* recognize his difference, that is, from the position where *we* become the ones to define the terms of difference. In this way, to paraphrase Mamo Saúl Martínez, *we* have never *dis-covered* who he is.

The analysis of the historical, social, ontological, and existential significance of this covering, or concealment of the *other*, is important because it also allows dis-covering, in the Mamosean sense of the term, that is, as a possibility for interlocution. Whereas covering over can be characterized as the blindness of those who obliterate, this blindness is violence towards those that are concealed. The systematic covering of the other is an expression of power—it is the force of a few affecting the lives of the many. This action is an aspect of racist practice; it entails bad faith, 'a choice not to admit certain uncomfortable truths about [one's] group and [a choice] not to challenge certain comfortable falsehoods about other people' (Gordon, 1999, 75). Mestizo critical thinking continues to be trapped in this dynamic. The problem is not limited to obliteration. When we discuss covering over, we do not necessarily see or hear the other, we might only be seeing the veil that covers her (cf. DuBois 1903). Ironically, seeing the veil can be limited in itself inasmuch as only one sense is used—sight. As is known, western knowledge tends to privilege sight as a means to knowledge, and thus connect seeing with understanding, so linking sight with mind. Other peoples in the world, however, base their knowledge on other senses, for example on hearing. In any case, by seeing the veil we might still not be dis-covering the other. For, what does it mean to be and think from under the vast veil that covers one up?[3]

As we will see in chapter 6, an initial approach to understanding what the Mamos refer to when they underline that they are essentially the same as they have always been shows that culture needs to be understood in terms of how peoples and groups *relink* in the world according to the changing environments. Identity, however, is something markedly different. It relates to being—in this case *being human*—in a world where we share responsibility in maintaining equilibrium in relation to the Mother. This distinction between culture and identity allows for an ontological understanding of how the Mamos of the Sierra apprehend who and what they are. Certainly, they do not deny change or any interrelations with other groups through history, including the history before conquest. What they maintain is that their essential role in the world, to live by the Law of Origin, remains constant. The whole realm of interaction—an extended subjectivity—that not only includes spirits, humans, elements, but also the realm of *aluna* (a concept discussed in detail in this chapter and chapter 6) is crucial to any deliberations concerning culture and identity. Any attempt at understanding the peoples of the Sierra without taking this immense realm of interaction is insincere: it ignores a constitutive ontological and existential dimension central to the engagement in decolonial historical realism. As happens in contemporary scholarship, the critique of essentialism works as a barrier to what the *other* actually says. It inhibits interlocution.

This antiessentialist attitude, and its effect of covering over, is one of the main causes of *others'* lack of interest—and angry rejection—towards whites, Mestizos anthropologists, or however else we, as members of the global elites, are identified. I do not suggest that essentialism is the best approach. I suggest, however, that radical antiessentialism works as closure of dialogue and delegitimization of struggles because of criteria that frequently prove to be beside the point of the struggles' claims. These criteria are, additionally, framed from within a colonial ontological order. Thus, it is often pointless for the subaltern to engage in discussions with those in the zone of being. Ironically, radical antiessentialist thought stems from anthropology's colonial history as a producer of knowledge about *essential others* in partnership with the idea of the civilizing mission that is predicated on the prior fashioning of someone as uncivilized. Is the nonsubaltern willing to allow herself to change, deeply and subjectively, by the subaltern?

The Mamos accounts tell us about the now in the past and the future, and about the past and the future in the now. What the Mamos themselves name the mythical history of the peoples of the Sierra is crucial to understanding their narrative and thought. The broad lines of this mythical telling are included in recent documents that the Mamos have written, and some lesser outlines are, among others, included in British documentary filmmaker Alain

Ereira's 1990 book, *The Elder Brother's Warning*. As Ereira notes, the details of this account are complex. He writes, 'The chapter headings alone take nine nights, and then for nine times nine nights the great epic of creation is spelled out in detail' (Ereira 1990, 110). Despite its generalities, I privilege Ereira's work for the following reasons: first, it has been written in collaboration with Ramón Gil from the Council of Mamos. Secondly, it is also consistent with the Mamos' written records, which are familiar from my own conversations with the Mamos. Finally, in his telling, Ereira is not motivated by academic scientific requirements to respect to the criteria of specific scholarly disciplines. This allows his work flexibility to relate without filtering it through discussions on validity, which are framed from within dominant rationality. Ereira's writing is reflexive; it considers published sources and accounts with the assessment of a Colombian anthropologist. This gives his work valuable transparency. It is important to mention that Ereira's work centers on the Kogi. Nevertheless, as we will see, the history of the four peoples is interrelated in many important ways. Other documents used in this context, and in the rest of the chapter, center on providing a historical overview of the major changes and continuities since the colonization to this time are comments or presentations made by Arhuacos, Kogis, Wiwas, or Kankuamos, as well as academic sources.

FROM *ALUNA* TO *GONAWINDÚA*

The Mother is intelligence. She is a transcendent intelligence literally encompassing all that is, including the creative forces of life, spirits, the micro and macrocosmic. Everything that exists, from stones, mountains, humans to fish, birds, mobile phones, and airplanes were first made in *aluna*—otherwise they simply would not exist:

> In the beginning there was only aluna. . . . The Mother concentrated, the nothingness which was the original sea of thought, spirit and fertility pondered and conceived the idea of the world. It began with a womb, a world-house, which was cosmos. This was the great egg of the universe. In aluna, [the Mother] then conceived nine levels, nine worlds, within this womb. They were her daughters. Each world has its own character, its own color, its own soil: her children had their own personalities. The mysteries of creation are to be understood as a process of aluna dividing, by an effort of concentration, into separate spiritual bodies. She also conceived of sons, among them Serankua. The Dawning began with the definition of these powerful beings, whose existence defines the Mother as a being too. (Ereira 1990, 111)

By defining and embodying sons, the Mother conceived and defined masculinity and her own femininity. In eight of these nine worlds/daughters, the earth was infertile; only the world of black earth was capable of fecundity. The black earth daughter was Seynekun, and within the encounter between *Serankwa* and *Seynekun* in aluna, the creation of the human being happens. Serankwa is the organizing principle and the principle of authority—he is the one that assigned functions to each of the beings in the world, and established the norms and principles of harmony and conviviality—still in aluna.

Seynekun is the organizing principle of the 'management, practice and use' of earth and all that exists. She also encompasses the vision of *development* of the four peoples (Cuatro Etnias 1999). In addition, Serankwa's part in the creation of the physical, material world was that he 'crossed two threads of cotton'.[4] This action established the equilibrium between the four cardinal points, the four guardian-peoples of Sierra Nevada de Santa Marta and the world.[5] In the center of this cross, the peak of Gonawindúa emerged where the stone that serves as the axis that gives consistency to the planet and the cosmos was created ('se estableció la piedra', Cuatro Etnias 1999). Gonawindúa means 'quickening the world' *and* 'the mountain where the world began, the law-bringer' (Ereira 1990, 112), and refers both to our physical and material world and to the central peak in Sierra Nevada. The peoples of the Sierra Nevada conceive of their territory as the Heart of the World, because it is in this specific place that the world began:

> Here [at the center of the cross that Serankwa made] the Mother stuck her spindle and spun it, turning the world on its axis, spinning out the thread which is time as well as space, and which heaps up in the cone of the Sierra, and which then develops, in an ever-widening spiral, into the whole of the world.

In this way, every being is connected to this point of origin in the Sierra and, ultimately, to the Mother. The links in the interrelatedness of being and life have to be protected and a fine balance must be kept in order to guarantee the continuity of life.

Humans already existed in aluna, but it was in the conjunction between Serankwa and Seynekun that humans were created in Gonawindúa. Humans came into existence to look after the world, as the four guardians who would live according to the Law of Origin—*Se*—and thus keep the fine balance of continuity of life. The four peoples—Arhuaco, Kankuamo, Kogi, and Wiwa—are all as important to the balance of the world as the four cardinal points and the four elements. The peoples often use the metaphor of a table to explain their role in the world and in relation to each other: if the table is the world, then the four peoples are the table legs. If one is weakened, the whole Sierra—and thus the world—is also brought out of balance. The world is out of balance in multiple ways that nevertheless interconnect. Regarding the four peoples, the weakening of the different groups, and especially the Kankuamos, has been a serious problem of imbalance for the 'heart of the world' in the last century. While entering into a detailed account of the history of the Kankuamos, or of any of the groups in itself, is beyond the scope of this book and might be irrelevant to the peoples themselves, it is important to mention that they all are involved in a process of self-strengthening and that, in the context of the equilibrium of the world, this process is crucial. It is, however, not without problems and tensions (Figueroa Pérez 2001; Pumarejo and Morales 2003). The Mamos are pivotal to this process.

After having created the four peoples to guard the equilibrium of the world, Serankwa created more humans—the younger siblings to the four peoples. That the four peoples refer to us outsiders as younger siblings is not, as is often believed, derogative. To the Mamos, the younger sibling is often the most spoiled one, which means that she is loved, but also that negative actions are tolerated with love. The idea of the younger sibling contains, however, other dimensions than those referred to by Ereira: including a critical stance like Aimé Césaire's, when he pointed to how colonialism negatively affects both colonizer and colonized. To elaborate, without healing the corruption of the younger siblings, the problems of the disequilibrium of the world cannot be solved. In any case, the younger siblings were created later; they had 'butterfly mind, which paid no attention to the Mother's teaching; the Kogi say "he changed color, from red to green and other colors"'. The younger siblings were given 'a different way of knowing things, a can-do, technological knowledge, and exiled to lands designated for him across the sea' (Ereira 1990, 113). As Ereira additionally notes, we must be careful not to form conclusions in which this mythical history is confused with the biblical narrative of creation.

The creation in aluna is not only about creation of the world. Rather, aluna is also part of the continuous creation of the world. This idea is central to understanding the temporal dimension in the thinking of the Mamos: no process is ever finished, everything is in the making and, as such, the future is here as much as the past and the present. No process can be without its possibility of existence in aluna, and without that, which has already been but continues being, in one form or the other, in aluna. This temporality also suspends the (mostly) chronological order of the biblical creation narratives, which suggests an inherently different principle at work in religions that have written texts as their basis. While open to new interpretations, once written, the written text remains the primary reference. By contrast, oral accounts are more adaptable to reformulation and often less concerned with a moment of

Immaculate Conception, so to speak. Orality also links with memory and community in a different way than literacy. According to the Mamos, the spoken word is much stronger than the written word. While orality indeed is dependent on community, the written word can be accessed by communities but is not reliant on these.

Additionally, while Adam and Eve are expelled from the Garden of Eden as a punishment, the younger siblings are expelled from the Sierra in order to defend the world: the younger siblings' way of knowing, useful in some situations, implies deafness to the teaching of the Mother in other contexts, and this makes them dangerous. And indeed, the younger siblings' return meant the implementation and defense of the death project. The younger siblings are, nevertheless, no less sons or daughters of the Mother, and neither they nor anything that exists in the world is *strange* or *external* to the world of the Sierra (Bocarejo Sueseún 2002; Ereira 1990, 113–14). One of the reasons for the discrepancies between some anthropologists and the Mamos, I suggest, lies in the failure of the former to consider that the Mamos do not regard anything as essentially alien. It is also important to take this into account if we are to make an initial approach to the ways in which conquest and colonization happened as localized globalism, that is, from and on the peoples of Sierra Nevada's location.

PACIFYING THE *OTHER*

Some thirty-three years after the arrival of Christopher Columbus to Guanahani (one of the Bahamas), and at the time when the Spanish friar Bartolomé de las Casas probably was starting to write his three-volume work *The History of the Indies*, the colonization of the Sierra Nevada de Santa Marta began. Although relations of exchange and exploitation had been established between Spanish conquerors and the peoples of the mainland from the very beginning (Sánchez Mojica 2009, 188; Reichel-Dolmatoff 1951, 3–14), the city of Santa Marta was not founded until around 1525. Being part of the Caribbean and a vital entry point to the continent, the place became crucial to the conquerors. As a junction of the colonizers on the mainland, Santa Marta briefly became an important portal for colonization. Significantly, though, in 1538, just thirteen years after the colonizers founded the city of Santa Marta, it no longer had a central role in the colonial geopolitical configurations. The colonial intake of Peru meant that Santa Marta increasingly existed by virtue of potential territorial expansion of the colonizing powers, and less for the sake of its possible colonizing activity (Uribe 2000, 3.1).

The colonizers used the common denominator of *Tayronas*—an adaptation of the designation Teyuna—to refer to the peoples that lived in Sierra Nevada. According to the Mamos, Teyuna is a name that involves the four peoples and it means and *is* the four peoples. As Sánchez (2008) claims, Teyuna is also the name of a specific sacred place—the place that was discovered many years later as the Lost City—and it refers to the spirit who created the caretakers of the different elements. This may suggest that Teyuna as a deity operating in aluna becomes materialized in the four peoples in this sphere of reality. Given the different ruins of cities that have been investigated in the region, the presence of the Teyuna in the Sierra has been traced archaeologically to the seventh century AD. These cities were probably populated until the 1550s to the 1600s. According to the Mamos, each city had its own specialty crops. The different cities were also materially interdependent, and this ensured a diversity of food and materials, including craft materials. This system was part of ensuring the greater balance and was also sustained according to the Law of Origin. As Ereira notes, the Spaniards came to characterize this exchange system rather wrongly as *trade* according to their own conceptions of private ownership, accumulation of wealth, and individual freedom. Furthermore, according to the Mamos, the arrival of the colonizers—whom they often refer to as 'Christopher Columbus'—was announced. It took place at a time of conflicts among the Teyuna who were split in groups, some of whom did not live by the Law of Origin.

We also know that the Teyuna exercised military resistance against the invasion carried out by the younger brother—either more or less jointly organized or in isolated episodes by some specific groups (Uribe 2000, 3.1; Langebaek 2007). Beyond the obvious reasons of the unfair treatment to which they were subjected, or those that were related to resistance against cultural colonization (Langebaek 2007), one may suggest, with the Mamos, that this resistance was also part of the attempts of the Teyuna to protect the heart of the world. To counter the indigenous resistances, the combined use of dogs, horses, and firearms became a Spanish military tactic. Also, as in many other parts of the colonized territories, the Spanish eliminated the elements of livelihood by burning villages and crops (Uribe 2000, 3.1). According to the Mamos, during this period the indigenous population in the Sierra started to migrate inwards to the mountains, approaching the Mamos that, by rank, lived in higher and more isolated places. Carlos Uribe (2000) and, to some extent, Carl Langebaek (2007), argue that the Tayrona culture disappears by the late sixteenth century and the beginning of the seventeenth century. This is, however, debatable if we consider the distinction between identity and culture with which the Mamos operate, a distinction which we will return to in chapter 6. In any case, in the late sixteenth century the

Mamos have a significant centrality within the communities of the Sierra (Langebaek 2007, 167). By 1538, when the Spanish functionary Jerónimo Lebrón writes in a report to the Crown on the status of the city of Santa Marta, the situation of the colonization in that place is unfavorable. The resistance and depopulation of the indigenous peoples hamper the exploitation of gold mines; there are conflicts among the colonizers, increasing pirate raids in the city, and corruption.[6] Consistently with the dominant thought of his time, Lebrón proposes the enslavement of indigenous people, including the children, based on their belligerence and, in general, the detrimental character that the region presents to colonizers (Langebaek 2007, 7).

The history of the Catholic missions is inseparable from the history of the conquest of frontiers and the subjugation of the indigenous population in the colonies (Daza 2006, 1; Castro 2007). The increasing granting of responsibility and power to the missionaries to 'preserve' the indigenous peoples through separatist policies also meant the decline of the physical extermination of them (König 1998, 17). In many cases, most notably in some Jesuit missions, this also meant that the indigenous peoples were better able to preserve their habits and customs, their languages and social structures than had they been left to the mercy of the colonizers and conquerors. In Sierra Nevada, the missions were also important agents of colonialism and lasted from 1693 until well into the twentieth century (Friede 1963, cit. in Pineda 2000; Langebaek 2007, 331). Since then, the so-termed indigenous territories within the colonized lands emerged in the form of villages, communities, indigenous reserves, and other concentrations (König 1998, 17). Spanish aggression in the late sixteenth century, which aimed at abolishing resistance, proved a hard blow to these communities. Additionally, the relative peace of the secondary role that the Santa Marta region now played after the displacement of power to Peru does not apply to those indigenous persons who were in the *encomienda* system.[7] According to the complaints of Bishop García Miranda, the indigenous peoples were tortured, enslaved, starved, and subject to many other acts of aggression. The commissioners (*encomenderos*) had no interest in the conversion of the indigenous peoples to Christianity, and the friars were often indolent (Langebaek 2007, 197–98).

In the seventeenth century, the general situation of the peoples of the Sierra seems to have followed a similar path. The colonial powers continued to raid indigenous villages, and there are also more or less systematic efforts to eliminate their spirituality, for example, by ruining sacred sites and the offerings (*pagamentos*) found there (Langebaek 2007, 224–331; Pineda Camacho 2000). As we will see in later chapters, this method of destruction had also been employed in relation to the conquest of Al-Andalus in the Iberian Peninsula some years earlier. To the Mamos, the incursions against sacred sites seriously damaged the efforts to maintain the equilibrium of a world in a precarious situation. In these incursions against the peoples' spiritual work, however, Christians relied almost entirely on the efficiency of their coercion and possibly collaboration of the 'natives' to bring them to these sites (Langebaek 2007).

For the Spanish, the eighteenth century was marked by economic depression and also by the armed resistance of other indigenous groups of the Province of Santa Marta—the peoples that the Spanish called *Chimilas*, *Motilones*, and *Guajiros* (Uribe 2000; Langebaek 2007; Luna 1991). Both in Santa Marta and throughout the rest of Latin America, the pacification of these groups was one of the administration's priorities (Faverón Patriau 2006). In this context, in the 1740s, the Spanish powers started a population strategy, especially in the territory of the Chimilas: they forcefully brought convicts to the region from Bogotá to populate the area and make pacification easier. Settler colonialism set in with full force, and the processes that were to bring about the institution of *mestizaje* were in play.

In the eighteenth century, the colonial authorities founded many of the villages that are now known as indigenous settlements. This is true of Atánquez, where Saul Martínez lives and which is known as the capital of the Kankuamo, and also of Nabusímake—now known as the capital of the Arhuaco. In its attempts to protect their property, including the indigenous populations, the Crown removed power from the encomiendas and encomenderos and granted power to the Church. The management of these villages was thus placed in the hands of the ecclesiastical authorities. One of the problems encountered by the missionaries in Sierra Nevada, especially after the founding of the above-mentioned villages, was that the indigenous peoples rarely came to live in them. They cultivated their pieces of land for most of the year, in concord with the principles of the Law of Origin, only occasionally travelling to the villages. Excepting the Kankuamo, who, however, also often move from the villages to their pieces of land, the indigenous people of the Sierra do not dwell in villages. Rather, they live moving from one piece of land to the other, taking care of and harvesting the crops that grow in the different altitudes. They also travel to the villages at certain points of the moon's cycle to meet and address community issues.

In spite of the missionary invasion of parts of the Sierra, and despite the economic depression in the province, the reprieve that the indigenous peoples of Sierra Nevada thereby gained was only partial. The colonial powers continued to advance colonization, and resistance to colonialist measures likewise continued throughout the period. The perseverance of the colonial endeavor in this period is illustrated through the tribute system that, according to Uribe (2000, 3.1), was employed from the beginning of the eighteenth century; all indigenous men between seventeen and eighteen years old and fifty-four (called *useful Indians*; *indios útiles*) were to pay tributes to the Spanish Crown. Those additionally classified as *infirm* and *handicapped* paid less tribute, or none at all. The few Spanish men who lived with *Arhuaco* women (at this point the four peoples of Sierra Nevada appear to have been named Arhuaco) were also subject to the tributary system, although their fee was half of that of Arhuaco men. This shows how the act of mixing with the indigenous populations implied the degradation of the hierarchical status of the Spanish. The children of these relationships, together with those Spaniards born of Spanish parents but on the soil of the colonized territories, were to highlight their mestizaje as the true race of the Americas and claim independence on these grounds.

INDEPENDENCE AND REPUBLICS

In the context of the making of the Republic throughout the nineteenth century, Sierra Nevada de Santa Marta had, once again, a marginal position in relation to the urban Creole[8] and Mestizo centers of Santa Marta, Riohacha, and Valledupar. To paraphrase Uribe, in this period the system of government and control of the indigenous population ceased to operate due to the larger political project of independence (achieved in 1819) and its consecutive wars. Consistent with the developments in the age of revolution in Latin America, the ethnic and racial origin of the indigenous peoples of the Sierra begins to be downplayed, as the Mestizo national identity is cultivated. For the indigenous peoples, this might indeed have mattered very little inasmuch as they were still an unrecognized, subhumanized *other* that needed to be civilized (read whitened) to become Mestizo. However, the investment in a Mestizo identity, and the ideas of racial equality discussed in that period, specifically meant that the tributary system no longer operated. Uribe additionally demonstrates that, in the census of the villages on the northern, north oriental, and oriental sides of the Sierra, the population no longer is divided in relation to their tributary status, and 'indigenous' and 'nonindigenous' are no longer used as categories in this sense.

In the mid-nineteenth century the relative quiet experienced in the Sierra was an effect of the Wars of Independence. When the wars began to end, waves of people came to the Sierra to 'organize, classify, discover, evangelize, civilize, discipline, experiment, study, and exploit' (Uribe 2000, 3.2). As in other parts of Latin America and the world, in the territories that came to be known as Colombia, the globalized localism of progress was an idea linked with a specific ethnicity: the Anglo-Saxon. Between 1850 and 1890, the Liberals in power instigated immigration of 'hard-working, civilized and entrepreneurial' Europeans (Uribe 2000, 3.2). In the new political order, the Province of Santa Marta was designated a sovereign state, the Sovereign State of Magdalena. As in other places, the local government did not hesitate to adopt legal and practical measures for immigration or, more precisely, the 'establishment of foreign colonies in the territory of the state' (Uribe 2000, 3.2).

It is possible to trace parallels between these efforts at colonizing and civilizing these territories through the immigration of Europeans, and the efforts involved in pacifying and colonizing the territories in the previous century by populating the lands with people brought from other regions, as was the case of the region of Boyacá where my father's family originates from—a locale in which colonization was subcontracted to Germans. Undoubtedly, both are known strategies of settler colonialism. According to Uribe, however, there is scant information about the efforts towards foreign colonization in the region of Sierra Nevada between 1850 and 1890. The available facts show that efforts to encourage immigration were not successful, and besides that, the State of Magdalena lacked the resources to continue with this endeavor. In 1871, the State of Magdalena legally relinquished the Sierra Nevada and the Serranía del Perijá (that borders to Venezuela) to the central administration of what was then called the United States of Colombia. However, the mission of the central state, which entailed civilizing, organizing, and adapting the territory for foreign colonization, also failed, and by the end of the nineteenth century, the 'political and spiritual' control of the territories of Sierra Nevada and Serranía de Perijá was relinquished once more to the Catholic missionaries (Uribe 2000, 3.2).

Among the devastating projects affecting the indigenous peoples in and around Sierra Nevada are the *orfelinatos* (orphanages). From 1910, the missionaries in the National Territories based their efforts on the concept that indigenous children, in order to become educated, acculturated, and civilized, must be removed from their families and cultural heritage. Uribe notes that the idea of the orphanages 'implied, of course, that the indigenous children were "orphaned" for not being Christian'. It also implied that the children were prevented from having contact with their parents and other adult members of their 'tribes', and were physically punished for speaking their own languages.[9] When the education in the orphanages met its objectives, all the indigenous people would become like the 'civilized', that is, 'they would cease to be "Indian"' (Uribe 2000, 3.2). The policies and practices of cultural annihilation and epistemicide in the orphanages meant that indigenous peoples not only learned to read and write (poorly), but were acculturated into 'proper' gender relations and roles (Uribe 2000, 3.2; Figueroa Pérez 2001). Missionaries annexed large pieces of land and started farms in which the children worked, instigating economic development, including the banana industry (Figueroa Pérez 2001; Peñaranda 2005). Missions also followed *blood dissolution* policies. The so-called orphans were married interethnically to gradually dissolve different ethnic groups through processes of whitening. The concept of blood dissolution spoke to the missionaries' ideas of culture and race—not to those of the subjugated. The peoples of Sierra Nevada, according to the Mamos, had always married interethnically, also with people outside the Sierra. Perhaps, like some Palestinians, the peoples of Sierra Nevada, faced with the perseverance of the colonizing project, did have more children and 'mixed' less with outsiders, as a means of resistance. The fact remains, however, that the orphanages had devastating effects upon the peoples of the Sierra to the extent that, among the Mamos, this recent period is referred to as the one having some of the most serious epistemicidal results.

SETTLERS

Waves of migration to the Sierra were constant in the twentieth century, a significant reason being displacements caused by the continuous war and genocide in the Republic of Colombia, as it has been called since 1886. The *colonos* (settlers) have exploited the indigenous people of Sierra throughout the last century in a relationship where, as Uribe suggests, the colonos have been the middlemen between the indigenous peoples and the regional powers. Some indigenous individuals collaborated in these exploitative relationships (Figueroa Pérez 2001); this is also an issue that the Mamos have broached in my conversations with them. The exploitation of indigenous groups, in addition to the theft of territory, has consisted of systems of debt hidden as salaried work; for example, by paying the indigenous laborer in advance with goods such as alcohol, cattle, cloth, and the like so that the indigenous laborer ends up being obligated to the settler (Uribe 2000, 4.1). Around the 1970s, the same period of time where the indigenous organizations in Sierra Nevada begin to consolidate, some of the colonos start to cultivate marijuana, and in the 1980s coca (Uribe 2000, 3.2, 4.1). As to many other indigenous peoples throughout Latin America, the coca plant—*ayu* or *ayo*—is a sacred plant to the peoples of Sierra Nevada, who use it in many different contexts. The violence involved in the exploitation of the ayo, to the Mother and to the peoples of the Sierra, is inestimable. Indeed, the abuse of ayo is yet another example of how violence against the indigenous peoples is concurrently symbolic, structural, physical, epistemic, economic, and political.

Laboratories for the preparation of cocaine emerged, and the Sierra was constituted as one of the main drug-trafficking routes. It is important to mention, in this context, that the emergence and effects of the drug trade in the Sierra is a localized globalism with deep colonial roots. When the younger brother found out how to make cocaine by using *ayo* and mixing it with chemicals in 1860, he was not only being aggressive to the Mother. He was also participating in a process of becoming of something fatal that would come to play a central role in the Colombian wars of the twentieth and twenty-first centuries. The younger brother's own prohibitions against the uses of this poison, aimed globally, have had distressing effects locally in the countries where it is produced, and in the regions where the plant is cultivated, processed, and sent on for consumption.

The change in crops in Sierra Nevada produced massive poverty and hunger among the colonos of Sierra Nevada and only a minority has gained any remuneration from the business of drug trade. Many colonos started to look more intensively for archaeological treasures to sell in order to survive (Uribe 2000, 3.2, 4.1). In the second half of the 1980s, however, the economies based on drug trade seemed to be partly dismantled and guerrilla groups entered the Sierra area, where they started to assume an organizing and regulating role. According to Uribe, in 2000, the Fuerzas Armadas Revolucionarias de Colombia (FARC—Colombian Revolutionary Armed Forces, the oldest guerrilla organization in the world) and Ejército de Liberación Nacional (National Liberation Army),

> attain their areas of influence in the occidental, south-oriental and north-oriental sides of the Sierra Nevada—that is, along the belt of the peasant settlements that circumscribe the indigenous reserves. Exempted from the control of the guerrillas is the peasant area of the northern side of the mountain, which corresponds, of course, with the area of influence of the drug-traffickers and their armed groups. (Uribe 2000, 4.1, translated from Spanish)

Government and paramilitary forces followed, and in the places where the warring forces collided, their presence has had destructive effects for the indigenous peoples and the colonos alike. As in many other parts of the country, people were forcefully recruited in these armies, some joined voluntarily, many were killed by them, many were displaced, and yet others silenced. Although persecution has not discriminated, the Mamos have been selected targets, and have had to withdraw inwards in the Sierra on several occasions in order to survive, or have had to leave the Sierra altogether for longer periods of time. Because of these dangers, Saúl Martínez has had to leave the Sierra. He lived in Santa Marta and Valledupar before going to Bogotá, where I met him in 2005. He returned to the Sierra in 2008, and lives now in Atánquez in Kankuamo territory.

POLITICAL ORGANIZATION

According to Astrid Ulloa (2004, 45), the first political organization among the peoples of Sierra Nevada happened in 1931 on the initiative of the Arhuaco, who formed the Liga Indígena de la Sierra Nevada (Indigenous League of Sierra Nevada) attached to the Federación de Trabajadores del Magdalena (Worker's Federation of Magdalena). In 1974, during the period of marijuana cultivation in Sierra Nevada, the Consejo y Organización Indígena Arhuaca (Arhuaco Indigenous Council and Organization, COIA) was formed with the aim to work on regaining control of the territory and to reclaim recognition and respect for their autonomy and culture. COIA became the Confederación Indígena Tayrona (CIT) in 1983. In 1987, the Organización Gonawindúa Tayrona (OGT)[10] was founded as a collaborative organization between the Kogi, Arhuaco, and Wiwa in order to interact effectively with the Colombian state institutions and provide better communication channels between these last and the Mamos, guaranteeing in this way the respect for the Law of Origin. With it, the Kogi, Arhuaco, and Wiwa authorities sought to emend a problem in the CIT, which did not work according to the Law of Origin. The OGT has been primarily based in the city of Santa Marta. Through the years, it has interacted in different ways with state institutions and national and international actors and NGOs, among them Alan Ereira. In the late 1980s and early 1990s, two more organizations emerged: the Organización Wiwa Yugumaiun Bunkwanarrwa Tayrona (OWYBT) and the Organización Indígena Kankuama (OIK) (Ulloa 2004, 48–50).

The Arhuaco, Wiwa, Kogi, and Kankuamo organizations are the links between the Mamos and state institutions. The representatives of these organizations towards the state are not Mamos, but elected *cabildos gobernadores*, who are to work closely with the Mamos and according to the Law of Origin. The collaboration between the four peoples is currently formally framed by these organizations. The Consejo Territorial de Cabildos (CTC) has allowed the consolidation of the four peoples' civic organization, among others, by obtaining the formal legalization of part of their ancestral territories. As Natalia Giraldo Jaramillo (2010) points out, the civic authorities emerge due to the need to establish effective channels of communication and negotiation with external institutions, and in many ways their organizational structure 'obeys the hierarchization found in western organizations, using juridical figures such as a general assembly, central directive board, cabildo gobernador, general secretary' (Giraldo Jaramillo 2010, 188). The civic authorities, however, are to operate in close connection with the Mamos, who are also organized in the Council of Mamos. The Council of Mamos is pivotal to guaranteeing proper readings and interpretations of the Law of Origin, as the Mamos possess expertise in this regard. The role of the Council of Mamos is not only to avoid single Mamos' abuse of their position of authority as interpreters of the law, it is fundamental to the equilibrium of the Mother. This equilibrium requires the four peoples' engagement and collaboration with each other and, as explained with the metaphor of the table, the Council of Mamos is the organizational consequence of this intimate interdependence among the four peoples and the Mother.

The political organization of the four peoples of the Sierra needs to be viewed within the framework of the offensive struggles. In a concrete (western) sense, they start to coordinate politically in the 1970s and 1980s.[11] As Ulloa (2004) demonstrates, their organizations have experienced many transformations, displaying a significant degree of adaptability to the different legal frameworks within which they have had to act and defend their territories and also showing their respect for the Law of Origin. Furthermore, not only the legal parameters have been changing; their political demands

> are the consequence of loss of territory . . . due to contact during conquest in the XVI century, the inflow of waves of colonization by the end of the XIX century and the beginning of the XX; to the processes of evangelization and the marijuana bonanza in the decade of the 1970s; to the coca boom in the decade of the 1980s; and to the current presence of paramilitaries, military and guerrilla groups. (Ulloa 2004, 47–48)

Additionally, conditions for the four peoples of the Sierra Nevada are framed by institutional logics imposed over the territories, such as the creation of the Tayrona National Park in 1964, the Sierra Nevada de Santa Marta park in 1975, and of course the three departmental and sixteen municipal borders that involve the territory (Ulloa 2010, 82). All these historical developments must be seen in terms of a global perspective, so as not to lose sight of the ways in which global expressions of hegemonic power come into play in specific localities, and the means by which the offensive struggles open fissures in hegemonic power.

An example of one of these breaches has been the continuous negotiations in relation to the Sustainable Development Plan (Plan de Desarrollo Sostenible) proposed by governmental authorities in the 1990s.[12] The plan highlights the centrality of the role of the Arhuaco, Kankuamo, Kogi, and Wiwa in the territorial and environmental management of the Sierra Nevada de Santa Marta, emphasizing in this way the validity and importance of their knowledge and autonomy. After approximately ten years of work around the plan, the four peoples of the Sierra suspended it due to inconsistency and lack of dialogue from governmental authorities, and decided instead to initiate an autonomous plan. The Sustainable Development Plan, and the yearlong debates around it, are excellent markers of the ways in which more subtle power struggles occur. However, as was the case with the Sustainable Development Plan, there is a great distance between that which is stated in print and the practices that accompany these kinds of projects. Additionally, the most common character of development projects continues being classic, environmentally devastating imposed projects that obey the interests of transnational corporations and capitalism.

In Colombia, these plans continue to be executed, overruling the legally established criterion of having the consent of the peoples in whose territory the schemes will occur, as stated in Colombia's 1991 constitution with criteria referring to economic development and the interests of the nation. The levels of violence that these projects entail are extremely high. Indeed, the policies of Colombian governments that, since the 1990s, have involved the economic opportunities for international investment have been enforced by the strong militarization of the areas of interest to international corporations. Almost 30 percent of the armed forces have been allocated to protect the corporations, often in direct war with the local populations. According to international observers, 'the regions which are rich in resources are the source of 82% of human rights and international humanitarian law violations, 83% of the killing of union leaders, and 87% of forced displacements' (Massé and Camargo 2012). The Sierra Nevada de Santa Marta is a territory rich in resources, and there is no reason to believe that it will not continue being target of these practices. The recent (2014) approval of fracking in Colombia, and its devastating effects on the Mother, should not be underestimated either.

There is also the consideration that the different policies and interventions that have been waged in the Sierra against the four peoples have, as one of their effects, the generation of double consciousness among many of them. In many respects, one can argue that there is a specific interest by the elites in the perpetuation of these internal conflicts among the indigenous peoples. As Figueroa contends, the contemporary process of '*reethnization*' of the Kankuamo 'signals the paradoxical behavior of the state that, in its search for legitimacy, visibilizes social actors while, at the same time, promotes new regional conflicts through the advancement of policies such as the "sanitation of reserves" which renders illegitimate the presence of "settlers" or "peasants" [in these areas]' (Figueroa Pérez 2001, 193, translated from Spanish). As we will see in chapter 6, however, the problem is more involved than Figueroa's detailing of it, when considering the ideas of the Mamos, the relationship between the offensive and the defensive struggles, and the difficulties of double consciousness.

TOWARDS DIS-COVERY

In the Mamosean philosophy, we are all sons and daughters of the Mother. Although among us there are people who act in bad faith and lack consideration for the Law of Origin, according to the Mamos no one can be rejected. As Saúl Martínez expressed it during a telephone conversation in October 2009, 'The sun does not shine only upon some people, it shines upon everyone without considerations about who they are.' When talking about my research with my Colombian peers, I have sometimes been asked what I think of the four peoples' reference to the little sibling being like a cockroach. While I have never heard this analogy used among the people from the Sierra with whom I have talked, it can be used to illustrate some of the problems of communication imbued with racism of the younger siblings towards the older ones. To the younger sibling, being compared to a cockroach is a terrible insult, and one might conclude that this analogy proves that the four peoples do not regard us as human (insomuch as they liken us to an insect). However, I suggest that this analogy, if used, does not imply that the younger siblings are classified as subhuman or nonhuman.

The principles of categorization that the Mamos employ between that which is human and the other beings is radically different from taxonomies that we, the younger siblings, employ. In this sense, if they indeed use the notion of a cockroach to refer to us, they are most probably using it as a means to describe our predatory (consumerist) tendencies, and our tenacity in the practice and defense of the death project. Seen against the background of the historical overview presented in this chapter, the analogy is perhaps unsurprising. But there is more to be said about this. Disregarding the issue of talking about the disrespectful and exploitative younger sibling or the cockroach analogy, both notions contain a powerful point, which has also been anticipated by Aimé Césaire when urging us to first study 'how colonization works to decivilize the colonizer, to brutalize him in the true sense of the word, to degrade him, to awaken him to buried instincts, to covetousness, violence, race hatred, and moral relativism' (Césaire 2000, 35). There are a number of key elements to understanding what occurred when the younger brother arrived in the land of the peoples of Sierra Nevada de Santa Marta. As the Spanish initially *covered over the other* (covering over understood in the Dusselian sense), the peoples of the colonized continent may have done something similar—and this is matter for discussion. It may be that the Teyuna have *re-cognized* in the invaders the younger brother, that careless and disrespectful human being beloved of, and spoiled by, the Mother. In this context, I use *re-cognition* taking into account the distinction found in the Danish language between *genkendelse*, which involves prior knowledge of someone or something, and *anerkendelse*, which may involve the first but requires acknowledgment and respect. In the sense used in this specific context, I refer to re-cognition as simply previous knowledge of the existence of the other.

Although theoretically the re-cognition of the Teyuna of the younger brother can be similar to the implicit re-cognition in the covering over as Indian of the Spanish, the re-cognition of the Teyuna cannot be understood as a simple covering over. This is not possible because the power relations between the Spanish and Teyuna were unequal in terms of technologies in relation to the extinction of the *other*. It is also impossible because the world-view of the Teyuna—to the extent that we can assume, as I do, that it has fundamental similarities to that of the Mamos and the four peoples of Sierra Nevada in the twenty-first century—does not permit this covering over. Mamosean philosophy contains a central component, which assumes that difference is essential to life. This component is shared with other indigenous peoples, and is by academics often translated into the principle of *equality in difference* and *pluriversality*. However, to simply state that indigenous peoples operate with these principles is also an act of covering over. The translation implies a generalization that in and by itself obliterates the plurality it seems to describe. This is why dis-covery, as employed by Martínez, is essential.

NOTES

1. Among the scholars are Bocarejo Sueseún (2002), Figueroa Pérez (2001), Langebaek (2007), Peñaranda (2005), Pumarejo and Morales (2003), Pineda Comacho (2000), Reichel-Dolmatoff (1961), Rodríguez and Busintana (2007), Sánchez Mojica (2008), Ulloa (2004), and Uribe (2000).

2. Encubrimiento is, in the English version of the book (Dussel 1995), translated as *covering over*. I use *covering over* and *concealment* interchangeably when speaking about encubrimiento.

3. DuBois (1903, 4): 'Then it dawned upon me with a certain suddenness that I was different from the others; or like, mayhap, in heart and life and longing, but shut out from their world by a vast veil.'

4. http://www.tairona.org/pueblos.html. Accessed in July 2009. Webpage for Organización Gonawindúa Tayrona, the organ of communication of three of the four indigenous peoples of Sierra Nevada: Kogi, Arhuaco, and Wiwa. Cuatro Etnias (1999).

5. As Dussel (2008, 120n78) notes, the cross has symbolized the four cardinal points to many Amerindian peoples, which, like in 'the far Orient', are also holy to the Mamos. The sign of the cross, which is used among Christians, can, according to Mamo Martínez, also be used among the four peoples, signifying each of the four elements—earth, fire, wind, and water.

6. Piracy is undoubtedly significant in the context of global history and the national and international order. Piracy connects to the use of nonstate (or nonofficial) violence, to the configuration of the global economy, and also connects to the distinction between moral and immoral, legality and illegality, and to contemporary drug production and trade. For an introduction to piracy in the Caribbean, see Zambrano (2007).

7. The encomienda system was a technology of settler colonialism. It functioned as land grants, provided by the Crown to specific colonizers. The lands included the peoples living there, who had to pay mandatory tributes to the colonizers. In return, the colonized were to be instructed in the Spanish language and the Catholic faith, and to receive so-called protection.

8. Creoles were people of Spanish and Portuguese descent born in the colonies, and second to Europeans in the social/racial hierarchy.

9. Indeed, the life story of Mamo Ramón Gil refers to these issues (Peñaranda 2005). Mamo Arwa Wiku (Arhuaco) equally refers to the *orfelinatos* as 'closed prisons'. See 'Entrevista con el mamo arhuaco Arwa Wiku' at http://nasdat.com/index.php?topic = 145-9.0;wap2. Accessed April 2010. Note that a similar practice took place in Australia between approximately the 1920s and the 1970s. (The children taken are known as the Stolen Generations.)

10. See also Gonawindúa at http://www.corazondelmundo.co/?q = node/64. Accessed July 2014.

11. For a historical overview of these organizational processes, see Ulloa (2004). For a more general and legally oriented overview of indigenous organizational processes and struggles in Colombia, especially in the 1990s, see Laurent (2005).

12. See Ulloa (2004) for an excellent overview of the most significant developments in the context of the Sustainable Development Plan. In addition, Ulloa's study is interesting in its examination of the ways in which power is challenged or reinforced in the context of the interrelationship between ecological movements and the indigenous peoples. See also Ulloa (2010).

Chapter Three

Race, Rights and Development

The colonial notion of *race* is an anthropocentric principle of categorization. This notion emerges concomitantly with the categories *human* and *nature*, and as such race also lies at the heart of the dominant notions of both human rights and development. These colonial categories are, notwithstanding, taken to be ontological truisms that are very rarely questioned. As we will see in this chapter and the next, however, a decolonial historical realism allows the demonstration of the particularity of these ideas, as well as the ways in which they are coupled to coloniality and the death project. As the entwinement between racism, capitalism, patriarchy, and the depredations of nature, coloniality works through dualistic categories such as human-nature, mind-body, reason-emotion, tradition-modernity, man-woman and secular-spiritual. These dualistic categories must not only be seen in combination, but also as the products of processes of domination heralded by specific agents in concrete historical contexts so as not to lose sight of the ways in which they organize the world into ontological truisms attached to coloniality. As the political undertaking attached to coloniality, the death project is the exercise of the power of whiteness, including its capacity to dispose over life and death as these are defined and hierarchized from within its colonial ontology.

The central contours of the death project were established in the context of six processes of extermination historically simultaneous to the rise of Europe as global imperial power: 'in a period of ten years the witch hunts had begun, the last Muslim stronghold in Western Europe had been captured, the largest expulsion of Jews from Christian soil had been accomplished, colonial penetration of America was well under way and the African slave trade was established' (Wright 2001, 59), and legal measures to expel Roma populations had been inaugurated (Motos Pérez 2009).[1] These six historical moments are pivotal to the configuration of coloniality in two ways: on the one hand, they were constitutive of whiteness and its institutions (Fanon's *zone of being*)

51

and, by this, they also created the realities and places of enunciation of those they sought to erase. In other words, they were constitutive of race. On the other hand, in the context of these genocides, the technologies of the death project were developed in tandem with the creation of narratives of homogeneity and belonging that were to territorially dis-place and/or re-place peoples not only from their lands, but from history and knowledge production. They were also to detach the very territories from their freedom. Among these death technologies is the law. In other words, the processes of extermination mentioned above were intimately connected to the development of law including legislature, judiciary, and its other instruments as we know it today. All had pivotal ontological effects; they generated a reality that established the zone of nonbeing. These processes of extermination were processes where whiteness started to emerge as overdetermination and overrepresentation, as the display of a specific form of hegemonic power, namely, colonial power. In this overrepresentation and overdetermination lies not only law, but also the very notion of development, including its corresponding temporality.

Concretely, in this chapter we explore how the idea of race that emerged in the sixteenth century proved pivotal to the ideas of Rights of People in conjunction with an early version of the idea of development. By including the period of the first modernity, and thereby taking into account the role that the Spanish empire, Latin America, and the Caribbean played in this concern, we are better positioned to examine the establishment of human rights and development. The analysis of the early history of the globalized localisms of (emerging) human rights and development suggests that they are elaborated in the context of the *defense* of the emerging death project. In overall terms, this chapter as well as the next are engaged with a decolonial historical realism that allows us to approach a nuanced understanding of the ways in which human rights and development are embedded in the struggles that were catalyzed by the violence of colonialism. I do not offer a historical revision of the last five hundred years. Rather, I present some of the profound implications that a shift in the temporality of reason entails.

Consistent with the effort to shift the temporality of reason and the call for a decolonial historical realism, this chapter presents the history of human rights and development mostly as it has been conceptualized by my people, so to speak, especially those among the Mestizo population, who have engaged in thinking through the decolonial perspective. But it also examines the interconnections between Europe and the Americas as these emerged as a result of colonial processes taking place from 1492. This is consequently another layer of the entangled histories of globalization and localization, of dominance and colonialism that looks into a different level of localization and coloniality than that presented in the previous chapter. From the region of the Sierra Nevada de Santa Marta, we direct our focus to the region of Latin America with a specific interest in Colombia. The Mamos remain, however, present in this chapter and the next through their assertion that human rights and development are not new ideas and practices, and their insistence that they cannot be understood apart from one another. It is thanks to the Mamos, and not to my own people, that I undertook this investigation into the common histories of human rights and development. Interestingly, there are shared elements in the historical analyses of the Mamos and those of decolonial scholars. As we open up this level of history, however, we also approach a more nuanced understanding of how, indeed, the resistance of some, in this case the Creole and Mestizos, continues the oppression of others—the indigenous and African populations in the Americas. Indeed, they could be viewed as obverse sides of the same coin.

SIX PROCESSES OF EXTERMINATION

The problems related to human rights have been analyzed predominantly in relation to their links to coloniality, their Eurocentric character, and the geopolitical workings of these in their current institutionalized forms.[2] The Mestizo decolonial perspective has mainly centered on studying what happened to the Christian Spanish elites' theocentric organizing principle when it was brought to the Americas and transformed to a racist hierarchization principle in the encounter with the indigenous populations (Lander 2000; Mignolo 2000). Other scholars, however, have underlined the importance of looking more in depth into how the proto-racist and proto-national discourse that came with the Christian Spanish elites to the Americas was transformed by the genocidal events in the latter continent, returned to Europe, contributing to its rise and hence also to the configuration of the hegemonic global power relations that are still with us today (Santiago-Valles 2003; Wynter 2003). Walter Mignolo, building upon already existing studies that suggest the 'interrelated histories of modernity/coloniality', explored the following connections:

(a) the conceptual re-configuration of previous mutual conceptualizations between Christians, Moors and Jews; (b) the new configuration between Christians, Indians and Blacks in the New World; (c) the interrelations between (a) and (b); and—last but not least—(d) the translation of race into racism that took place in the sixteenth century that was (and still is) strictly related to the historical foundation of capitalism. (Mignolo 2006, 18)[3]

Shelley Wright (2001) and Silvia Federici (2010), among others, similarly explore the historical interconnectedness of different colonial pasts and presents, adding the dimension of gender to their analyses by taking into account the witch hunts, a dimension also contemplated by Ramón Grosfoguel (2013). Although a thorough discussion and analysis of the differences and similarities between these sources remains yet to be done, these explorations point towards my reading that the historical interrelations between the witch hunts, the end of Al-Andalus, the conquest of the Americas, and the transatlantic slave trade are highly significant contextual elements to the shaping of the death project, and with it, the ideas of human rights and development.[4] The lack of consideration about the genocidal practices aimed specifically at the eradication of Roma populations within those same 150 years is, however, saliently absent (Fernández Garcés et al. n.d.), as is the lack of attention to the extermination of the Mother through these processes.

Malleus Maleficarum (*The Hammer of the Witches*) was first published in 1486 and became the basis for later investigations attached to the witch hunts. It is crucial to dwell on this document for a moment and highlight that the text ties women to witchcraft, sorcery, and the Devil (Wright 2001, 51)—and that in this misogynist process, women who were not (proper) Christians, who carried alternative knowledges and spiritualities, were targeted. Dualisms as mind-body and human-nature were already in operation, organizing the logic that come to underlie the depradations of nature. *Malleus Maleficarum* can also be seen as a precursor to the processes of indigenization that entailed racialization and feminization, which was to become evident in the context of the conquest of the Americas. Additionally, it is important to note that 'the treatise was widely publicised through the new technology of printing and laws prohibiting witchcraft were enacted throughout Europe beginning in France (1490), the Hapsburg empire, England, Scotland, Russia and Denmark' (Wright 2001, 51). The role of *Malleus Maleficarum* and of the legal documents that followed in its wake is important because it gives force to the argument that the feminization of the colonized other is not a consequence, but a point of departure, of coloniality (Ochoa Muñoz 2014, 110). The European institutionalized misogyny is central to the configuration of racism, and is neither external nor sequential to it. Significantly, it produces legal, political, and physical death.

Within the same period the witch hunts were spreading across Europe, the events that led to the final conquest of Al-Andalus took place. While the power logic in play in Al-Andalus allowed for the coexistence of multiple identities and spiritualities within one form of political authority, the expulsion of the Jews and the conquest of Al-Andalus by the Spanish Christian monarchs in 1492 must be seen as the imposition of a correlation between one identity, one political authority, and one religion (González Ferrín 2006).

This imposition must be considered from within the context of the spread of the misogynist practices mentioned earlier. Here, we find the beginning of the notion of the nation-state as a proto-racist and patriarchal discourse, as well as providing the limited frameworks that hamper any understanding of spirituality in the minds of secular westernized subjects until our time, which also influence the inability to pay attention to the Mother. The expulsion of Jews from Christian territories materialized with the *Decreto de Granada*, expedited on 31 March 1492. Months earlier, on 2 January 1492, the conquest of Al-Andalus at the hands of the Catholic Crown reached its culminating point. These processes produced the idea of purity of blood in conjunction with a specific way of conceiving spirituality (the idea of the 'pure' Christian) through which human beings were hierarchized theocentrically (Wynter 2003), and the dominating Christians hierarchized the spiritual, granting ontological status only to their own interpretation of the Christian deity. Together with the genocidal practices against the Roma people (since 1499) that applied criteria of sedentariness, productivity, and servitude (Fernández Garcés et al. n.d.), these intra-Iberian processes of extermination influenced other emerging European empires and were further developed and adapted to the domination of other peoples. With the conquest of the Americas, which was initiated with Columbus's travels in October 1492, the criteria of hierarchization of purity of blood-spirituality, sedentariness, and servitude combined with the ideas of the human as property-owning man who is an entity separate from nature. There is no reason to doubt that people who were sent to conquer the territories we now refer to as the Americas shared the theocentric imaginary that was used to legitimize the genocides against the Semites in the conquest of Al-Andalus. This is the imaginary by which it made sense to the Spanish elites to engage in philosophical discussions concerning whether the indigenous populations in the Americas were human—they had, in the eyes of the Christian conquerors, no god. We will discuss these issues in more detail in the remaining parts of this chapter, where we will also see how, as Maldonado-Torres (2007) has noted, in this moment in history we find the emergence of the doubt about the humanity of others, which is at the basis of the colonial attitude that grounds racism. As Ramón Grosfoguel (2013) states, with the conquest of the Americas, the doubt no longer concerned whether people were praying to the right or the wrong god. Now, their humanity as such was considered questionable. In relation to this way of thinking, and according to the interests that were in play with the colonization inside the Iberian Peninsula as well as in the territories across the Atlantic, several new criteria were added to the definition of who was a human being. The aggressive persecution of two categories of people, the 'Semites' (Muslims and Jews) and the 'Gypsies', starting from 1499 add further dimensions to this discussion. In 1499, the Catholic Crown signed the first 'anti-Gypsy law', a legal document that required the Roma become sedentary and economically productive, predominantly through agriculture (Motos Pérez 2009). The last royal 'anti-Gypsy law' was issued in 1788.

The first legal documents targeting the Roma population are tied to the normativity of the emerging capitalist system. Inspired by Foucault and Agamben, Isaac Motos Pérez suggests that the first 'anti-Gypsy law' semanticizes the sociocultural organization of the Roma as criminal; it is both a death sentence and a way of forcing people into a specific way of life. Inasmuch as it includes strategies of discipline and regulation, the law is biopolitical. However, because the Roma population is only included in the law in terms of their exclusion and the negation of their existence, it cannot be situated within the framework of the norm but rather in the framework of exception, as the Agambean *Homo Sacer* (Motos Pérez 2009, 69–73). By contrast, and consistent with the conceptualization of the death project, my point is that the negation of existence is the framework of the norm and of law. The directive shows that the developments surrounding the Catholic Crown's imposition of a correlation between one identity, one political authority, and one religion was concomitant with the imposition of a specific way of life harmonious with the productivist logic. This observation is evidenced by there being within this period a reorganization of the monetary system on the part of the Spanish monarchs (de Francisco Olmos n.d.). Significant to the processes of extermination of the Semites is the first law for the forced conversion of the *moriscos* (Moors) of 1502 (Fernández Garcés et al. n.d.). In this stage, the discourse against the Semites changed—now they were not people who prayed to an inferiorized god, but 'subjects without souls', that is, not human. The category *human* had already impacted the genocidal practices in Europe, and had as one of its effects that the enslavement of the Semites, most of who had converted by force, significantly increased. This resulted in many rebellions until, in 1609, the converted Semites—mostly converted Muslims—were expelled. Conversion was no longer an option—now they were not classified as humans to begin with (Grosfoguel 2013). The idea of purity of blood had acquired new dimensions, inasmuch as the Semites who converted were now subject to a biopolitics—the principle of purity of blood—that doubted the authenticity of their conversion (Wynter 2003).

The establishment of the transatlantic slave trade naturalized the colonial criteria of inferiority, linking racism and capitalism. In other words, racism became the foundation for the logic of capital and exploitation of labor, and, as we will see in the next chapter, years later this reasoning also underlined the rationale behind the elites' decision to abolish slavery (Mignolo 2000; Suárez-Krabbe 2013b). In the Caribbean, the extermination of the indigenous populations was almost comprehensive. This annihilation preceded the acknowledgment of the Indians' humanity and came at the expense of the different populations in Africa—who were then brought to the Americas to replace the former as workforce. Africa was also subject to the overall racial logic of power, and indeed came to be constructed as the continent without history. The genocide of the enslaved Africans proceeded from an imperial certainty about the Africans not being human at all (Wright 2001, 46–61) and to engage in discussions about their humanity was not even an option. The enslaved African populations were constructed as people who were unproductive in any areas, but whose *raison d'être* was to be subjected to exploitation and violence. Hence, being enslaved became rationalized as a natural attribute of theirs, more so than an actual condition of oppression (they were slaves, not enslaved persons). This adds yet another dimension to the racist discourse, and affects all the subjects who are now being rendered inferior. Now, all racialized subjects are subjected to exploitation and violence, and not to emancipation and regulation (Santos 2007). In this sense, they are subjected to necropolitics. This condition remains true also after the formal abolition of slavery in the eighteenth century. As Wynter (2003, 297) has noted, the establishment of the transatlantic slave trade 'provides a model for the invention of a by-nature difference between "natural masters" and "natural slaves"'. In other words, with the transatlantic slave trade the conditions by which the *other's* inferiority is naturalized are used as the legitimation to continue oppression.

The death project was applied to *other* knowledges and ways of being in the world that existed among large segments of the populations of Europe, the Americas, and Africa, including their relationship to territory and other spiritual and natural beings. Besides women, the targets of these practices inside Europe were Muslims, Roma, and Jews. The gender dimension of genocide became essential in relation to the white normative dimension of the definition of gender in which the modern western family came into being:

[T]he contraction of this new type of family (from the sixteenth to the nineteenth centuries) from its former and extended-family modalities, and its ability to recede as a purely economic unit were both materially enabled by (a) the coerced labor of wage workers and peasants in Europe; (b) the colonial surpluses being extracted from colonized labor (slave, peon, and/or—historically to a lesser extent—wage based) in the plantations and mines of the Americas; and (c) by how the latter forms of labor (i.e., 'b') became the conditions of possibility for the enterprises mobilizing the former types of labor (i.e., 'a') by providing raw materials, markets, investment capital, and models for deploying, organizing, and disciplining labor. (Santiago-Valles 2003, 61–62)

As we know, these processes have come to play an important role in the ways in which white ideas about equal gender relations are used to legitimize contemporary racist practices inside Europe, and genocidal practices outside Europe. The discourses that try to save brown women from brown men are salient, as are the racist practices of the white feminists inside Europe (Leets Hansen 2011).

THE CROWN, THE CONQUEROR, AND THE CHURCH

Fifty years after Columbus's arrival in the Americas, the different criteria that had been created in the six processes of extermination combine to form the idea of race, that is, they combine to form the category of the human. This is evident in the Valladolid debates that took place approximately between 1550 and 1551, and centred on the question about the humanity of the indigenous peoples where the discussions pertained to criteria for rationality, private property, nearness to nature, religion, and economic organization. Indeed, the above recounting of the processes of extermination that took place in this early point in the history of coloniality provides the necessary contextual elements to understand how the law is tightly connected to the legitimation and exercise of appropriation and violence to the benefit of the colonizer; the death project in its historical connection to development through race, in the period of the first modernity. In the remaining parts of this chapter, I concentrate on the ideas of the time, as it is important to understand this connection without leaving its context aside. Among those who consider the significance of period of the first modernity to human rights thought many argue that the Dominican friar Bartolomé de Las Casas, his colleague Francisco de Vitoria, or both of these men are the precursors of international human rights thinking (Carozza 2003; Maestre Sánchez 2004; Rubio Angulo 1979). In a concrete sense, they are right. Anthony Anghie (1996, 2004) and Daniel Castro (2007) validate this argument. They also demonstrate how these ideas were imbued in the legitimation and justification of imperialism; they developed in tandem with the continued execution of the death project. The role of Las Casas and Vitoria in Latin American history is frequently debated. Positions that emphasize the discourse of these thinkers and almost sanctify them, as well as positions that totally condemn them, abound. It is not my intention to wade through these positions. Las Casas's thought, especially, has been an important element in the context of the legitimation of independence struggles in Latin America (Carozza 2003; Guardiola-Rivera 2010), and has been significant in human rights environments, as well as to liberation theologies. Las

Casas's legacy is telling within the context of subsequent struggles against colonialism and global inequalities, predominantly those of the Latin American elites. This legacy is important in illustrating the trickster status of Mestizo identity, which principally stays within the logic and institution of whiteness. *Indigenismo* is central in this context. Indigenismo is an expression of *mestizaje*; it is a position that exercises whiteness in the name of the defense of the indigenous populations. It can be traced back to the early decades of colonization of the Americas, and has involved study of the indigenous peoples, defense of their rights, and valorization of their cultures at the same time it has exercised the power to define them as peoples, and to determine their 'political' projects (Huinca Piutrín 2013, 110–14). Indigenism is closely interlinked with what Herson Huinca Puitrín calls *simpaticismo criollo* (Creole sympathism). To paraphrase Huinca Piutrín, Creole sympathism has tried to break the colonial relationship between colonizers and colonized by intending to be sympathetic with that which it classifies as 'indigenous' or 'indigenous people'. While Creole sympathism is an attitude where researchers position themselves as people who try to understand the colonized without having experienced the traumas imposed on colonized peoples, the situatedness of the Creole sympathizer will unveil her colonial character, and she will be seen as a colonizer by those who have been subjected colonization, no matter how sympathetic she otherwise appears to be (Huinca Piutrín 2013, 110–11). Las Casas's thought needs to be understood from within the framework of Creole sympathism and indigenismo; indeed, as an early expression of these. Ironically, Las Casas's thought is also often mentioned as being the main source of the construction of the Black Legend, whereby the Spanish empire was depicted as being brutal and inhuman— implying, of course, that Las Casas was lying and unjustly attacking the Spanish empire.

Sylvia Wynter, one of a number of commentators, argued that it was predominantly in the realm of ethics and law that 'Man's' ontological nature was debated in the sixteenth century (Wynter 2003; Maldonado-Torres 2007; Mignolo 2000, 2009; Rubio Angulo 1979). It was in ethics and law that the idea of racial-gendered difference as ontological gained currency. The Valladolid debates between Ginés de Sepúlveda and Las Casas during 1550 and 1551 are illustrative of the ways in which the rights of people are part and parcel of the legitimation of war. While Sepúlveda's thoughts spoke of a hierarchical order between humans based on the allocation of degrees of rational capacity to different races, those of Las Casas are founded on the notion of spiritual perfection (Wynter 2003). Both sets of ideas concern how Spanish presence in the colonies should be enacted, and not with whether Spanish invasion and colonization in itself was legitimate. Hans Joachim König's characterization of the different hegemonic positions during conquest and colonization proves useful in broadly presenting these discussions. Taking into account recent scholarship relating to this subject,[5] I maintain it is through the eventual convergence of the positions of the Spanish Crown, the Conqueror, and the Church (König 1998, 13–14) that we obtain grounds for human rights and development as the globalized localisms that currently exist. In other words, some fifty years after conquest, the complete ontological and epistemological foundations are established for human rights and development. König's characterization also allows us to see how the elites of the time (for example the three hegemonic positions) did not necessarily constitute a homogeneous group. In the 1500s, they could be considered emerging global elites. They were transatlantic because their ideas were oriented to and emerged from Spain/Europe and the Americas,[6] and they were elites because their power was intrinsic to the exercise of violence in the continent, including their appropriation of lands and goods—that is, the accumulation of capital (König 1998; Quijano 2000a, b).

In brief, the Crown's interest was to preserve and take care of the indigenous populations. This position was partly due to theologically based humanist considerations, understanding these last from within the context of the human as a colonial category. It was also founded on the recognition that the Crown regarded the population as part of the value of the conquered territories, and that it depended upon the exploitation of the *Indians'* labor in order to receive tributes. The logic of the Crown was, as we have already seen in relation to the Roma populations in the Iberian Peninsula, predominantly productivist: economic growth was a 'rational and unquestionable objective' (Santos 2005, 162). While the Church did not call into question the notion of Euro-Christian superiority, at least in some of its expressions, it argued that the Indians were intelligent beings able to *develop* into good Christians. By contrast, at the core of the conquest of Al-Andalus in Spain, known as the *Reconquista* (it reached its zenith in 1492), there was a defense of an excluding and hostile Christianity. As we noted previously, during the conquest of Al-Andalus, this hostile Christianity was predominantly anti-Semitic; that is, it acted especially against Jews and Muslims. Whereas this hostile Christianity was also a factor in the conquered lands across the Atlantic, there were also members of the Church, and mainly those from the Dominican and Jesuit orders, who propagated a friendlier, more *sympathetic* version of Christianity. Las Casas represents this latter version.

Missionaries were concerned that the practices of the conquistadors and colonizers towards the indigenous peoples could result in extermination and that the conquistadors and colonizers otherwise obstructed the evangelizing mission of the Church (König 1998, 15; Castro 2007). The position of the Church included, with respect to the Americas, a hierarchy of knowledge and spirituality (Christian superiority), linear temporality (either the indigenous peoples represent an innocent Edenic past, or they can become good Christians), and a logic of social classification (they are Christian *in potentia*) (Fernández Herrero 1992; Rubio Angulo 1979; Serrano Gassent 2002). Finally, the position of the colonizers and conquerors was predicated on the desire for the rapid enrichment and access to power; productivist logic also used by the Crown. Rapid wealth production and access to power depended directly on the exploitation and/or eradication of native populations. The colonizer's and conqueror's viewpoint was that the indigenous populations were born for enslavement because of their supposedly wild customs and intellectual weakness—the social classification based on a linear temporality here clearly combines with feminization. Karina Muñoz Ochoa (2014, 106) distinguishes between infantilization and feminization indicating how the condition of being an infant is transitory; whereas the condition of being a woman is permanent inasmuch as women 'remain tied to the "protection"/dependency to the male/adult, now in his quality as a husband.' Within this distinction, she contends that in all the positions present within the debates concerning the status of the indigenous populations in the Americas, feminization was in play. However, as we will see, if feminization is solely defined in contradistinction with infantilization, this is not the case; rather, feminization needs to be understood as a way in which notions of peoples' closeness to *nature*, including their *other* spiritualities and knowledges, interlink with ideas regarding *development* or *perfection*.

THE QUESTION OF WAR

With the previous section providing necessary background, a brief examination of the elements of the international debates on the status of the indigenous peoples in the conquered territories as expressed in the Valladolid debates of the 1550s is apposite.[7] These debates must be read not so much as an exploration of the quality of being human than as a process of categorization closely connected to the question of war whereby the qualities regarded as essential to the being-ness of the Spanish Church, the conquerors, and the Crown are formulated as the criteria to define the lesser humanity of others, and thereby legitimizes the practices of the death project. In the context of these debates, the idea of the human being emerges as a category that does not capture the humanity of all human beings but which, instead, dehumanizes all those who are not constituted as Christian, European, property-owning, productive, and masculine. Included in this imaginary is the modern/colonial notion of nature. Besides these processes of categorization, rights are made to the benefit of the colonizer and his efforts to dominate all others. According to Sepúlveda's position, the indigenous peoples were subhuman others who had to comply with more *advanced* peoples and their laws. If war was required to meet these aims, then war had to be waged. Sepúlveda, who never visited the Americas, expressed his thinking in the following terms:

> But see how they deceive themselves, and how much I dissent from such an opinion, seeing, on the contrary, in these very institutions a proof of the crudity, the barbarity, and the natural Slavery of these people; for having houses and some rational way of life and some sort of commerce is a thing which the necessities of nature itself induce, and only serves to prove that they are not bears or monkeys and are not totally lacking in reason. But on the other hand, they have established their nation in such a way that *no one possesses anything individually, neither a house nor a field, which he can leave to his heirs in his will,* for everything belongs to their Masters whom, with improper nomenclature, they call kings, and by whose whims they live, more than by their own, ready to do the bidding and desire of these rulers and *possessing no liberty.* And the fulfillment of all this, not under the pressure of arms but in a voluntary and spontaneous way, is a definite sign of the service and base soul of these barbarians. They have distributed the land in such a way that they themselves cultivate the royal and public holdings, one part belonging to the king, another to public feasts and sacrifices, with only a third reserved for their own advantage, and all this is done in such a way that they live as employees of the king, paying, thanks to him, exceedingly high taxes. . . . And if this type of servile and barbarous nation had not been to their liking and nature, it would have been easy for them, as it was not a hereditary monarchy, to take advantage of the death of a king in order to obtain a freer state and one more favorable to their interests; by not doing so, they have stated quite clearly that they have been *born to slavery and not to civic and liberal life.* Therefore, if you wish to reduce them, I do not say to our domination, but to a servitude a little less harsh, it will not be difficult for them to change their masters, and instead of the ones they had, who were barbarous and impious and inhuman, to accept the Christians, cultivators of human virtues and the true faith. (Sepúlveda 1996, 109-113)[8]

Note that a criterion for establishing the degrees of humanity that Sepúlveda's text presents is that of the ownership of private property, implying sedentariness and the negation of the territory. Additionally, the indigenous peoples' method of government is erroneous, and the peoples servile and unfree because they do not revolt in spite of being subjected, according to Sepúlveda, to unjust rule. Reducing[9] the Indians would be to their advantage, because they would be released to a less harsh government—the Spanish one. In short, Sepúlveda's position obeys the interests of the conquerors and the crown; it provides legitimation for colonization and exploitation. Sepúlveda frames his argument in secularized terms that especially favor the productivist logic. Sepúlveda clearly feminizes the indigenous people in Ochoa's sense; he relegates them not to an infantile state, but to a status quo where they only exist as servants (Ochoa 2014, 106).

Las Casas's position rejects war as a means to civilize the *other*. Instead, the *other* must be won by reason, and *otherness* must, at least in principle, be respected. Las Casas advocated for colonization without direct physical violence. In his early activities, Las Casas's ideas concerning peaceful colonization implied, for example, a sympathetic settler colonialism: building fortresses in the conquered territories where the colonizers had still not arrived. This would allow the missionaries to remain close to the Indians, win their loyalty, and,

> trade for gold and silver and pearls and precious stones, [and in each fortress have a few members of the religious orders that would be in charge of preaching the Gospel] this way it would be possible to obtain as much gold and things of values as the Indians have [and] to earn their love and friendship, having earned their goodwill, in due time build fortresses inland making it possible to uncover their secrets and with the industry and diligence of the missionaries the people could be progressively converted and begin confirming the truth of the Spaniards' friendship and in turn teach them about the kindness and the justice of the king so they could be easily won over and of their own free will become his subjects granting him, with full awareness of it, their obedience. (*Historia de las Indias*, cited in Castro 2007, 5)

Las Casas's later work concentrates in condemning the encomienda[10] system, denouncing atrocities committed against the indigenous peoples in the Americas, and refuting his own early position in favor of enslaving Africans. Also, he appears to have been less interested in providing legitimation for his ideas concerning evangelization based on the idea of profit. Las Casas's ideas underwent important transformations. He also increasingly centred his attention in writing communications to Spain in defense of his ideas, and concerned himself less with the planning of specific projects to be carried out in the colonized territories (Castro 2007, 63–104).

Along with a number of others,[11] Enrique Dussel (2008) has argued that Lascasean ideas entail important contributions to interculturality; this latter understood as a method of decolonization. In my reading, these ideas are at best limited to having a transformative *potential* towards interculturality and, in any case, imbued in Creole sympathism. Las Casas neither took the necessary measures to become involved with *the other*, for example by learning Indian languages (Castro 2007), nor assumed the, at least to us, logical consequences of his own ideas; that is, the negation of the 'universal' superiority of Christianity (see also Ochoa Muñoz 2014). Additionally, Las Casas did not question the right of the Spanish to be in the colonies. What he disputed were the methods and goals of colonization. As already mentioned, this position is in many ways similar to that of contemporary decolonial Mestizos. One of the methods of colonization Las Casas opposed was war, as illustrated in the following quotation:

> Those that arriv'd at these Islands from the remotest parts of Spain, and who pride themselves in the Name of Christians, steer'd Two courses principally, in order to the Extirpation, and Exterminating of this People from the face of the Earth. The first whereof was raising an unjust, sanguinolent, cruel War. The other, by putting them to death, who hitherto, thirsted after their Liberty, or design'd (which the most Potent, Strenuous and Magnanimous Spirits intended) to recover their pristin Freedom, and shake off the Shackles of so injurious a Captivity: For they being taken off in War, none but Women and Children were permitted to enjoy the benefit of that Country-Air, in whom they did in succeeding times lay such a heavy Yoak, that the very Brutes were more happy than they: To which Two Species of Tyranny as subalternate things to the Genus, the other innumerable Courses they took to extirpate and make this a desolate People, may be reduced and referr'd. (Las Casas n.d., *Brevísima relación de la destrucción de las indias*)[12]

Being against war, however, is not by far the same as struggling against the death project. The death project can easily be defended and implemented without use of physical force, and my suggestion is that Las Casas was an important precursor to this kind of practice as it is evident in indigenismo and Creole sympathism. The idea of the *noble savage* and the more recent related concept of the *ecological native* (Ulloa 2004) are also part of this tradition. Indeed, to Las Casas, the primary defining feature of his attitude concerning the indigenous peoples was paternalism. As such, I contend contrary to Ochoa (op. cit.), that Las Casas's position was not feminization but an infantilization of the indigenous peoples. Las Casas's Christian project entailed a conception of the Indian as being *potentially better* Christians than the Spanish due to their innocence and, to some extent, because of their suffering. To Las Casas, that the Indians were *not* Christian did not mean that they did not have all that was necessary to *become* Christians. Instead, the indigenous peoples' innocence was similar to that of Adam and Eve in the Garden of Eden. Feminization, by contrast, did not entail sympathetic colonial idealization. Las Casas's position appears to have been that, without the obstruction that the conquerors posed to the evangelizing mission, the indigenous people would almost automatically convert to Christianity, leaving the status of perpetual dependency characteristic of feminization. The evangelizing mission was in this sense a mission to *develop* the Indians, so to speak, based on the idea that when properly instructed the *other* naturally endorses the values and beliefs of the colonizing power, becoming a good version of it:

Thus, when some people of such wild kind are in the world, they are as untilled land that easily produces bad weeds and useless thorns but has within itself such natural virtue that when tilling and cultivating it, it will provide domestic, healthy and rewarding fruits. (Las Casas n.d., *Apologética Historia*, vol. 3, chap. 48, cited in Rubio 1979, translated from Spanish.)

Indeed, in many ways the early evangelizing missions resemble development projects—from soft projects that are considered development from below (similar to some Paraguayan Jesuit missions) to dedicated development projects (corresponding to the encomienda missions in northern Colombia).

MODERN SUBJECTIVITY

Wynter (2003, 269) defined the Valladolid debates as a dispute

between two descriptive statements of the human: one for which the expansion of the Spanish state was envisaged as a function of the Christian evangelizing mission [according to a theocentric conception of the human], the other for which the latter mission was seen as a function of the imperial expansion of the state [according to a new humanist and ratio-centric conception of the human].

The heritage of thought that Sepúlveda represented prevailed. However, at least in relation to human rights and development, important modifications to such thought meant a more elaborate concentration of the interests of the Crown, Conqueror, and Church—nonetheless, with the Conqueror's position remaining the predominant defining influence. The next section, on concealment of the *other* and international law, shows how this is the case through a presentation of the thought of Vitoria. Before engaging in that discussion, however, it becomes imperative to examine the existential meaning of the colonizing endeavor and its relation to modern subjectivity. Indeed, it is through this examination that my contention—along with that of the Mamos—that human rights and development can be traced to these early colonial times, acquires force.

There is a direct link between colonial and modern subjectivity. Dussel noted this historical connection in the early 1990s, arguing that the Cartesian *ego cogito* was preceded by the *ego conquiro*; the *I conquer* of the first modernity (1995). Dussel's approach to the I conquer considers the historical processes outlined below in the context of the conquest and colonization of the Americas and the Caribbean. As we know, at first the Spaniards had not realized that they had arrived at lands previously unknown to them, but believed that they were in Asia. Along with other Latin American scholars (O'Gorman 1991/1957), Dussel calls this period, which extends from 1492 until 1502, the period of the 'invention' of the Asian in the Americas. This point is important because it implies that the people who were to be named *Indians* were not dis-covered as different, but as the same, that is, an already established *other*—that of the Asian Indian. In this way, America became the site onto which the same—from a European perspective, the already known—is projected. Dussel conceives of this phenomenon as *encubrimiento del otro* (covering over of the other). Mamo Martínez's statement, 'They have conquered and colonized us, but they never discovered us', explored in chapter 2, provides a corollary to Dussel's formulation. Covering over will be decisive in the subsequent negation of the colonial side of modernity, the creation of the zone of nonbeing, and also of the impact of these processes in Mestizo identity.

The second decisive process to the formation of the I conquer occurs between approximately 1502 and 1520, when the colonial powers realized that they had not landed in Asia but in a previously unknown territory. This factor is a catalyst to the existential experience of an Occidental Europe as a 'discovering universality' at the center of history. After all, they did not only 'discover' a 'New World'—of equal importance, they produced their own world as an 'Old World' in the specific sense that they began to conceive of Europe as the place where history starts. By extension, this meant the justification of the Old World extending geographically to the New (Dussel 1992). This notion was necessary to the development of ideas concerning the inhabitants of the 'New' territories as people without history, a conception that consequently allowed for succeeding thought that, according to the linear temporality, establishes the *other* as always lagging behind, in a state of feminine being-ness. As Ochoa (2014) implies, feminization also entails a *denial of coevalness* (Fabian 1983) but, as suggested in relation to the witch hunts, feminization, at least in its intersection with racialization, needs to be understood as a way in which notions of peoples' closeness to nature, including their spiritualities and knowledges, interlink with ideas regarding development or perfection. Feminization-racialization localized these *other* histories and people, and universalized the European.

After the 'invention' and subsequent 'discovery' of America, Dussel highlights the I conquer. In line with Hans Joakim König's characterization of the position of the conqueror and colonizer, Dussel's I conquer seeks to erase the *other* through exploitation and violence. It represents an enslaving ego; the I conquer also represents a male and phallic ego. To state that the I conquer stance actualizes a gendered ego is to emphasize, once again, that racist configurations of power cannot be understood without taking into account patriarchal configurations of power (Lugones 2007, 202). The notions of gender and sexuality with which Spanish men had arrived in the Americas (where there were exceedingly few Spanish women) changed fundamentally with the emergence of the I conquer. With the I conquer, the masculinity of Spanish men was not solely constructed in their relationship with the Spanish women, but also in their relationship of (sexual) violence with the indigenous and also later with African men and women (Silverblatt 1987; Wynter 2003; Ochoa Muñoz 2014). The eroticism practiced in the colonies by this phallic ego was part of a practice of domination of the body through the sexual colonization of women and the forced labor of men (Dussel 1992, 50). Mestizos are predominantly the offspring resulting from this eroticization. The notion of appropriate gender applied to white European, Christian, and bourgeois women and men, that is, to those in the zone of being, which came to be characterized by biological and sexual dimorphism, heterosexualism, and patriarchy (Lugones 2007, 190). In the zone of being, the category *man* orders white bourgeois men's and women's lives and, simultaneously, determines the modern/colonial significance of all men and women. Moreover, the zone of being is heterosexual, and heterosexuality permeates the racialized patriarchal control over production (including knowledge production) and collective authority. At the same time, the category *man* characteristically ignores race and naturalizes gender. Its fundamental dependence on the zone of nonbeing is also distinctive.

According to Maria Lugones (2007, 195–96, 206), the coloniality of gender had two principal effects on white bourgeois women. First, women were women as long as they were regarded as sexually pure and passive, thereby fit to reproduce bourgeois, white males' class, colonial, and racial position. In accordance with dichotomist biological distinctions, the white woman was characterized by her reproductive role as well as by her sexual passivity and purity. Second, because of their 'nature', women were excluded from the collective sphere of authority, knowledge creation, and control over the means of production. Purported weakness of mind and body were important components in the reduction and isolation of these women from most of human experience (Lugones 2007). Those relegated to the zone of nonbeing are, in turn, confined in a space organized by the logic of appropriation, violence, and control.[13] People in the zone of nonbeing are nonhuman or subhuman; they do not have a gender and are forcibly subjected to sex, labor, and death. Other existing modalities of gender and sexuality are also relegated to the zone of nonbeing. As they do not qualify as human according to white, male criteria for humanness, they were and are not endowed with a sexuality, but were and are ascribed an extremely aggressive sexual disposition. They were (and are) also not classed as men and women, but as males and females— although the biological distinction between these categories remains blurred. Whether a Mestizo woman can pass as white or be included into whiteness, in turn, depends among other things upon whether she lives and practices gender and sexuality according to the coloniality of gender or not.

As Lugones observes, it is important to note that the race and gender relations in coloniality imply that some principles of social organization, which tend to be universalized by white feminism, only apply to the zone of being—the same zone from which these feminist readings of society emerge. These are, first, the division between public and private social spheres and, second, the upholding of appropriate gender differences, such as the dichotomy between men and women. This race-gender normativity functions to emphasize differences between those inside and outside of the zone of nonbeing. With these elements in place, it is, however, especially by virtue of Nelson Maldonado-Torres's examination of the I conquer that we approach an understanding of the existential significance of this early subjectivity. Maldonado-Torres complements Dussel's reading of the I conquer by combining and further developing Mignolo's idea about the *coloniality of being*, the Fanonian elaborations concerning the *damné* and the zone of nonbeing, and Lewis Gordon's work pertaining to the existential phenomenological dimensions of antiblack racism.

According to Maldonado-Torres (2007, 245), the Cartesian methodic skepticism is preceded by the 'racist/imperial Manichean misanthropic skepticism'—or 'imperial attitude'—of the I conquer that questions the humanity of the conquered. Maldonado-Torres emphasizes the crucial significance of the doubt, or the questioning, of the Manichean misanthropic skepticism because of its centrality to understanding the existential dimensions of the I conquer for the conqueror and the conquered. Indeed,

[m]isanthropic skepticism doubts in a way the most obvious. Statements like 'you are a human' take the form of cynical rhetorical questions: Are you completely human? 'You have rights' becomes 'why do you think that you have rights?' Likewise, 'You are a rational being' takes the form of the question 'are you really rational?' (Maldonado-Torres 2007, 246)

By doubting the obvious, these questions are expressions of bad faith. In this sense, when asserting the humanity of the indigenous people, Las Casas was rejecting bad faith. However, he succumbed to another form of bad faith by seeing the indigenous people not as who and what they were, but as what Las Casas wanted them to be. Disregarding the issue of Las Casas's misrecognition, Maldonado-Torres's accentuating of the importance of misanthropic skepticism's questions proves crucial. It is this doubt that relegates the *other* to the zone of nonbeing, where she is expected to remain or constantly prove her *being*.

The Misanthropic skepticism provides the basis for the *preferential option for the ego conquiro*, which explains why security for some can conceivably be obtained at the expense of the lives of others. The *imperial attitude* promotes a fundamentally genocidal attitude in respect to colonized and racialized people. Through it colonial and racial subjects are marked as dispensable. (Maldonado-Torres 2007, 246, italics retained)

Thus, Maldonado-Torres continues, what Sepúlveda did in the context of the Valladolid debates was merely expressing ideas that were already becoming part of the common sense of the colonizer (Maldonado-Torres 2007, 247). This common sense was already patriarchal, racist, and colonial, and it radicalized and naturalized the nonethics of war (Maldonado-Torres 2007, 247, see also Maldonado-Torres 2008a). Inasmuch as the imperial attitude was also displayed in relation to the conquered territories that were seen as Terra Nullius that, similarly to the colonized subjects, was to be penetrated exploited and domesticated, the death project had already emerged.

The Manichean doubt had become common sense by the time that the Pope, in 1537, declared that the indigenous populations were humans. As Breny Mendoza argues, the formal recognition of the indigenous populations as human beings must be understood within the framework of the process of legitimation of colonial occupation through evangelization. Naturally, within the existing frameworks of thinking, beings that were not human could not be converted to Christianity (Mendoza 2007). In this way, the declaration did not really make a difference (Maldonado-Torres 2007). Accordingly, the Manichean doubt was already at play when the Valladolid debates took place. This imperial common sense was never questioned by the Cartesian doubt either. Nor is this coincidental. Rather, as Dussel (2008) has shown, historically it connects to Descartes's education being influenced by Iberian philosophy. For example, his formal education took place in one of the schools founded by Ignatious de Loyola, the founder of the Jesuit order. Francisco Suárez, who, in turn, had been influenced by both Francisco de Vitoria and the jurisprudence and theological scholarship of the School of Salamanca, wrote one of the first texts that Descartes studied in detail. The connection between Descartes and Iberian thought is more invested than this—indeed, in the early modernity the Spanish and Portuguese ecclesiastical educational institutions were important, and extended to both sides of the Atlantic (Dussel 2008). Historically, then, there is no reason to suspect that Descartes was isolated from the ideas of his time, and a genealogy of thought in the Iberian/American direction is viable. According to Maldonado-Torres,

If the *ego cogito* was built upon the foundations of the *ego conquiro*, the 'I think, therefore I am' presupposes two unacknowledged dimensions. Beneath the 'I think' we can read 'others do not think', and behind the 'I am' it is possible to locate the philosophical justification for the idea that 'others are not' or do not have being. In this way we are led to uncover the complexity of the Cartesian formulation. From 'I think, therefore I am' we are led to the more complex, and both philosophically and historically accurate expression: 'I think (others do not think, or do not think properly), therefore I am (others are-not, lack being, should not exist or are dispensable)'. (Maldonado-Torres 2007, 252)

The following section explores the connection between the death project, the zone of nonbeing, and the imperial attitude in the context of Vitoria's thought—Vitoria being widely recognized as one of the founders of international law.

ENCUBRIMIENTO AND INTERNATIONAL LAW

By attempting to regulate the relationship between nations, international law can include doctrines and institutions including human rights and development—at least in the cases where these concern international and transnational issues, for example, in respect of Gaza, Afghanistan, Haiti, Colombia, and the like. Although often separated in theory, in practice international law and human rights and development are inseparable. An important figure in the discussions of the School of Salamanca on natural law, the rights of peoples (*jus gentium*), fair play, sovereignty, and just war, Vitoria can also be regarded among the first thinkers of the modern colonial capitalist world system. His deliberations included an exploration of the moral basis of trade based on profit (Gómez Rivas 2005; Koskenniemi 2010), and his thought connects to the second modernity through that of Hugo Grotius, Samuel Puftendorf, Gershom Carmichael, Francis Hutcheson, David Hume, and Adam Smith (Gómez 2005).[14] In significant ways, Vitoria's work condenses the positions of the Crown, the Conqueror, and the Church to form a reason, and an ethics, of war and his deliberations are harmonious with those of Las Casas and Sepúlveda. As Anghie has shown, Vitoria provides principles for the distinction between *natural law*, *human law*, and *divine law* in order to conceptualize the 'Indian question', that is, the legitimacy of imperial power regarding indigenous peoples in America. Importantly, in Vitoria's times, natural laws were those that were seen as naturally inherent in all human beings. Natural law was determined by nature, and thus it required the use of reason to analyze what is indeed the human nature and, from these analyses, to determine the rules that govern human beings. Within this distinction, he makes a crucial manoeuvre in situating questions having to do with ownership and property within natural and human law. While divine law, mediated by the Pope, is limited to the Christian world, natural law and human law transcend cultures. Inasmuch as they transcend specific cultures, they are universal—this is the basis of the *jus gentium* (Anghie 1996, 324–26, Vitoria 1981 [1539]).

The problem of cultural difference is central to Vitoria's ideas. He makes three decisive steps in relation to cultural issues that reflect the metaphysical, ontological, and epistemological strategies central to the concealment of the *other* in international law. First, Vitoria recognizes the difference of the 'Indians'. His arguments about the rational capacity of indigenous people show how they, within their own cosmological frameworks, are human—their use of reason is, for instance, reflected in their social, economic, and religious organization (Anghie 1996, 331). Second, Vitoria attempts to overcome difference through *jus gentium* and the characterization of 'Indians' as human beings who have a universal rationality, which allows them to understand and therefore comply with *jus gentium*. Third, because they are equal to the Spanish in having this capacity for universal reason, one can expect them to obey the universal standards. There is a problem in that these apparently universal standards are actually Christian Spanish standards (Anghie 1996, 332). The first two steps in Vitoria's ideas conform to Lascasian thought as exemplified in this quote:

> [T]he true state of the case is that they are not of unsound mind, but have, according to their kind, the use of reason. This is clear, because there is a certain method in their affairs, for they have polities which are orderly arranged and they have definite marriage and magistrates, overlords, laws and workshops, and a system of exchange, all of which call for the use of reason; they also have a kind of religion. Further, they make no error in matters which are self-evident to others; this is witness to their use of reason. (Vitoria, *De Indis*, cited in Anghie 2004, 20; see also Vitoria 1981 [1539], 36–37)

The third step takes a different approach from Lascasian thought, and moves towards the ethics of war:

> If after the Spaniards have used all diligence, both in deed and in word, to show that nothing will come from them to interfere with the peace and well-being of the aborigines, the latter nevertheless persist in their hostility and do their best to destroy the Spaniards, they can make war on the Indians, no longer as on innocent folk, but as against forsworn enemies and may enforce against them all the rights of war, despoiling them of their goods, reducing them to captivity, deposing their former lords and setting up new ones, yet withal with observance of proportion as regards the nature of the circumstances and of the wrongs done to them (Vitoria, *De Indis*, cited in Anghie 2004, 24; see also Vitoria 1981 [1539], 76–79).

Whereas Vitoria's argument concludes by not only denying the difference of the 'Indians', it also uses their assumed sameness and equality with the Spanish to deny them sovereignty. It is precisely because the 'Indians' are ontologically equal to the Spanish that they have to obey 'universal' norms—for example, those that dictate the right of the peoples to travel and explore other lands, trading in a fair manner with their equals and spreading the Christian religion (Anghie 2004, 20–21; Vitoria 1981 [1539], 72–76). In other words, Vitoria's humane equality masks oppression based on difference with a veneer of Spanish philosophical, cultural, economic, and political life. These Spanish forms of life dictate the terms of *jus gentium*. The commonsensical nature of the imperial attitude addressed by Maldonado-Torres is in operation.

The obvious—that is, that the indigenous peoples cannot and will not become like the Spanish—is produced as their inability to comply with the laws of *jus gentium*. Bad faith is in play. The indigenous peoples are violating the 'universal' laws, and consequently incurring a transgression that legitimates *just war* against them (Anghie 1996, 326). Indeed, this is the naturalization of inferiority, and the inferiority itself is the rationale for a just war (see also Dussel 2008, 166; Maldonado-Torres 2007). The similarities between this rationale and that which was at play in the witch hunts are not coincidental. The greatest difference is that, through the notion of just war, participation in the death project is now mandatory. Indeed, the indigenous peoples end up existing as violations, and not simply violators, of 'universal' law and cannot implement just war themselves. Just war is, in this definition, a Christian's right, so the indigenous peoples would have to convert to Christianity before being able to conduct war justly (Anghie 1996, 330). The humanistic equality defended by Vitoria conceals difference and unequal power relations under a veil crafted from the Spanish colonial perspective about philosophy, culture, economy, politics, and spirituality. This veil is part of the lie that I am critiquing—it is an aspect of *The Emperor's New Clothes*. These Spanish forms of life dictated the terms of the rights of peoples, not only legitimizing the death project, but making it a requirement if one were to be included in the zone of being.

It is easy to find contemporary cases in which the same logic is apparent, and applied to legitimize the death project. Cultural difference is now readily recognized—and in terms of human rights, new generations of rights have been formulated to respect this cultural difference. This difference, however, is foundational to the universal declaration of human rights—a declaration that claims that cultural difference is not fundamental. Rights thinking has created, legitimized, and sustained nonbeing. However, cultural difference is of itself essential because it provides key elements in thinking about the construction of a different world. This will be exemplified in later discussions of the notion of *common-unity* as it is understood by the four indigenous peoples in Sierra Nevada de Santa Marta. Significantly, in the same manner in which Vitoria in his time—and from his specific cultural place—decided that to think rationally means to understand, accept, and obey the colonial practices of the time in all their dimensions (hence his conclusion that as rational beings indigenous peoples must obey the rights of peoples), in this same way the dehumanization of the other in the present does not happen through a public denial of their humanity. Politicians and public officials do not justify the commission of atrocities because the people against whom they will act are not human. Rather, the legitimation of atrocities occurs precisely through the logic that Vitoria also employed, in which some assumptions about people, the state of things, and what is possible and realistic (and what is not) are used as ontological truths.

The 'universal standards' that decide if the life of a given population is respected are standards that also defend the death project. Cultural difference is subordinated to this logic. Which leads to the question: why does Vitoria emphasize the humanity of the indigenous peoples in some parts of his discussion, while he in others excuses just war against them? According to the Spanish, the 'Indians are' potentially ontologically equal to them. However, the ontological definition occurs within Spanish Christian epistemological frameworks—there is an *encubrimiento* at the centre of the definition: what for the Spanish is a *potential* is, at the same time, a *negation*. By which I mean that a potential to sameness is a negation of difference. This concealment makes it possible to grant meta-legal status to the war against the 'Indians'. International law and the doctrine of sovereignty contain this ambiguity—which is obscured or explicitly negated (*encubiertas*) in studies of international relations and international law (Anghie 1996). These foundations continue to perform a central role in relation not only to 'humanitarian' intervention (Anghie 2004), but also in relation to human rights and development practice. Additionally, in this covering over, we find the necessarily interdependent origins of what we recognize as human rights and development: that is, the institutionalized and legally imposed hierarchization of people upon colonial, and Euro-male-centric criteria of what it means to be human, and the constant questioning of the *being* of *the other*.

The hierarchization of human beings is at the core of racism. It implies that those who approve of the white, male, bourgeois, and Christian-dominant standards of defining what a human being is evaluate all those people who do not fit into these standards and discuss their degree of humanity, thus defining what kind of practices can be carried out against them—often under the banner of 'humanism'. In colonial times, as now, the farther a person is from those standards, the less 'human' this person will be regarded. Social and material life is organized according to those hierarchies by applying such criteria. In the colonial eras, these discussions were held on the basis of what the Spanish authorities thought were important characteristic features of a human being: spirituality as it was practiced by the Spanish Christian elites; Spanish economic, social, and political organization; sexuality practiced as the Spanish did; and rational thought—defined as thinking as an elite Christian Spanish man with private property. Within this racist reasoning, Vitoria's thought defends that power relations among humans divide into public law jurisdiction and private ownership (Koskenniemi 2010, 44). This division developed into a 'kind of universal sociology or philosophical anthropology' that became foundational for the idea of universal law (Koskenniemi 2010, 47). To rephrase, it is this 'universal' philosophical anthropology that is also the basic rationale for human rights and development.

NATURE AND MOTHER WORLD

The thought of Vitoria proves useful in explaining another important facet of the death project, and the role that dominant practices of human rights and development play in this concern. This aspect has to do with the invention of *nature* and its close relationship with the denial of Mother World as our existence. The Mother is not the same as nature; it is the being that contains all beings. Actually, the idea of nature presupposes the negation of Mother World because it is based on the separation of the human and the natural, and on the secularization of thought. The Mother cannot be understood from the dominant secular rationality because s/he is a living being that operates across all spheres of life, also those known to us as the subconscious and spiritual and, most significantly, in *aluna*. To explain how the denial of Mother World happens, and how that denial is an essential part of the death project, it is interesting to return to the distinction that Vitoria makes between natural law, human law, and divine law. Vitoria places questions about property and ownership (including land) within the scope of natural and human laws that transcend cultures and are, therefore, universal. The divine laws, however, apply only to the Christian world and are dictated by the Pope. Vitoria's maneuver to separate the natural and human law from divine law in this context has to do with secularism. On the one hand, Vitoria dismisses, so to speak, the Pope as the beginning and end of the law, and as the highest power on earth. As we saw earlier, this dismissal in practice means that Christian ethical standards that had previously limited the colonizing project, however slightly, were now in a different area, that of the divine, which did not influence the field of human and natural law.

As we know, the secular principle reached a peak with Descartes's formulation of the principles of method. This is significant because with it we enter a new era with the colonial scientific tradition, which, seeing itself being free of spirituality, is now fully understood as man's tool to own and manipulate nature. In Quijano's words:

> The idea of 'exploitation of nature', associated with the idea of 'race' as a 'natural' condition within the species, departs from the racist episteme of Eurocentrism, that is, a foundational and inherent element of coloniality of power. And you do not need to surrender to the mystification of the idea that before coloniality of power, our species always lived in 'harmony with nature'. This notion is in any case one of the basis of Eurocentric mystification: the idea of 'nature' as something 'external' to us. (Quijano 2009, 31)

With these remarks on secularism, I am not defending the dominant Catholic Church and its projects then or now. Although the Catholic spirituality has had counterhegemonic expressions, the denial of Mother World has important antecedents in the practices of the Catholic Church, most notably in relation to its attempts to annihilate those who it regarded as heretics, both within and outside Europe. In practice, the Catholic Church has been complicit with the death project when trying to annihilate those groups of people who, in some way or the other, recognize and defend other relationships to and ontological notions of the divine—for example the so-called witches (inquisition), indigenous peoples (conquest), Roma populations, African peoples (transatlantic slave trade), Muslims and Jews (during the Reconquista), and also the Mother World (development).

Secularization can be seen as a logical consequence of the dominant Christian faith, including the Protestant faith that has already conceived the divine outside our world, as the creator, judge, and ultimate authority with some chosen mediators on earth. It is also remarkable that this creator has a gender—male. That logic is very different from other ways of relating to the divine, as in Candomblé, or in the thinking of many indigenous and African or African diasporic groups in the world, for whom the divine, so to speak, is an intrinsic part of the human, the natural, the social, and so on. In recent years, studies about the coloniality of nature have emerged from within the Mestizo decolonial perspective, pointing to how environmental problems cannot be understood only as pertaining to an entity outside of the social, political and cultural spheres and outside of global power relations.[15] Broadly stated, the coloniality of nature addresses the very creation of the idea of nature that presupposes the separation between the human and the natural, and the colonization and destruction of nature and their continuity in time as constitutive to capitalism. In line with these insights, and from the basis of my work with the Mamos, there emerges also the following essential observation: nature is a modern/colonial, secularized idea that prevents us from understanding the material and immaterial dimensions of Mother World. I refer to these dimensions when using the term *spirituality*. As I use it here, the spiritual is to do with the relatedness of everything as vital force of all that exists; we could also call it god, Serankwa, or the Mother. Finally, it is important to notice the political dimensions attached to these observations: Many nonsecularized traditions do not operate according to the logic of an entity that is separate from that which it created. This is significant in onto-logical terms and it affects the delimitation of the political field. The par-ticipation of the Mother in the political is inconceivable in Eurocentric secularized dominant reason and, as such the possibility of other futures, that is, of political projects that go against the death project, are discredited for being irrational. We return to this discussion in the second part of the book that centres on the geography of reason.

TOWARDS THE SECOND MODERNITY

The idea of gender-race was pivotal to the ideas of rights of people in con-junction with an early version of the idea of development. A central element in their evolution is the imperial question highlighted by Maldonado-Torres on the humanity of the *other* and subsequent elaborations based on this inter-rogation. These elaborations were to become central elements in the making and consolidation of the global elites. While it is impossible to establish a genealogy from the thought of Vitoria and his contemporaries to current human rights and development based on the ideas presented in this chapter, I suggest that it is possible to do so complementing this reading with further alternative reassessments of history. In brief, the link is suggested by the fol-lowing: the transatlantic elites that emerge in the eventual convergence of the positions of the Spanish Crown, the Conquerors, and the Church precede the global elites. Although they occupy different positions in the colonial hierar-chies, they share a conquering and colonial common sense—here exemplified by Vitoria. This common sense is founded upon the negation of the *other* and of difference and proves pivotal to the construction of the ethics of war and the exercise of the death project. It provided the epistemological and ontolog-ical grounding for the ways in which the global elites produced the zone of nonbeing and, to use Santos's terminology, the ignorant, the residual, the inferior, the local, and the nonproductive (Santos 2005, 160–62). The nega-tion of otherness was, additionally, denied through the establishment of Span-ish imperial criteria of what being human meant—thus, the indigenous peoples could only exist as human according to criteria that defined human-ness as a lack of *otherness* in which the opposite of the *other* is Spanish. Together with Maldonado-Torres and Dussel, I suggest a link between the I conquer and the ego cogito by mentioning that Descartes—as well as Grotius and probably many others of their coevals—studied texts written by Iberian scholars. These scholars conceptualized reality despite the significant challenges that the 'discovery' and colonization of the Americas posed to them. In the next chapter, I bring some examples of how *otherness* disappeared as a factor in subsequent thought. This provides further evidence in affirming that the Manichean misanthropic skepticism that became common sense in the early period of the first modernity was not questioned by the Cartesian methodical doubt.

Additionally, the *other*, and the offensive struggles, were crucial actors in the context of, for example, the emergence of ideas of racial equality—indeed an important component in some early Latin American constitutions (Carozza 2003). The role of these offensive struggles was, however, to be negated in the subsequent considerations on human rights and development by the global elites. There is a historical hole, so to speak, between the first Latin American constitutions in the nineteenth century and the institutionalization of human rights and development in the mid-twentieth century. The Black Legend played an important role in the displacement of imperial and colonial power to northern Europe, a displacement that was already under way in the time of Grotius and Descartes (see Gómez Rivas 2005), which precisely meant that the contributions of the Iberian empires were obscured by dominant history. However, along with the English Magna Carta and the French Declaration of the Rights of Man, some of the first Latin American constitutions were used as inspiration in the context of the elaboration of the Universal Declaration of Human Rights.

Finally, a constant lack in the dominant historical accounts, in both the first and the second modernity, concerns the *other*. This is a significant absence to scrutinize because it implies investigating the role that those who were covered over had in relation to important events that were to affect directly the further elaboration of ideas pertinent to human rights and development. Of course, this implies considerations including covering over and *silencing the past* (Trouillot) happening at different levels—thus also how the Latin American Mestizo elites were *covered over* by the subsequent imperial powers. However, the struggles of these elites have for the most part been complicit with the global articulations of power through the practice of internal colonialism, racism and the death project. By focusing on these processes, the next chapter takes yet another step in the investigation of the ways in which the dynamics between emancipation and the subsuming, or neutralization, of emancipation by hegemonic powers are a constitutive part of the globalized localisms of human rights and development, which in that sense continue to veil the offensive struggles. Mestizaje plays an important role in this regard.

NOTES

1. See also Fernández Garcés et al. (n.d.), Suárez-Krabbe (2014), Mignolo (2000, 2006), and Grosfoguel (2013).

2. For analyses of human rights in relation to their links to coloniality, see Mignolo (2000, 2006, 2009), Santos (1995a, b, 2000), Wright (2001), and Wynter (2003). Deliberations concerning the Eurocentric character of human rights are to be found in Herrera (2005), Ishay (2004), and Jackson (2005). Studies that center on the geopolitical workings of human rights in their current institutionalized forms include Douzinas (2000, 2007) and Herrera (2005). Some important contributions to the more recent debates concerning human rights as seen from a Third World perspective are to be found in Barreto (2012).

3. The texts upon which Mignolo elaborates his thesis are Aníbal Quijano, "Colonialidad y Modernidad/Racionalidad," *Peru Indigena* 13 (29): 11–20; Aníbal Quijano and Immanuel Wallerstein, "Americanity as a Concept: Or the Americas in the Modern World-System," *International Journal of Social Sciences* 134 (1992): UNESCO, Paris; and Sylvia Wynter, "1492: A New World View," in Lawrence Hyatt, Vera and Rex Nettleford, *Race, Discourse and the Origin of the Americas: A New World View* (Washington and London: Smithsonian, 5–57).

4. In Suárez-Krabbe (2014b), I show how these genocides were important in shaping the place of enunciation of decolonial social movements and immigrant populations in Europe, simultaneously being key to understanding the narratives of belonging that European countries tell about themselves, and by which they legitimate racism. In it, I incur in the error pointed by Fernandez Garcés et al. (n.d.) of omitting the genocidal practices against the Roma populations in my considerations.

5. These sources are: Anghie (1996, 1999, 2004), Arias (2008), Carozza (2003), Castro (2007), Dussel (1995, 2000, 2004, 2007, 2008), Espinosa (2007), Faverón Patriau (2006), Fernández Herrero (1992), Ferro (2005), Gledhill (2000), Gómez Rivas (2005), Grosfoguel (2009), Guardiola-Rivera (2010), König (1998), Langebaek (2007), Lugones (2007), Maestre Sanchez (2004), Maldonado-Torres (2007, 2008a), Mamigonian and Racine (2010), Mignolo (2000, 2005, 2006, 2009), Mora (2009), Quijano (1992, 2000a, b), Rist (1997), Serrano Gasser (2002), Wynter (2003), and Zambrano (2007).

6. On how the ideas of the elites of the times were oriented to and emerged from Spain/Europe and the Americas, see Dussel (2008).

7. Jaime Rubio Angulo (1979, 93–120) made an important overview of the main themes around which these discussions revolved.

8. Translation into English retrieved in September 2010 from http://www.columbia.edu/acis/ets/CCREAD/sepulved.htm.

9. Similar to the *encomiendas*, the reductions, *reducciones*, were Spanish settlements whose purpose was to assimilate the indigenous populations into Spanish culture and religion. The Indians were to live near the Spanish in reductions of *encomiendas* in order to learn their ways of life and work.

10. As explained in chapter 2, the *encomienda* system functioned as land grants, provided by the Crown to land settlers. The lands included the peoples living there, who had to pay mandatory tributes to the settlers. In return, the colonized were to be instructed in the Spanish language and the Catholic faith, and receive so-called protection.

11. Among contributors who find Las Casas important to elaborations on interculturality are Rubio Angulo (1979) and Guardiola-Rivera (2010).

12. Translation of this quote retrieved in September 2010 from http://www.gutenberg.org/cache/epub/20321/pg20321.html.

13. Whereas Lugones herself writes of the light and the dark side (2007), I prefer Fanon's more existential distinction between zones of being and nonbeing (1967).

14. Gómez Rivas (2005) traces the connection as follows: Grotius, who undoubtedly has studied Vitoria and other thinkers from the Iberian scholasticism, was a great influence on Samuel Pufendorf (1632–1694) who, among others, worked in Sweden and Germany. Pufendorf influenced the thought of Gershom Carmichael (1672–1729), who worked in Scotland, and disseminated the ideas of Locke, Leibniz, Descartes, Grotius, and Pufendorf. Carmichael, in turn, influenced Hutcheson (1694–1746), who studied in Scotland and was the teacher of David Hume (1711–1776) and Adam Smith (1723–1790).

15. For elaborations concerning the coloniality of nature, see, for example, the compilation of texts in Alimonda (2011).

Chapter Four

Rights and Rebels

Understanding the dynamics between emancipation and the subsuming or neutralization of emancipation by hegemonic power implies observing how the death project is effectively challenged or reinforced. The reassessment undertaken in this chapter suggests that the offensive struggles were crucial to vital changes in terms of ideas and legal issues of the phase of the Latin American independences and of republic building at the end of the eighteenth century and the beginning of the nineteenth. While this period is engaging in itself, it is particularly so in the context of reviewing the global configurations of power in this current century and the legacy of my people, the Mestizos. In this historical moment, the global elites become more cohesive among themselves, and they also continue to deny, or indeed render obsolete, the offensive struggles that, however, powerfully influence their thought and political practice. The impact of the offensive struggles was negated in the subsequent global elite thought on human rights and development. The criticisms that came to be known as the Black Legend had already been advanced, especially during the Enlightenment.[1]

The Black Legend involved the representation of Spanish colonialism as being anachronistic and particularly cruel. As a Protestant backlash towards Catholic colonial Spain and Spanish imperial practices, it obeyed the imperial interests of northern European (British, Danish, Dutch, French, German) and North American colonialisms, implying that they, by contrast to the Spanish, were humane and *modern* (Beverley 2008, 599). Among the common assumptions of the global elites was an understanding of the *others* being in an earlier stage in the history of humanity; more specifically, at an earlier stage of northern European history. For indeed, the Black Legend effectively cemented of the imaginary wall which would for centuries deny the transatlantic nature of western ideas since the conquest and colonization of the Americas, and, create a north–south divide within Europe as well (Santos

2002a; Mignolo 2005; Dainotto 2007). The Black Legend is important because with it the racialization of Europeans by Europeans is consolidated. This is not surprising if we take the six processes of extermination detailed in chapter 3 into account, inasmuch as they generate a south inside the north from the very beginning. But the Black Legend also allows the European metaphorical north to disregard the constitutive events that shaped it, which took place with the Iberian colonial expansion. And so, the Black Legend has also contributed to ignoring the critical ways in which Iberian colonialisms' intellectual and political practices shaped the northern practices. The negation of southern Europe additionally implies that the people who can be said to be the descendants of those who were targeted in the six processes of extermination in the initial stages of the first modernity are, to differing degrees, also negated.[2]

The north–south divide between European nationalities has for the most part not been a racial divide, but an ethnic divide. Many of the reactions that we see in these southern European countries to the current economic crisis are informed by bad faith, in the sense that Europeanness-as-whiteness has been the tacitly accepted telos. The southern European countries have looked towards the north and identified with it, although they can never become the north, which is also constituted by ethnic discrimination towards the south. In accepting the frameworks of the northern versions of history, southerners have tended to ignore the historical processes that led to their situation being as it is, and that have granted them racial privilege in relation to racialized subjects; those whose oppression is compounded by racism. Finally, the Black Legend is one of the reasons why many human rights students depart from the assumption that these mainly are a product of the seventeenth and eighteenth centuries' northern European thought, particularly tied to Hobbes (*Leviathan,* 1651) and Locke (*Two Treatises of Government,* 1690). The rights narrative commonly is constructed chronologically from the English Bill of Rights in 1689, through the US Declaration of Independence in 1776, and the Declaration of the Rights of Man and of the Citizen in 1788 that stems from the French Revolution. According to this narrative, these declarations culminate in 1948 with the Universal Declaration of Human Rights and the subsequent 'generations' of rights (Balfour and Cadava 2004, 282; Jackson 2005, 166; Douzinas 2000, 2007).

This historical narrative is part of the three layers of negation upon which colonialism was legitimized, the first layer being the covering over of the *other.* The second layer was the Cartesian *ego cogito,* which concealed the covering over of the *other,* and was built upon the *I conquer.* The third layer is an extension of these negations whereby Spain (and southern Europe) themselves are located in a border zone. They are relegated to a position 'between Prospero and Caliban' (Santos 2002a). In this sense, ironically, the rationality that legitimized the Iberian elites' genocides and epistemicides came to haunt them as well, and is still in play, as in the logic behind the denomination PIGS (pejorative abbreviation for Portugal, Italy, Greece and Spain).[3] Reassessing the history of human rights and development in the second modernity implies penetrating those three layers of negation. The revision of this historical period suggests alternative links and influences in history, and in doing so, proves that there is still much to research in this area. I can only indicate some of these links and influences. Thus, the reassessment presented centers on exploring the role that the *other* played in history, the processes of cohesion among the global elites, and, within these, the covering over of the relevance of Spanish and Latin American contributions to the ideas of human rights and development.

THE *OTHERS: OUR* PAST

The ideas, processes, and discussions in the sixteenth century were inertial in relation to the notions and discourses of rights that emerged in the seventeenth and eighteenth centuries. From the end of the seventeenth century, the idea of progress whose central mechanism was reason started to dominate European thought (Rist 1997, 37). A brief review of some of the important writings of the time is illustrative in this regard. Two defenders of (Christian) reason as a means to progress were Georges-Louis Leclerc Buffon (1707–1788) and Marie-Jean-Antoine-Nicholas Caritat Marquis de Condorcet (1743–1794). Both Buffon and Condorcet were critics of slavery and of colonialism, and Condorcet additionally spoke in favor of women's rights and the independence of European colonies. According to Condorcet:

> These vast lands are inhabited partly by large tribes who need only assistance from us to become civilized, who wait only to find brothers amongst the European nations to become their friends and pupils; partly by races oppressed by sacred despots or dull-witted conquerors, and who for so many centuries have cried out to be liberated; partly by tribes living in a condition of almost total savagery in a climate whose harshness repels the sweet blessings of civilization and deters those who would teach them its benefits; and finally, by conquering hordes who know no other law but force, no other profession but piracy. The progress of these two last classes of people will be slower and stormier; and perhaps it will even be that, reduced in number as they are driven back by civilized nations, they will finally disappear imperceptibly before them or merge into them. (Condorcet, *Sketch for a Historical Picture of the Progress of the Human Mind*, cited in Loptson 1998, 126)

While Condorcet employed a rhetoric closer to that of Las Casas—who similarly, and in accord with the tendencies of his time, had proposed three different types of so-called barbarians (Rubio Angula 1979, 105–7)—the paternalistic framing of Condorcet's ideas can also be compared to that of Sepúlveda's:

> It will always be fair and according to natural law that those people are subjected to the rule of princes and most intelligent and human nations, so that by their virtue and the prudence of their laws, lay down their barbarism and reduce themselves to a more human life and to the worship of virtue. (Ginés de Sepúlveda, cited in Dussel 2008, 166, translated from Spanish)

The feminization-racialization discussed in the previous chapter is also at play here. However, in contrast to the sixteenth century, in the eighteenth century, concerns with colonialism and the colonized subjects were gradually suppressed, giving way to issues which at best addressed questions of how to *humanize* the other.

In many instances, reference to the indigenous peoples in texts from the eighteenth century is used to exemplify earlier stages of the existence of the men writing these texts. This is the case with David Hume's *Treatise of Human Nature* (1739), Adam Smith in his *Lectures on Jurisprudence* (1760s), and maybe the most well-known example, the work of Jean-Jacques Rousseau (1712–1778). Merete Falck Borch's annotation regarding Rousseau's thought is especially illuminating with respect to the idea of progress and the covering over of the *other*:

> The picture that Rousseau created of contemporary indigenous peoples as representing the golden age of human development has been seen as the ultimate illustration of the tradition of the Noble Savage, though some scholars question this by pointing to the fact that Rousseau's realism prevented him, in fact, from depicting this existence in the truly idyllic fashion commonly associated with the Noble Savage myth. Strictly speaking . . . the happiness of [the indigenous peoples'] intermediate stage [of human development] was not even the product of man's natural existence but of his slow progress away from it; Rousseau was thus not celebrating the primitivism of "savage man" but the particular level of his human development. (Borch 2004, 251)

Like Las Casas before him, Rousseau seems not to have been interested in the indigenous peoples as *others*, but more as illustrations of the stages in human (European, Christian, male) development. However, as Enrique Dussel (1983, 287) notes, there is a difference in Las Casas's ideas concerning the indigenous peoples and the later ideas of the noble savage:

> To determine whether the Indian was able to receive faith was important in the context of justifying or delegitimizing the Spanish encomendero's dominion over the

peoples of America. All this within a first preindustrial and mercantile capitalism. By contrast, the question of the bon sauvage, by the end of the XVII century and in the XVIII century, had as its horizon the right of the Europeans (principally the English and French) to dominate the new colonies, but now from the capitalist system which shortly after will be industrial (and, from the end of the XIX century, imperial). (Translated from Spanish)

With the Industrial Revolution in nineteenth-century Europe, the British Empire reaches its greatest strength. Besides the previously mentioned processes, other examples of the notions relating to the ontological construction of human and humanity include the publication of Charles Darwin's *Origin of the Species* in 1859, and John Stuart Mill's *On Liberty* in 1859 and *Utilitarianism* in 1861. Darwin's theory on the origins of the species effectively challenged the idea that the different races had different origins, but not the idea that these could be thought of as hierarchically different through an idea of progress or evolution throughout history—social evolutionism. As we know, anthropology regarded other societies as windows to the past, contributing to the consolidation of the binary opposition between tradition versus modernity.

RACIAL EQUALITY IN THE AMERICAS

In 1776, the Europeans who—under the Spanish and English colonization of the region, had come to what currently is the United States—declared themselves independent from British colonial power and affirmed the rights of 'Men'. Their Declaration of Independence did not acknowledge African-descendent slaves as men, and it portrayed these Europeans as vulnerable to the 'merciless Indian Savages, whose known rule of warfare, is an undistinguished destruction of all ages, sexes and conditions'.[4]

On the one hand, it is clear that 'the people' to whom the declaration refers were only a few human beings who regarded themselves more or less as the incarnation of their own notion of civilization (in its latest stage of progress). On the other hand, it indicates that the 'Indian Savages' are not real people due to their supposedly violent nature and destructive behavior. Enslaved persons were invisible in the text of the declaration. In this document, rights cover over colonialism and coloniality and not only the *other*. As Anthony Bogues notes,

> When the political ideas of civic republicanism profoundly shaped the [US] American Revolution, they did not challenge racial slavery in the United States. For many of the key figures in the [US] American Revolution, the definition of slavery

revolved around the lack of self-government, and the corruption by the English
crown of the "rights of English men." (Bogues 2012, 211–12)

The Latin American Creole and Mestizo elites' independence movements
relied on similar discourses. However, while the US elites disguise their own
colonial activity through the belittling of indigenous peoples on the grounds
of alleged primitiveness, the Latin American elites would highlight the indigenous virtues by returning to some of the ideas of Las Casas, for example.
As discussed in chapter 3, this practice became known as indigenismo.
Before turning to revisit the subject of the struggles of the Latin American
elites, it is important to dwell on the similarities and differences in the context
of the creation of the nation-states in the Americas. These differences will
play a significant role in the configurations of power in the region, and in
their relationship with Europe.

Colonization in British America was initially characterized by the occupation of relatively small territories, where the indigenous populations did not
live. This implied that the indigenous peoples were not colonized at this
point; they were, instead, recognized as nations with whom the European colonizers had commercial relations and, in some cases, military alliances (Quijano 2000a, 229; Borch 2004). For this reason, prior to independence,
colonial and racial relations existed predominantly between white Europeans
and enslaved Africans in British America. Undeniably, the African enslaved
population, although demographically a minority, would be pivotal for the
economy of the colonial and later the national society. The relationship
between the European colonizers and the indigenous nations also influenced
the process of becoming of the United States. According to Shelley Wright
(2001, 39),

> For the drafters of the US Constitution democratic models within Europe were
> scarce, whereas models of democratic governance in Indian Country were common.
> Not only the Iroquois and other northern groups but also the 'Five Civilised Nations'
> of the southern [US] American colonies (Cherokee, Chickasaw, Choctaw, Creek and
> Seminole) provided more accessible models than did the nations of Europe. George
> Washington, Thomas Jefferson, Benjamin Franklin and others had frequent inter-
> course with Indians during negotiations, wars, peace settlements and land deals from
> the mid-eighteenth century onwards.

There is historical evidence that shows that indigenous forms of government
and social organization influenced, at least partially, the political thinking of
the European white elites in what is now the United States. However, this
influence needs to be understood from within the deeply colonial historical
process in which it took place. As such, it was more an exercise of assimilation of some ideas into whiteness, and an enterprise to defend the death project. Indeed, with the creation of the United States—an alliance between the

European colonizers in North America—the indigenous peoples began to be excluded as well. The European colonizers, who positioned themselves as colonial populations being oppressed by the British colonial power, start to conquer the indigenous peoples' lands and almost exterminate the indigenous populations. The conquering of the territories meant that access to land in the United States was balanced among the European population by the demographic majority (Quijano 2000a; Borch 2004).

In broad terms, the processes of the construction of the nation-state in that which is now Latin America can be divided into four different types, according to the effects of colonization in the territories.[5] First, there are the countries where the indigenous populations were almost or completely annihilated and replaced with people of African descent, who became the demographic majority. This is especially the case in the countries of the Caribbean. Second, there are the countries where the attempts at the extermination of the indigenous peoples diminished their demographic representation considerably, and that, at the same time, had had significant immigration from Europe. The nations of the southern cone (Argentina, Chile, and Uruguay) are the best examples of this. These countries were considered particularly prosperous by the end of the eighteenth century, leading to exceptionally large European immigration, and consequently a European-descendent elite. The processes of homogenization of the nation-state happened through the exclusion or extermination not only of indigenous and African-descendent peoples, but also of Mestizos (Quijano 2000a). Thirdly, there are those countries, including Mexico, Peru, Ecuador, most of Central America, and Bolivia, where the efforts of the elites involved cultural homogenization, and so concentrated efforts at the cultural genocide of indigenous and African-descendent peoples. Finally, there are the countries that promoted the idea of racial democracy but that were constituted upon the racial discrimination against and domination of their limited indigenous populations and also of the African-descendent people. Among these are Colombia, Brazil, and Venezuela. These different nation-state projects imply that the societies in Latin America and the United States are different, and that these differences need to be considered. However, there are other traits in history that involve the construction of a distinct *Latin* American identity that are equally important to take into consideration. Before doing so, it proves imperative to highlight the fact that the Haitian revolution was not only the first revolution of independence; it was also the only revolution to actually break with coloniality and racism:

[T]he 1805 Haitian Constitution formally confronted the 'great chain of being' conceptions of human beings that undergirded Western thought during this period. It did so by arguing that God had scattered human species all over the world to show both his glory and diversity, and that people of African descent had been considered outcast because of slavery. Its explicit opposition to Africans as inferior was the recognition by the revolutionary slaves of one dimension of racial oppression. It was a dimension that was never recognized by any other revolution of the period. The preamble therefore shattered racialized thinking of the period. What is also intriguing is its appeal to a "supreme being." All the revolutionary declarations of the period made the same appeal. However what was different in the Haitian case is how that appeal made God an active being. (Bogues 2012, 224)

It is important to underline that the Haitian revolution is the exception that confirms the rule, as well as to note that it is, first and foremost, one of the most powerful contributions of the offensive struggles of the time. It is also significant to highlight that it breaks with racism and displays a different understanding of, and relationship to, god.

Altogether, the independence movements in the first half of the nineteenth century in the Spanish and Portuguese colonies were connected to European imperial conflicts over economical and political control of the conquered territories and the Atlantic commercial circuit. They materialized simultaneously with French usurpation of power in Spain and Portugal in 1807–1808. When the French armies occupied large parts of Spain and King Ferdinand VII had been imprisoned, the Spanish Empire underwent some important changes. Although the crown's authority was not explicitly questioned, the cities in Spain and the colonies started to organize into local governments. Contextually, the Spanish authorities gradually relinquished power to the Creole elites (people of Spanish and Portuguese descent born in the colonies, and second to Europeans in the social/racial hierarchy). In 1810, the Constitutional Courts in Cádiz were established in order to decide upon a constitution for the monarchy, for a grand Spanish nation including its colonies in the Americas. The Constitutional Courts quickly recognized indigenous citizenship largely because the idea of their 'legal liberty and nominal equality' was already established in the Spanish legislation of the time (Lasso 2007, 35). They did not recognize, however, the same rights for people of African descent who were free (*pardos*). Enslaved people were also not discussed in this context. According to Marixa Lasso, recognizing that the *pardos* had the same rights would mean that the demographic majority would lie with the (Latin) Americans, because few of them could prove the purity of their bloodlines. Ascendance to free Africans could consequently be claimed by almost all (Latin) Americans. In this manner, questions of racial equality acquired centrality not only in these debates, but also in regard to the construction of the nations in the Americas. That these questions were debated does not mean, however, that the covering over of the *other* was in any way questioned or overcome. Indeed, in face of the Spanish arguments about the danger of the racial heterogeneity in the Americas, the elites instead initiated justifications about the positive characteristics of the racial diversity in the Spanish territories, which, they contended, were not marked by the brutality that characterized the French colonial regime in Haiti (Lasso 2007).[6]

In addition to these developments, some revisions of the history of Latin America and the Caribbean, concerned with the period of independence and republicanism in the nineteenth century, suggest that the partial recognition of racial equality in a number of Latin American countries was the effect of the offensive struggles of the time (Dussel 2007, 201–6; Lasso 2003, 2006; Romero Jaramillo 2003). Indeed, by the end of the wars of independence in 1824,

> the constitutions of all the nations in Spanish America granted legal racial equality to their free populations of African descent and a nationalist racial ideology had emerged that declared racial discrimination—and racial identity—divisive and unpatriotic. (Lasso 2006, 336–37)

In the context of the processes of independence and republicanism in *Gran Colombia* (now Venezuela, Panama, Ecuador, and Colombia plus small portions of Costa Rica, Peru, Brazil, Guyana, and Nicaragua), racial equality was in several instances a condition put forth by indigenous and formerly enslaved leaders in exchange of their support in the independence struggles (Dussel 2007, 201–6; Lasso 2003, 2006; Romero Jaramillo 2003). Within the Caribbean Gran Colombia,

> Afro-Latin Americans were not mere 'cannon fodder'; they participated and influenced the political debates about citizenship in the revolutionary period, sometimes pushing the elites to acquiesce to radical measures they had not initially contemplated. (Lasso 2006, 337–38)

The degree of the support to the independence struggles of the indigenous people vis-à-vis the free blacks can be questioned when considering that the Spanish empire granted the indigenous peoples citizenship, while denying it to populations of African descent. To some of the indigenous populations in Latin America (as well as to some of the Creole elites), the protection of the Spanish Crown appeared a better outcome than that offered by the idea of independence. However, the different indigenous rebellions throughout the continent in this period demonstrate that the indigenous peoples, at least in some cases, were engaged in the search for the construction of a different society than the one offered by the colonizers and their descendants (Faverón Patviau 2006; Hernández 2008). Significantly, the indigenous and Afro-Latin Americans on occasion were in a position to negotiate conditions to the elites.

This was related to their being the demographic majorities whose support was necessary to wage the independence wars. Additionally, their rebellions, large and small, had decisive effects in this context. Among the most significant of these rebellions were the Tupac Amaru rebellion in the Viceroyalty of Peru between 1780 and 1782, and, as already mentioned, the Haitian revolution between 1791 and 1804. Indeed, news of these and other rebellions travelled throughout the continent and was discussed not only among indigenous and black leaders, but also among the global elites of the time (Dussel 2007; Lasso 2006).[7] The effects of these revolutions were powerful, generating terror and insecurity among the elites. Many elites feared that the idea of racial equality could mean chaotic conditions, similar to those faced by the elites in Haiti (Lasso 2003; Romero 2003). In Caribbean Gran Colombia, some of the elites started to negotiate the idea of racial equality with the formerly enslaved leaders. However, the perception of racial equality as entailing mayhem and disorder, implying the loss of control of the means of production of goods, including lands, can be a reason why, in the end, the Creole elites chose to identify more with the elites from the north than with the people who had enabled their revolutions (Dussel 2007). According to Marixa Lasso, at that historical point,

> [t]he ideal of racial harmony and equality had the potential either to empower those who were disenfranchised or to keep them in their place. The question was who controlled the concept. The answer was not immediate, but was itself a product of contestation as *pardos* sought to express racial grievances in the name of achieving racial equality, while elites criminalized those grievances, claiming that the ideal had already been achieved. (Lasso 2006, 341)

These inherently colonial and racist outcomes link to the fear of losing property and privilege in the newly established republics. The legacy of the 'mystified ideas of humanity and progress' also remained (Quijano 2000b). As Francesca Gargallo (2009) has argued,

> Mestizaje is the social structure that holds that it is an advance for women that engage in advocacy in the favor of liberal individualism or conservative familism to emphasize their own degree of intellectual development and the right to defend their own position in society. Equivalently, it is the social structure that allows the construction of a single subject of citizenship to the American republics, a male and Western(-ized) subject.

Like in other newly independent territories in Latin America, in Colombia's early republican period the idea of racial equality transmuted into the idea of the *Mestizo raza* as a universal race in which the quality of being Colombian could be created. This idea prepared the ground for attempts in Colombia to whiten the population. Even though Mestizo identity implies whitening some and blackening and indigenizing others, the racial hierarchies continue to play an important role in mestizaje. As implied in Gargallo's quote, mestizaje is not simply a racial institution; it is also the institutionalization of specific forms of sexuality and gender.

LATIN AMERICA AND RIGHTS

The idea of Latin America evolved among the Creole and Mestizo elite populations who were now identifying with European histories (Mignolo 2005). The belief that the only way possible for the course of history to unfold was towards European modernity, civilization, and progress inherited from the initial moments of conquest and colonization had become the perceived natural order of things. To the Creole and Mestizo elites, Latin America, as an extension of the new central axis of European imperial powers and intellectual centers of Germany, France, and the United Kingdom, was the domain of the *Latin* race (not of the American indigenous, nor of those of African descent). Postrepublican Latin America took shape reproducing and adapting colonial hierarchies and social organization to conform to the interests of the new elites, that is, through internal colonialism and mestizaje. The idea of purity of blood, which had been brought to the conquered territories from Spain and Portugal, now became fundamental for the hierarchical social-racial differentiation that justified Creole domination over other groups. In this hierarchy, the Creoles were followed by the Mestizos (indigenous-European descent), the Mulattos (Afro-European descent), the Indios (descendants of the indigenous populations), the Zambos (Afro-Indian descent), and the Negroes (Afro descent). Creole and Mestizo identities emerged in a doubled way; as geopolitical consciousness in relation to Europe, and as racial consciousness in regard to the other populations in the colonies (Mignolo 2005).

The questions and concerns among the Creoles and Mestizos were subsequently markedly different from those of the Afro-descendent and indigenous peoples. While the Creole/Mestizo experience in Latin America, as that of the US Americans, is marked by its participation in colonial and imperial projects—and concurrently by their being imperial and colonial subjects—the colonial histories of the people of African descent are entrenched with the African diaspora, slavery, resistance, *cimarronismo*, and rebellion, and the stories of indigenous peoples are embedded in these populations' relationship to, and rebellion and resistance against, Spanish institutions and settlements.

The offensive struggles have existed since the sixteenth century, and are to be found in many different manifestations and spheres in Latin America. Perhaps the best-known and oldest example is Guaman Poma's *The First New Chronicle and Good Government* (1615), a source that continues to have important standing in Latin American intellectual thought. In recent times, but with a clear connection to previous struggles of resistance, one can mention *Katarismo* in Bolivia, *interculturalidad* in Ecuador, *Zapatismo* in Chiapas, and the Mamos' struggle to protect the heart of the world. While these are offensive struggles from the indigenous populations, the ideas of, for example, the Process of Black Communities in the Colombian Pacific, exemplify offensive struggles from the Afro-descendent people, and *Chicana* thinking from the US-Mexican-indigenous female perspective.

In the late nineteenth century, the United States started to gain an important role with respect to Latin America. It achieved political, economic, and military control over Cuba, Panama, and Puerto Rico. The Roosevelt corollary to the Monroe Doctrine in the early twentieth century (1904), which stated the right of the United States to intervene in Latin American countries, marked the transition from European to US dominance in the continent. At the same time, it indicated a will to establish clear-cut boundaries between Latin and Anglo-Saxon America. Nevertheless, in practice these boundaries blur from the moment of their inception, namely, because one of the effects of US imperial activity in Latin America has been an increase in the Latino population in the United States (Mignolo 2005). Oscar Guardiola-Rivera (2010, 281) states that 'the real story is that many among the US' largest ethnic "minority" [the Latinos] are feeling the pressure to define themselves as black or white, and to choose whether they will struggle to achieve power, or serve it.' In retrospect, the argument of these scholars has been that the US Empire started to implode while it was still expanding. Recent US Census analyses, however, point in a different direction: the race and ethnic response changes between the 2000 Census and the 2010 Census (Liebler et al. 2014) shows that while approximately two million people had previously described themselves as Hispanic members of 'some other race', they now were identifying as 'Hispanic members of the white race'. About one million people switched in the other direction. This is an expression of precisely how mestizaje and *Latinidad*, like the mythical trickster Loki, plays out in two directions, and often accommodates whiteness.

The trajectory of the offensive struggles in Latin America is as long as that of the defensive struggles (see also Arias 2008). What happens in the process of becoming of the Latin American elites as part of the global elites is, however, simultaneous to an emergent Latin American consciousness that in some cases is also mobilized in the context of the offensive struggles.

The point is not that the expansionist and racial ideals of white [north] American elites, imitated by white Creole elites south of the border, have disappeared. Rather, the effect of the mobilization of Latinos [and other colonial and racialized subjects] in the north and Indians, Afro-Latin Americans and others in the south, reduce the political impact of such ideals. (Guardiola-Rivera 2010, 280)

By the end of the nineteenth century and the beginning of the twentieth, critical reflections among some members of the Latin American elites on the colonial and geopolitical idea of Latin America were concerned with the colonial legacy and the inceptions of new colonialisms. They involved a search for understandings of history and society based on different rationales from the ones dictated by European thought, and reproduced by Creoles and Mestizos. These critical reflections, however, have often been an expression of the Lascasean legacy in the Mestizo identity—involving Creole sympathism and a self-construction as the good, indigenous friendly or indeed indigenized person—than an actual change in the politics of being of mestizaje.

The period of the Latin American independences is woven into the general decline of Spain as a major colonial power, the ascendency of northern Europe, and, indeed as Simón Bolívar pointed out, the rise of the United States as imperial powers. While the independence movements explicitly used the idea of racial equality, the Haitian movement represented a rupture with white supremacy, and the elites in the United States ignored race. As the French Revolution and the Declaration of the Rights of Man and the Citizen attest, the concerns for racial equality had been absent in these latitudes for some time. Contrary to the idea of progress and to, for example, the debates on the rights of people in the sixteenth century, consideration about the colonial aspects of issues concerning citizenship and (in)equality were increasingly absent from elaborations of the ideas of rights (Mignolo 2000, 29). These ideas became, more and more, detailed within the epistemological frameworks drawn by the 'proto-national and national limited and sovereign' (Santiago-Valles 2003) as principles of social organization, and by the configuration of the citizen within these structures. In order to fit into the category of the citizen, a person had to conform to requirements regarding religion, blood, color, gender, knowledge, government, property, etc. as defined by European male elites. According to the dominant imaginaries, the colonized still had to progress towards maturity before they themselves could be expected to start processes that marked civilized societies including that of defining rights.

The ideas of the French Declaration of the Rights of Man and of Citizens, of the US Declaration of Independence, and those of the Latin American self-determination movements and constitutionalist endeavors were varied continuations on a theme that began to be discussed with the management of the colonized lands of the Americas (see also Césaire 2000). These all were, in diverse ways, concealing the 'imperial/racist Manichean misanthropic skepticism' or 'imperial attitude' (Maldonado-Torres 2007, 245) in relation to the emerging focus on the nation-state, and particularly in relation to the category of 'the citizen'—a condition not granted to all inhabitants. Paolo Carozza (2003) has argued that the reason the ideas of the French and North American revolutions resonated in Latin America is not simply a matter of mimicry: these ideas resounded in Latin America because they were based on the same legacies, dating back to the Spanish colonial endeavor. Although the African descendent and the indigenous movements had promoted some of the ideas concerning racial equality, it remains true that the revolutionary independence movements, in ideological terms, were the work of the elites. Indeed, in the years leading up to the (Latin) American revolutions, the Spanish Crown 'tried to abolish all professorships of public law, natural law and the ius gentium in the colonial universities and seminaries, and to ban all teaching of doctrines of popular sovereignty' (Carozza 2003, 299). As Mary Ann Glendon states,

> Though conventional history treats Latin American constitutionalism as merely derivative of [US] American and [north] European models, it is more accurately regarded as representing a distinctive fusion of moral and political traditions. The insistence on the correlation between human rights and duties, for example, has been a characteristic feature of Latin American political philosophy and constitutional law since the beginning of the nineteenth century. The universalizing, internationalist dimension of this heritage was furthered by the Inter-American Conference, established in 1890. (Glendon 2003, 33)

In this sense, it is more realistic to see the legacy of human rights as the variety of ramifications of mono-logic ideas concerning rights, sovereignty, and citizenship of the global elites. These elites include those in Latin America, who, precisely in this period of history, begin to emphasize northern European myths about civilization and modernity. In doing so, they obscure the participation of Spain, Latin America, and Africa in world history, including the history of ideas. That Latin American elites contribute in the construction of these historical blind spots is an expression of internal colonialism (González Casanova 1992), and these blind spots will continue to reinforce my peoples' tendency to defend the death project.

HUMAN RIGHTS AND DEVELOPMENT

> I would suggest that it is no accident that the worst period of European misogyny coincided with the first major waves of colonisation, or that it was accompanied by

death in the 'New World' itself. Although persecution, murder and the destruction of whole populations are not peculiar to early modern Europe the objects of this hatred are. From the fifteenth century onwards the most virulent hatred against a range of groups broke out resulting in the deaths of millions of women, Jews, gypsies, indigenous peoples and Africans mainly by or at the instigation of Europeans. The Nazi Holocaust has a long and terrible history behind it. (Wright 2001, 52)

In this quote, Wright reiterates some of the major points presented in the previous chapter regarding the six processes of extermination in the early period of the first modernity. She also restates what Aime Césaire had already noted years ago in his *Discourse on Colonialism*. The Holocaust was yet another expression of the death project. The Holocaust targeted Jews and all kinds of *others* inside Europe: Roma people, Poles, 'communists, gays and lesbians; the mentally and physically disabled; political agitators; pacifists; anyone deemed deviant by the German state' (Wright 2001, 18). The Holocaust has also a direct line to Al-Andalus where anti-Semitism was directed both against Jews and Muslims. Additionally, as a final solution, the Holocaust was not the only one. Besides the German genocide in Namibia in 1883 (Olusoga and Erichsen 2010), another 'final solution'—that of transferring European Jews out of Europe—had been contemplated by the Nazis at an early stage, and was developed by the British Empire:

> Given the British Empire's colonial control of the sacred land of Jews, Christian and Muslims in Palestine, they began after the 1917 Balfour Declaration and with the support of the European Zionist movement to massively export huge numbers of European Jews to what is defined by these monotheistic religions as the Holy Land. This began a process of settler colonialism where Zionism as a form of Jewish nationalism in Europe turned into colonialism. (Grosfoguel 2009, 95)

The Holocaust came to be rationalized as a deviation in Europe, and its perpetrators as fanatics that were operating irrationally. Indeed, the problem is not that dominant rationality has constructed the Holocaust as irrational. The problem is that it constructs the Holocaust as an exception, and not as an expression of the norm (Stratton 2003). Doing otherwise would contribute to dismantle the fiction that upholds colonial Europe.

The process of institutionalization of human rights and development crystallizes towards the end of the Second World War.[8] The United States, followed by the European countries that participated on the victorious side of the war, advocated their will to open the path to a new global order characterized by freedom, justice, and democracy—principles that were to apply to all spheres of community life—including economic life. Thus, in 1944, the leaders of the Allied countries met in Bretton Woods, New Hampshire, to discuss the structure of the new world economy, and the Articles of Agreement of the International Bank for Reconstruction and Development and the International

Monetary Fund were prepared and adopted. In 1945, the Allied powers also started another project: a Human Rights Commission composed of people thought to represent some of the world's major cultural backgrounds, religions and philosophies was assigned the work of drafting a declaration of human rights. To this end, the commission appointed UNESCO to research perspectives on human rights, an assignment which was conducted through the sending of questionnaires on notions of human rights to prominent people from UN member states. The commission used the material resulting from this survey in its search for a new 'universal' ethics, and three years later, in 1948, the General Assembly of the United Nations ratified the Universal Declaration of Human Rights (Ishay 2004, 16–18). As we know, the International Convention on the Elimination of All Forms of Racial Discrimination entered into force twenty-one years after the ratification of the Universal Declaration, in 1969, even though, for example, black activists from the United States, including W. E. B. DuBois, were involved in trying to ensure that the Universal Declaration addressed the profound problems of racism (in the United States and elsewhere). Their perspectives were not taken into account:

Although Eleanor Roosevelt, a member of board of directors of the NAACP (National Association for the Advancement of Colored People), was also a member of the American delegation to the United Nations, she refused to introduce the NAACP petition[9] in the United Nations out of concern that it would harm the international reputation of the United States. According to Du Bois, the American delegation had 'refused to bring the curtailment of our civil rights to the attention of the General Assembly [and] refused willingly to allow any other nation to bring this matter up. If any should, Mr. [*sic*] Roosevelt has declared that she would probably resign from the United Nations delegation.' The Soviet Union, however, proposed that the NAACP's charges be investigated. On December 4, 1947, the United Nations Commission on Human Rights rejected that proposal, and the United Nations took no action on the petition. (Dudziak 2000, 45)

Against this background it is enlightening to note that, in spite of reluctance from the US State Department, Eleanor Roosevelt, however, defended women's socioeconomic rights, insisting that these issues be included in human rights (Wright 2001, 74). Her reluctance to address racism is illustrative of white feminism and the ways it defends white privilege and the death project. Referring to DuBois's experience, Sean Elias adds,

Through these unsettling experiences with 'more sympathetic,' 'liberal' whites oblivious to rights abuses of white racism, DuBois realized that the human rights concerns of blacks, in the US and abroad, could not be entrusted to white political leaders, who knowingly or unknowingly "have historical strong interest in preserving their present power and income" that rests on white racism. (Elias 2009, 286)

Once again, we dis-cover the problem concerning the profound investment of some people, who otherwise present themselves as progressive, to the defense of the death project. These historical repetitions strengthen the argument that alternatives to human rights and development need to bypass people and institutions working within the framework of coloniality.

While Costas Douzinas (2000, 85–86) has argued that the formulations of the Universal Declaration resemble those of the French Declaration of the Rights of Man and of the Citizens (1788), other scholars look elsewhere when indicating the Latin American influence on the drafting of the same document (Glendon 2003; Carozza 2003). They refer to John Humphrey's accounts of drafting the Universal Declaration to underscore this point. Humphrey was the Director of the Division of Human Rights during the creation of the Universal Declaration, and author of the document's first draft. According to Carozza (2003, 285),

> Humphrey . . . fashioned the first draft of what would eventually become the Universal Declaration on the basis of various models that the UN Secretariat had collected. Among them were a model based on a Cuban-sponsored proposal at the San Francisco conference [that founded the United Nations in 1945], a proposed first draft offered by the Chilean delegation, and the earlier Panamanian draft. Humphrey described the latter as "the best of the texts from which I worked." Among the provisions that Humphrey drew from the Latin American models, those relating to economic and social rights stand out. As Morsink has shown with an article-by-article comparison, Humphrey took much of the wording and almost all of the ideas for the social, economic and cultural rights of his first draft from . . . the bills submitted by Panama (ALI) and Chile (Inter).

Carozza provides other examples that prove his argument regarding the importance of the Latin American contribution to the declaration. Latin American countries participated in the drafting process within meetings, and in many other ways; they also displayed certain homogeneity relating to conceptions of rights and their momentousness:

> [T]here was in fact a very strong and distinctive Latin American commitment to the idea of human rights in 1948. First, the region exhibited a dedication to international human rights generally at a time when the idea was still viewed with reluctance or even hostility by most other states. The Latin American voices resounded with a firm belief in the universality of rights and, especially, the equality of rights among all races and both sexes. Their understanding of rights consistently emphasized the social dimensions of the human person, from the family to the social and economic structures in which she realizes her dignity. And even while championing rights, they consistently sought to balance them with the language of duties, too. (Carozza 2003, 287)

Indeed, Carozza continues, it was because of the Latin American contributions that the liberalist/socialist dichotomy of the time—embodied in the United States and the USSR as world power blocs—was avoided and a balanced declaration, that neither overly emphasized collectivism nor individualism, resulted (Carozza 2003, 288).

Even though human rights and development were institutionalized in separate entities, the interdependence of these ideas remained constant, and the legitimation of coloniality and the death project a significant component. For, as the World Bank's first president, Eugene Meyer, described it in 1946,

> There is a marriage partnership between politics and economics in which divorce is an impossibility. And because of this marriage, it is as true that *there can be no enduring peace without a decent level of prosperity as that there can be no prosperity without peace.* . . . The essential objective of the Bank is to promote the international flow of longterm capital and to assure funds for the reconstruction of devastated areas and the development of resources in member countries. (World Bank 2005, 12, italics added)

These discourses and their institutions were to play decisive roles in the substitution of the remaining colonial administrations with the establishment of commonwealths and other governmental mechanisms. During the Cold War, the globalized localisms of human rights became a tool against those states that were considered ideologically unsound (Douzinas 2007), whereas they are now employed to execute the death project among perceived culturally or religiously wrong peoples and countries. Similarly, development was, and continues to be, an implement to supposedly help the peoples of the world reach the same level of progress (alignment to a capitalist market and world order) as northern Europe and the United States. Arturo Escobar has indeed shown how poverty and underdevelopment were part of a project that permitted the continuation of colonial exploitation, mainly through the institutionalization and the scientific-ation, so to speak, of development (Escobar 1996). What has come to be known as *Truman's Point Four*—the final part of the inaugural address delivered by the then president of the United States in early 1949—is seen as a turning point in the history of development (Escobar 1996; Rist 1997).[10] Here, the term *underdevelopment*, used for the first time in a text with wide circulation, illustrates how human rights and development continued to interlock; rights such as liberty and peace legitimized the civilizing missions and development practices, providing now-universal fundament to them. At the same time, the notion of underdevelopment was the new expression to refer to lack of humanity or subhumanity. Moreover, Truman's speech provides an important example of how human rights and development continued to be conceived in similar terms to those established during the colonization of the Americas, perhaps most notably through Vitoria's defense of just war. Reinforced by Truman's explicit rejection of 'the old imperialism', the speech epitomizes the replacement of European administrative colonialism—which for the most part had collapsed at the end of the Second World War—with US-driven neocolonialism carried by the notion of free markets, science, and technology as the solution to all evils. Truman's intervention can be read as an illustration of the expansion of the US-American sphere of influence as it becomes global.[11] As mentioned, this period of institutionalization was also a period of rapid developments in the scientific traditions and technological inventions led by the west, concomitant with important changes in productivity, which by extension meant an increase in the exploitation of nature. The humanism of the discourse promulgated after the Second World War and the subsequent decolonization of African and Asian colonies was followed by the creation of new discourses and practices, which contributed in securing First World productivity and subsequent consumerism.

In 1966, after years of pressure by representatives of countries from the south, the International Covenant on Economic, Social, and Cultural Rights was adopted. The covenant then entered into force ten years later, in 1976. There were disagreements on the nature of human rights and development among the representatives of nations from north and south. For example, the elites from the south pushed for the right for self-determination as a human right, meeting with strong objections from the elites from northern colonialist nations (Cmiel 2004). The force on the southern countries to prioritize international economic development goals was also to be the instigation behind the recognition of the right to development by the UN Commission on Human Rights in 1977, adopted by the General Assembly in 1986 (Steiner and Alston 1996, 1110–14; O'Manique 1992, 78). In this regard, the pressure used by elites from the south is in several cases both reproducing internal colonialisms and exploitative violences, and inherently subversive of the northern will to conceal the colonial nature of relations on a global scale. One can also argue that the elites of the so-called underdeveloped countries might just as well have been struggling for a bite of the cake in the context of the exploitation of their countries' resources. There is no doubt that in many cases the emphasis placed by the countries of the south on economic, cultural, and social rights was an attempt at regulating neocolonialism, and that of course, the elites in Latin America, with a longer experience of neocolonialism due to the subcontinent's longer period of independence, would share their stake in protecting themselves with the indigenous and African-descendent populations. This does not imply, however, that these elites were interested in the economic, cultural, and social rights of the indigenous and

African-descendent populations—if anything, the histories of the subcontinent suggest that this was not the case. The representatives of the Latin American countries in the drafting of the Universal Declaration and subsequent elaborations did not represent their countries' populations but, at best, were elites with sensitivity towards social and economic inequality.

The subsequent introduction of bills such as the Convention on the Elimination of All Forms of Racial Discrimination (entry into force: 1969), the Convention on the Elimination of All Forms of Discrimination Against Women (enforced from 1981), the Convention on the Rights of the Child (enforced from 1989), and the Declaration on the Rights of Indigenous Peoples (approved in 2007) into the hegemonic globalized localisms of rights and development must be seen within the frames of the offensive and defensive struggles. (Even though thorough analyses remain to be done on the questions of how and why these additions happened), there can be no doubt that these conventions reflect the ways in which the colonial category of 'human' has omitted racialized-feminized subjects, women, children, and the Mother. While ideas on progress and rights worked as justifications for colonialism in the first modernity, in the second modernity, ideas on progress (later termed 'development') and peoples' rights (later termed 'human rights') gradually divide their agendas; progress continues to justify the death project while the increasingly elaborated ideas on rights and human rights cover over colonialism and coloniality. The interconnectedness of these ideas remains, however, largely ignored in scholarship on human rights and development. Although researchers reference the problems of race, they do not acknowledge the embedded nature of race in the ideas of human rights and development. This connects to most of these analyses being made through the colonial patriarchal gaze that, among other blind spots, does not allow for an understanding of the ways in which race and gender intersect with the ontological construction of the categories human and nature. In this way, academics often ignore the role of human rights and development in the construction of the death project.

From the mid-1990s, the rights-based approaches to development have gained important strength in international cooperation institutions. They seek to incorporate the 'norms, standards and principles of the international human rights system into development work' (Mikkelsen 2005, 200). Development is regarded as being the missing link to human rights, and poverty is understood as a condition where a person's or a group's human rights, such as the right to food, participation, and freedom of expression, are unfulfilled. Consequently, poverty is the manifestation of exclusion and powerlessness. The rights-based approaches also imply emphasis on practices, which are respectful of human rights, and should then be important guidelines and guarantees for 'good development practice' (Mikkelsen 2005, 200). The rights-based approaches begin and are largely guided by the principles of human rights, and seek to adjust these in practice, that is, regarding specific contexts and development projects. This is one of the reasons why *development from below* practices are progressively more popular. Nevertheless, there are two major problems: first, development from below does not ask the ones below what development and human rights is, and it fails to question whether development and human rights are relevant. The ones above have expertise and experience in development, and continue to be the people to decide whether this or that plan, which has to be translated into a project, is a suitable development project. The definition of *who* and *what* the *others* are, and what future they wish for, is in the hands of the ones above. Among other interests, the peoples above, the global elites, have the money or access to the funds to invest in development, and the expertise to guarantee its success. Second, a related problem concerns the reality that human rights and development projects need not only to be translated into the language of the funding agencies, they also periodically have to show the agency that the project is advancing as planned, according to agency-defined aims. This means that projects that are innovative, explorative, alternative, or *other* have restricted access to the general development agenda, which is largely funded by northern national and global human rights and development institutions. Openness is relative, and the expertise of the practitioners makes the agenda, controlling the definitions, the methods, and the reasons for action (Powell 2006). Although unexpressed, the view of the ones subject to development as inferior remains as does the justification for having development projects emerging from below controlled and evaluated from above.

MESTIZOS AND DECOLONIZATION

With their global institutionalization, human rights and development continued evolve in a symbiotic relationship whose most important characteristic is the negation of coloniality. The negation of coloniality means, by implication, the negation of the possibility of *other* worlds and knowledges. The western man, as the developed producer of scientific knowledge, was to be the one to determine the desirable futures to be constructed, because he was the only one to possess the knowledge and expertise to do so in scientifically and rationally grounded terms. Not unexpectedly, the conception of what was and still is scientific and rational was not only determined by the global elites themselves; the terms upon which this notion is elaborated can be traced back to the Enlightenment and its universal aspirations as a thought paradigm that made other forms of thinking redundant, or unscientific.

Human rights and development functioned and continue to function in two ways. They constitute a utopia for the global elites, which simultaneously covers over its darker side: that it can only be attainable by these elites. In short, it favors the heterosexual western white man. Secondly, its attainability depends upon the persistence of coloniality and the death project in relation to the 'underdeveloped' south. In this way, emancipatory projects working on the basis of *other* utopias and against the death project are, within this logic, at best unrealistic, and at worst they come to constitute the selfsame problem that colonial utopias seem to overcome (Gordon 2004, 79). It is true that *other* uses and practices of human rights and development are partially permitted in the globalized localisms. Nevertheless, these are allowed as long as they offer only a view of, and not the realization of, *other worlds*. The contents of the hegemonic globalized localisms may be changed, but not the terms upon which they operate. While the terms do not alter, these *other worlds* will hardly be accepted—the present is shrunk to encompass only one specific conception of the world. Theoretical and practical concerns of human rights and development are conditioned by coloniality, which again defines the limits permissible to theory and practice. Certainly, then, changing the terms of the discussions is inherently corrosive, or indeed, transformative, of these. Inasmuch as human rights and development are also ideas and practices in which processes of identity construction and power relations are enacted and experienced, the discussion of *other* possible worlds and the reluctance to change the terms of the discussions may well be attached to an existential and ontological insecurity. Indeed, the idea that human rights are a meta-human, meta-political set of concepts and norms that protect us cloaks the aspects of human rights that are constitutive of the problems they themselves seek to protect us from. The belief in this cover story is a form of bad faith. While one can argue that human rights work, they do so predominantly for people who have already rights (Jackson 2005)—and especially for those in the zone of being. Existentially, the cover story of dominant ideas of human rights and development seems to connect many individuals to the modernist and modernizing utopias (Espinosa 2007) of human prosperity and equity. These utopias are similar to those by which conquest and colonization were justified and implemented. In this sense, the notions of human rights and development constitute a particular utopia about humanity, defined on the basis of the negation of the *other*. In other words, it is based on an inherently colonial racist-gendered conception of what being human means. Politically, the dominant ideas of human rights and development function as a framework that monopolizes political possibility to encompass only the horizons of possibility delineated by the rationality of coloniality.

The imperial attitude is key to understanding the role of subaltern struggles in the history of human rights. Indeed, while these struggles have impacted upon the ideas that were condensed as human rights, they have been concealed in the dominant narratives about human rights. The studies that show how the earlier Latin American constitutions were important inspirations in the drafting of the International Declaration of Human Rights in the mid-twentieth century suggest on these grounds that human rights themselves might be understood as creolized. Beyond the continuing power of the imperial attitude, this neglect reflects that those global elites who write histories have overlooked important elements of global history and taken for granted that the subaltern did not play any significant role in shaping this history. Consequently, if human rights are to be treated as a product of creolization, it is important to specify that this is a process that has happened at the expense of the subaltern and their voice. In other words, it is a creolization that occurs among elites, who have appropriated and whitewashed ideas stemming from the social struggles that they seek to cover over. For the most part, however, the idea of racial equality, and that of abolitionism, is widely believed to have emerged as a great concession of the white man, and not as the result of offensive struggles. This is a significant point to remember, as is the fact that the idea of racial equality, as adopted by the elites, has subsequently been used to prevent rather than foment radical social change.

It is important to place contemporary Mestizo thinking within this historical trajectory. Indeed, in the course of the last ten years or so, the decolonial perspective has taken great force, especially among the Mestizo populations in Latin America. Among its most crucial contributions have been the strengthening and mobilization of several social and political processes that are producing significant changes in the region. It has engaged in overcoming some of the problems of the previous contributions such as those of indigenismo and dependency theory, and politicized many social actors, bringing new perspectives and contributions to the arena. But if we look at our historical precedents, as Mestizo populations, there is also a great danger involved in this perspective that it replicates the dynamics of the Latin American independence movements and the processes of republic building. I have alluded to Mestizos as a Loki-like figure, which is neither god nor ettin, and is both god and ettin. Florencia Mallon (1996, 71) has accurately described how '[a]s a discourse of militant hybridity [mestizaje] is a counterhegemonic claiming of intermediate identities that, by its very indeterminacy and flexibility, escapes the use of ethnic and racial categorizations for the purposes of social control.' This is the case of Chicana Mestiza identity, for instance. However,

mestizaje also emerges as a discourse of nation formation, a new claim to authenticity that denies colonial forms of racial/ethnic hierarchy and oppression by creating
an intermediate subject, and interpellating him/her as 'the citizen'. As a discourse
of social control, official *mestizaje* is constructed implicitly against a peripheral,
marginalized, dehumanized Indian 'Other', who is often 'disappeared' in the process. (Mallon 1996, 71–72)

Mestizaje is counterhegemonic; it has also been an identity constituted upon
racial hierarchy, at the expense of indigenous and African-descendent populations, and it is also an institution of whiteness. Indeed, in numerous
instances, mestizaje has been used as a discourse for national or continental
unity against colonization and imperialism, but not against whiteness. Marisol de la Cadena (2006) distinguishes between Mestizo as an identity, and
mestizaje as a political ideology. This distinction is important to the extent
that it leaves room for a project whereby Mestizo counterhegemonic identity
can be detached from the white political projects of mestizaje. At the same
time, however, it is important to take into account the many ways in which
Mestizo identity and mestizaje continue being constitutive of one another,
among other things through the colonial politics of being.

The colonial politics of being, to which I provide a more detailed explanation in chapter 5, conceptualizes the identity politics of whiteness, so to
speak, among other elements by attending to how both colonizer and colonized identify with and interiorize the colonial naturalizations of superiority
and inferiority as part of their very notions of being. Here, I indicate the dangers that the Mestizo decolonial perspective simply continues striving for
emancipation at the expense of the *other*, and that its processes of liberation
'with' the indigenous and black populations do not carry any fundamental
capacity for change because the processes of liberation leave our legacy of
whiteness untouched. These dangers are a possibility and a tendency that we
must necessarily address. My point is that irrespective of the great contributions of the decolonial perspective it is a (predominantly male or male domi-
nated) Mestizo perspective that does not name itself as such. As with the
white perspectivity (Gordon 1999, 103), it does not seem to need naming
itself—and this is what inextricably attaches it to whiteness. However, as Mónica Moreno Figueroa (2010) has noted, the in-betweenness of mestizaje also
implies that its privilege is not a constant. It is precarious and can be taken
away. In the same way, the Loki-like nature of mestizaje is what allows having outbursts of whiteness among people who otherwise position themselves
as working for decolonization. This is perhaps the most important reason that
the decolonial perspective, and especially the men that herald this perspective
internationally, systematically relate to their own locus of enunciation, its
nature as an expression of a (male) Mestizo identity, and its own articulations

in the global hierarchies of power. This is a necessary exercise to assist the process of putting mestizaje at the service of decolonization, dismantling it as a colonial institution.

NOTES

1. Julián Juderías coined the term in his 1914 book, *The Black Legend and Historical Truth (La leyenda negra y la verdad histórica)* in reference to anti-Spanish propaganda.

2. Santos provides an analysis of this condition in the case of Portugal in "Between Prospero and Caliban" (2002a), and Dainotto in the case of Italy in *Europe (in Theory)* (2007).

3. For a comprehensive analysis of this, see Dainotto (2007). According to Robert Holloway, 'PIGS has been used as an abbreviation for Portugal, Italy, Greece and Spain since at least 1999, when they and eight other countries adopted the euro as a common currency'. In http://web.archive.org/web/20100420025605/http://blogs.afp.com/?post/2008/09/15/Pigs-in-muck-and-lipstick. Accessed 20 April 2013.

4. http://www.ushistory.org/declaration/document/. Accessed December 2010. For analyses of the complexity of attitudes towards the indigenous peoples in the British colonial territories, see Borch (2004).

5. This brief outline is inspired by a characterization made by Quijano (2000a, and follows it rather closely.

6. Anthony Bogues's (2012) excellent and powerful essay on the practices of freedom in 'the dual Haitian revolution' looks at these practices of freedom as political ideas radically different from—and alternative to—those present in western political thought. He calls the Haitian revolution 'dual' because it had 'two impulses. The first impulse was the abolition of racial slavery. The second was the establishment of an independent republic' (Bogues 2012, 218).

7. Interestingly, as Susan Buck-Morss (2000) suggests, it was also largely due to the Haitian revolution that Hegel acquired his idea of the relation between lordship and bondage.

8. The naming 'Second World War' is itself an expression of the overdetermination and overrepresentation of whiteness.

9. The petition known as National Association for the Advancement of Colored People: An Appeal to the World! A Statement on the Denial of Human Rights to Minorities in the Case of Citizens of Negro Descent in the United States of America and an Appeal to the United Nations for Redress (New York: NAACP, 1947) was prepared under the editorial supervision of DuBois, with contributions by Earl B. Dickerson, Milton R. Konvitz, William R. Ming Jr., Leslie S. Perry, and Rayford W. Logan. See Dudziak 2000.

10. The part of Truman's Four Point speech I refer to is the following: 'Fourth, we must embark on a bold new program for making the benefits of our scientific advances and industrial progress available for the improvement and growth of underdeveloped areas.

More than half the people of the world are living in conditions approaching misery. Their food is inadequate. They are victims of disease. Their economic life is primitive and stagnant. Their poverty is a handicap and a threat both to them and to more prosperous areas.

For the first time in history, humanity possesses the knowledge and skill to relieve suffering of these people.

The United States is pre-eminent among nations in the development of industrial and scientific techniques. The material resources which we can afford to use for assistance of other peoples are limited. But our imponderable resources in technical knowledge are constantly growing and are inexhaustible.

I believe that we should make available to peace-loving peoples the benefits of our store of technical knowledge in order to help them realize their aspirations for a better life. And, in cooperation with other nations, we should foster capital investment in areas needing development.

Our aim should be to help the free peoples of the world, through their own efforts, to produce more food, more clothing, more materials for housing, and more mechanical power to lighten their burdens.

We invite other countries to pool their technological resources in this undertaking. Their contributions will be warmly welcomed. This should be a cooperative enterprise in which all nations work together through the United Nations and its specialized agencies whenever practicable. It must be a worldwide effort for the achievement of peace, plenty, and freedom.

With the cooperation of business, private capital, agriculture, and labor in this country, this program can greatly increase the industrial activity in other nations and can raise substantially their standards of living.

Such new economic developments must be devised and controlled to the benefit of the peoples of the areas in which they are established. Guarantees to the investor must be balanced by guarantees in the interest of the people whose resources and whose labor go into these developments.

The old imperialism—exploitation for foreign profit—has no place in our plans. What we envisage is a program of development based on the concepts of democratic fair-dealing.

All countries, including our own, will greatly benefit from a constructive program for the better use of the world's human and natural resources. Experience shows that our commerce with other countries expands as they progress industrially and economically.

Greater production is the key to prosperity and peace. And the key to greater production is a wider and more vigorous application of modern scientific and technical knowledge.

Only by helping the least fortunate of its members to help themselves can the human family achieve the decent, satisfying life that is the right of all people.

Democracy alone can supply the vitalizing force to stir the peoples of the world into triumphant action, not only against their human oppressors, but also against their ancient enemies—hunger, misery, and despair' (Truman 1949).

11. The expansion of US dominance of course also entails conflicts with the old European power, for example, in the context of the Suez crisis.

Part Two

Geographies of Reason

The previous part of the book shifted the temporality of reason, looking into the different but interconnected histories that emerge from distinct power positions in the processes of colonization. While shifting the temporality of reason requires a decolonial historical realism that reads the history of colonization privileging entities and realities that have been localized or invisibilized, so shifting the geography of reason requires analyzing reality privileging *other* knowledges, epistemologies, and ontologies, at the same time remembering the diversity represented in *other* knowledges, and the fact that they have not been localized or invisibilized in the same way nor to the same extent. Pluriversalization does not mean looking into difference in order to set it aside; neither does it mean emphasizing commonality at the expense of difference. Indeed, this would simply be the reproduction of dominant rationality. Instead, pluriversalization requires careful attention to the complex processes that inform the struggles that defend the death project, and those that work against it. As such, as Boaventura de Sousa Santos (2014) emphasizes, equality needs to be emphasized whenever domination happens through its negation, and difference has to be highlighted whenever it is used as a means of oppression. In terms of geographies of reason, pluriversality implies dismantling dominant rationality and working against bad faith. One of the major problems in relation to shifting the geography of reason—especially for groups in more or less advantageous positions in the global hierarchies of power such as Mestizos—is that it is a matter that pertains the ways we think, feel, act, and react. It also means that our attempts to change do not equal that we have overcome coloniality. Our efforts, however, can mean that our grandchildren might be better equipped to overcome these problems. This part of the book discusses these issues scrutinizing knowledges, methodologies, identities, communities, common-unity, and pasts and futures. In doing so, it also spells out the alternatives to human rights and development as they look from the thinking of the Mamos.

Chapter Five

Towards Decolonial Methodologies

Anthropologists produce monologues, not monographs.

—Mamo Saúl Martínez

There is a point at which methods devour themselves.

—Frantz Fanon

[Disciplinary decadence] involves ontologizing one's discipline—literally, collapsing 'the world' into one's disciplinary perspective.

—Lewis Gordon

As part of hegemonic power, the university has largely been constituted as a site of formation of global elites who have contributed in the legitimation, justification and continuous elaboration of the death project. The death project is tightly knit into the global neo-liberal market and the colonial organization of the world. Enlarging upon these insights, and upon the work of Arturo Escobar (1996) and Edgardo Lander (2008), I emphasize, overall, that the global elites work in harmony with the death project by defining, managing, and classifying nonelites and the natural world in terms of their (possible) applicability or utility for the global neo-liberal market. The major organizations the members of the global elites work within are transnational. The most powerful include institutions such as the UN, the World Bank, the IMF, the European Community, international or national development agencies in the north, the mass media, multinational corporations, and the university.[1] I engage with a broad understanding of global elites, and include organizations of differing natures and scopes. This is to stress that those of us who have access to and work as specialists or in leadership positions within these organizations are a minority in a world that is much larger than the one we often imagine and construct among ourselves. With this characterization, my aim is not to ignore the vast diversity included in this category, as the global elites include national elites worldwide, as well as those of us who do not consent hegemonic power. By this, the category of global elites includes major cultural diversities, political projects, and positions. We are, however, elites because our power, in different ways and to different extents, extends beyond our 'immediate spatial-temporal coordinates' (Gordon 2006a, 46). In other words, these elites are global *and* heterogeneous.

The university educates many of the members of the global elites, and as mentioned often while working closely with the institutions named above. In all these organizations, expressions of racist segregation and hierarchization are visible; there are numerous ways of policing boundaries, overseeing surveillance, and attending to public relations in the interplay between them (Kohler 1995; Dalby 1998; Ben-Ari 1999). In academia, *border control* occurs, for instance, through the definition of specific requirements to research projects within calls for funding that fit the overall project of the global elites (Rossiter 2010, 4). *Patrolling* happens through the criteria established within the Eurocentric logo-centricism to determine what is scientific and useful knowledge and what is not, among other things, in the system of ranking of universities and journals that privilege 'western knowledge traditions and the hegemony of global English' (Ibid., 6). *Surveillance* in the university transpires, for instance, through requirements to faculty to publish in specific journals, most of which function as border patrols. Finally, the *public relations* aspect, concerned with the university's image within its community and as it presents to outsiders, is illustrated by 'racism without race' (Ibid.), and by the incorporation of dissent. By the incorporation of dissent I refer to the inclusion of *others* who, preferably, are loyal to the death project, or whose dissent is otherwise tolerated as long as it is not seen as a serious threat to the status quo. Additionally, conditions in the geopolitical south are framed by 'the dominance of foreign financial control, the role of aid donors and puppet regimes' (Dalby 1998, 138).

In the geopolitical south, some members of the university faculty constitute the puppet regimes. These are often persons who, despite being located physically in the south, enact a 'spiritual brain drain' (Fals Borda 1981, 80); that is, people who are intellectually dependent and uncritical and/or complicit with the legitimation of the death project. In Latin America, most of these members of university faculty are Mestizos. If the Eurocentric elites in the geographical north are those that manufacture the Emperor's clothes, the Eurocentric elites in the geographical south declaim that the Emperor is wearing beautiful attire. In doing so, they constitute part of the north and obey the logic of the defensive struggles. They are intellectually colonized (Fals Borda 1981, 79; Rivera Cusicanqui 2010). Funding from the geopolitical north— often in the form of development aid—oversees research so that it conforms to death-project interests. As an example, there is a document written by the interest group of the eight Danish universities entitled *Building Stronger Universities in Developing Countries* (Universities Denmark 2009). This document was the product of an invitation by the then Danish minister for Development Cooperation, Ulla Toernaes, to Universities Denmark to consider how they envision the role of the university in development cooperation. The working group that was appointed this task consisted of three deans, five professors, three associate professors, an associate dean, and a pro-vice-chancellor, that is, scholars occupying important positions of power in the Danish university system. The document is coherent in its use of the linear temporality that backs up the notion of the backwardness of the south and the advancement of the north. It also revisits the idea of the white man's burden. It states that '[w]ell-managed local universities are essential if low-income countries are to *develop into* modern knowledge societies' (Universities Denmark 2009, 6, emphasis added). The colonialist endeavor becomes clear when, according to Universities Denmark, the Danish universities must *assist* the southern universities in terms of *management*. The universities in the south must, in turn, strengthen the local 'capacity to effectively implement international aid programmes', and 'contribute to the establishment of a larger and more professional private sector' (Universities Denmark 2009, 6)—in other words, strengthen initiatives whose basic requirement is spiritual brain drain and the defense of the death project.

As a Colombian-Danish Mestiza scholar based at a Danish university, I realize that the position presented in the document by Universities Denmark is not representative of the otherwise varied positions among academics in the country. Numerous critiques exist of this development approach, as well as to the university reforms that seek to align the Danish universities to the logic of global neo-liberalism. These varied positions notwithstanding, and despite the critiques to the university reforms, it however remains true that these are the frames within which we, as scholars in Denmark with a concern with cooperation with the south, operate—including when we apply for grants. Significantly, however, these varied positions and critiques hardly make a difference in the global south as they seldom transcend their printed form. In the last couple of years, initiatives to decolonize the university have emerged at different universities in Europe, notably in the United Kingdom and Holland. These initiatives remain marginalized, and in the Danish context they are not really part of any of the discussions in the more recent student and staff mobilization against reforms implemented in 2014. The elites from the geopolitical south have often been docile in the face of the colonialist practices of the university, and have worked towards being included in the global elites (Fals Borda 1981; Escobar 1996; Avilés 2008). Orlando Fals Borda's characterization of the spiritual brain drain or intellectual colonialism emphasizes how the university's programs are constituted by epistemic violence. The spiritual brain drain is a variation on a theme addressed in different contexts and locations through history. Among the most famous are Malcolm X's representation of the *house negro* and the *field negro*, and Audre Lorde's critique of *the master's tools*. These concepts address different dimensions of repressive violence and exploitation, of power and complicity with power. They also complement the ideas of bad faith, double consciousness, and the zone of nonbeing.

The university helps form actors that work in the defense of the death project, such as economists and other functionaries in international development institutions, politicians, employees in transnational extractivist corporations, schoolteachers and university professors. Although on a much smaller scale, it also helps form actors who engage in a diverse array of offensive struggles such as activists, teachers, and human rights defenders. Above all, the university—and by definition that includes the work of its researchers, teachers, and theorists—cannot be detached from the world at large. There is no such thing as the ivory tower, only the pretense that whatever happens inside the university is inconsequential. It is precisely because what we do, or omit to do, has consequences that it is important to position oneself carefully as part of it. Fals Borda, a Colombian Mestizo intellectual, provides an initial step to explain this positioning. He was conscious of his own role as a scholar within power structures that he regarded as relevant at the time of his writing (the 1970s). In doing so, he recognized that the social sciences often require the scholar to account for reality in its ambiguities and nuances. However, he also noted that there is an intrinsic danger in applying a preoccupation in ambiguity and nuance as a principle of scientific research without having positioned oneself socially according to the *ideal of service*. The ideal of service implies position taking in society along with those groups whose interest is beyond themselves and who struggle for the benefit of *all* (Fals Borda 1981, 58–59, fn. 42). As I employ Fals Borda's idea, it implies thinking and acting less as I, and more as we—a *we* that is not limited to anthropocentric relationships.

This consideration is decisive because it points to how, applied without the ideal of service, the principle of considering the ambiguities and nuances of reality functions as a depoliticizing tool. Such thought can dispose us to maximize *some* nuances and ambiguities, while blinding us to others. Significantly, this thinking can direct attention away from the continuity of colonial violences and exclusions and from the systematic way in which these are supported and legitimized. Fals Borda's call to position ourselves according to the ideal of service is insufficient insofar as it does not guarantee the avoidance of a covering over. As such, the ideal of service must pass through the acknowledgment of several fundamental facets of oppression. The zone of nonbeing, which Fanon used to refer as the lifeworld to which the colonized are condemned, is a zone that is continually created and recreated through the social sciences and the humanities (among other actors) that engage in the defense of the death project. In this sense, the zone of nonbeing is the space that not only contains deletion, but also the very possibility of transformation; the offensive struggles. The offensive struggles such as the ones inaugurated by W. E. B. DuBois and Frantz Fanon emerge from that zone. The struggles of the Mamos entail struggles against the death project's relegation of the Mother to the realm of nonbeing. However, it is also important to remember that, anthropocentrically (sociogenetically), the zone of nonbeing continues to produce subjects who, as Fanon detailed, are deceived and crushed by the power of the zone of being. This means that we do find subjects striving to *be* through the negation of themselves; for example striving to be white or to be black as white continuously defines black or indigenous (Fanon 1967; Gordon 1999; Gordon and Gordon 2010).

One of the effects of the zone of nonbeing is what DuBois, studying the problems of antiblack racism in the nineteenth-century United States, called *double consciousness*. DuBois defined double consciousness as 'this sense of always looking at one's self through the eyes of others, of measuring one's soul by the tape of a world that looks on in amused contempt and pity' (DuBois 2008, 4). The expression 'double consciousness' catches some of the ways in which the representations fabricated in the zone of being concerning the *other* force those in the zone of nonbeing into a reality that is not theirs—that is, into identities imposed on them, while they are more or less consciously aware of this fact. They are condemned to live a lie, to *be* a lie or, in other terms, a negation of themselves. These elements are also part of bad faith, and point to the deceptive nature of the zone of being which includes the covering over of the other, and consequently recreates the zone of nonbeing. Bad faith is also at play among Mestizos, and *in* the zone of being. To name and locate bad faith is to reject the lie about social reality and humanity that justifies racism and violence by calling them what they are not (protection, fact, solidarity, scientific, methodology, humanism, inclusion, concern, decoloniality, etc.) (Gordon 1995, 1999).

Naming the presence of the global elites, and locating ourselves as scholars within this group, is one of the ways to approach the relationship between the methods that we, as academics, learn, and the ways in which we engage with these methods. These methods imply taking part in a process of identification, which has white normativity and the negation of the other at its core. We learn an institutionalized normative identity by adopting and employing particular approaches, and this process of learning implies the forgetting of several aspects of reality. This chapter addresses these dimensions embedded in knowledge production, and then formulates the guiding principles that I have used in my work with the Mamos. These dimensions are political; they link with power and force, and to notions of time, to ontology, and to existence. The struggles against the death project are largely delegitimized or produced as absent in dominant knowledge construction, and this ties the latter to the death project, colonizing the political field so that it only contains the horizon of possibilities presented by the rationality of coloniality.

THE COLONIAL POLITICS OF BEING

The university continues producing knowledge from a single ontology that is coherent with the spatial, temporal, and political dimensions required to legitimize and maintain the death project. From an existential vantage point, the dominant academic endeavor passes through people's continuing commitment to the death project, that is, the colonial politics of being. The colonial politics of being refers to the ways in which the structural (coloniality) is also existential and material. In order to understand this connection, it is necessary to proceed via Lewis Gordon's distinction between reason and rationality. Gordon's distinction provides further insights into the structures of thinking—or the master's house—that require the enactment of the colonial politics of being. If the house is rationality, the elements that structure the house are the methods, whereby the house gains maximum consistency. Once built, nothing can contradict the methods, not *rationally*, because the house itself determines the spaces of thinking—logic—and of course no *rational* being would tear down the walls of *his* own house. Rationality demands self-consistency, and it achieves this consistency through the construction of general theories and the application of their methods. These ways of seeking consistency, or of staying inside and defending the master's house, is in Gordon's words, an 'effort to colonize reason' (Gordon 2011, 98). Reason, on the other hand, exceeds rationality; it leaves and can dismantle the master's house, and so it is also thinking which is able to embrace contradictions. If it is not able to do so, it cannot evaluate itself (Gordon 2011, 97).

Rationality is lazy, whereas reason is living thought (Gordon 2006b). Rationality can only be what it is because it is integral to wider power relations, based on racism and coloniality, at all levels of social life. Rationality views its own present as if it were the universal future and, as we have seen in the chapters concerning the temporality of reason, denies coevalness to others. Thus, rationality's present is limited to only containing itself—the present is only that which is within the walls of the master's house.

According to its linear temporality, the house itself *is* the present, in constant movement to its far-off future. The past in rationality is behind, and it is an *other*. In relation to this *other*, the house represents itself as the future. Additionally, the master's house is constituted on the basis of creating anything which demands its destruction as that, which is *The Problem*, and as such either outside of the house (something which is past, hence overcome or inexistent others), a fissure in the house created by unruly children (something immature, to be corrected), or it can even accommodate any activity that demands its destruction as decoration on its walls. In any case, to be inside the house, we are required to identify with its project and its structures. This is a strong requisite embedded in the idea of scientific method: it is something we acquire when we learn processes, concepts and theories. By learning rationality, we are required to unlearn to use reason. So while we might indeed learn to be critical, this critical skill is in most cases framed within the walls of the master's house and we become critical without using reason. This allows for the existence of scholars who, for instance, acknowledge racism and coloniality while at the same time inhibit their recognition of the profound implications and effects of these problems. In other words, rationality is not necessarily dismantled by its acknowledgment of the existence of violence, of racism, and the death project. Rationality is embedded in a specific ontology, and it pertains to existential processes as well. Following Sylvia Wynter, I conceptualize these last processes as the colonial politics of being, a specific and powerful expression of identity politics attached to whiteness.

An important constituent to the structure of the master's house is composed of the continuous mobilization of methodological and conceptual equipment as if it *were* the world at large. In Gordon's words:

> many disciplines lose sight of themselves as efforts to understand the world and have collapsed into the hubris of asserting themselves *as the world*. Locked in their own circumscribed regions—beyond which is simply the end of the world—they shift from articulating their own limits and conditions of possibility to the assertion of their legitimacy in deontological terms—in terms, that is, that are categorical or absolute, in terms that do not require purpose. (Gordon 2006b, 8, emphasis retained)

The ways in which we utilize our conceptual and methodological apparatus are often harmonious with the production of a specific normativity—white male identity, including white male knowledge—based upon the negation of the *other*. This critical aspect, the colonial politics of being, is in play in Mestizo identity, and continues to be a largely ignored aspect connected to whiteness, and to academic knowledge production. While the critique of modern subjectivity is in no way a new phenomenon, its colonial character and the ways in which it is constitutive of who and what we, as intellectuals, are, continues to be downplayed. I argue that the negation of the colonial subjectivity constitutive of modern subjectivity (as described in previous chapters) is not only a conceptual blindness; it is an exercise of power through the negation of the other. It is a central aspect of identity politics attached to whiteness. Indeed, the colonial discourse has legitimized itself through the idea by which an ontological difference is instituted between the colonizer and the colonized, implying that both colonizer and colonized identify with and interiorize this structure as part of their very notions of being (Losada Cubillos 2014). In Wynter's writing,

> Although Foucault, in his analysis of the processes by means of which the classical episteme was replaced by our own, had proposed that these epistemes be seen as being discontinuous with each other, what he oversaw was that such a discontinuity, like the earlier discontinuity that had been effected by the classical episteme itself, was taking place in the terms of a continuous cultural field, one instituted by the matrix Judeo-Christian formulation of a general order of existence. That, therefore, these shifts in epistemes were not only shifts with respect to each episteme's specific order of knowledge/truth, but were also shifts in what can now be identified as the "politics of being"; that is, as a politics that is everywhere fought over what is to be the descriptive statement, the governing sociogenic principle, instituting of each genre of the human. With the result that as Christian becomes Man1 (as political subject), then as Man1 becomes Man2 (as a bio-economic subject), from the end of the eighteenth century onwards, each of these new descriptive statements will nevertheless remain inscribed within the framework of a specific secularizing reformulation of that matrix Judeo-Christian Grand Narrative. With this coming to mean that, in both cases, their epistemes will be, like their respective genres of being human, both discontinuous and continuous. (Wynter 2003, 318)

In other words: the historical discontinuities highlighted by Foucauldian studies are from the outset framed from within the continuity of the colonial category of *human*. As outlined in chapter 3, that category rests upon the doubt of the humanity of others—the imperial attitude (Maldonado-Torres 2007). Subsequent to Wynter's analysis, I suggest that the imperial attitude must be understood as part of a larger 'politics of being'. More precisely, it is a colonial politics of being. Its ontological dimension generates and simultaneously invisibilizes nonbeing; its existential or identity dimension is whiteness. As a result, the colonial politics of being does not conceive of reality beyond the zone of being. This of course implies that the colonial politics of being is sustained through a specific way of conceiving reality that requires Eurocentrism, racism, and the defense of the death project. In this sense, the colonial politics of being is the existential face of white supremacy. Through this way of conceiving reality and being in the world, a vast region of nonbeing is constructed, a no-reality of no-knowledge where the only valid moves are those that attempt to enact the colonial politics of being. It is important to underline that even though the negation of the *other* happens because the reason (rationality, in Gordon's terms) that sustains it has been part of a rooted common sense whose violence only comes to the light when those subjected to this violence name this condition, the colonial politics of being is a practice of active negation—it is not unavoidable, but rather chosen.

The negation of the colonial politics of being has vast implications not only for the academic field but also for the field of social action and in relation to the struggles against exclusion, racism, and oppression. This is because, by not recognizing the colonial politics of being, the zone of nonbeing generated through it is also negated. By implication, not only the people who do not fit into the Eurocentric, white, and colonial frameworks of knowledge (and being) are neglected, but also their realities and their theories about these realities. Ultimately, this grounds the multiplicity of paternalisms by which academics tend to grant themselves teleological, ontological, and epistemological privilege. As Gordon has noted, within this way of doing science, one can be an African (or Latin-American indigenous man or woman) *and* an academic, but one cannot *legitimately* think academically from an African-centered or an indigenous-centered viewpoint (Gordon 2006b, 64). To succeed in the invisibilization of its nucleus of enunciation and of its creation of nonbeing, the colonial politics of being must pass through bad faith. Additionally, the colonial notions of being (existential, discursive, and ontological) also permeate economic and political relations, and to a large extent they legitimize and justify inequalities beyond the temporal reach of administrative colonialism. From this perspective, for example, development is to be seen as a singular historical experience (Escobar 1996) based on a single *ontology of politics* that inhibits the very possibility of thinking alternatives (de la Cadena 2010). Anthropology is useful to exemplify how these mechanisms operate in academic knowledge construction.

ANTHROPOLOGY, EVIDENCE,
AND AUTHORITY

Several debates within anthropology concerning its relationship with the *other* revolve around the question of knowledge, specifically anthropological knowledge, and the status of this knowledge in relation to *other* knowledges. To an extent, anthropology is one of the few disciplines to broach the issue of how *other* knowledges destabilize the anthropologist's knowledge (Hastrup 2004). This particularity connects to anthropology being, traditionally, the only discipline in which relatively long interaction with a nonwestern *other* has been fundamental. In contemporary anthropology, fieldwork no longer necessarily occurs in remote locations. Anthropology at home—within the anthropologist's particular society and social group—has become a common practice, leading to important changes within anthropological theory and obviously also within the field of anthropology itself, which is, nonetheless, viewed as a transnational, international, or global discipline (Ribeiro and Escobar 2006). In this context, it is interesting that many of the debates concern the question of the nearness or the distance of the anthropologist to the subject of study. Through this questioning, anthropologists also reveal concerns about the theoretical and disciplinary *integrity* of the expert, meaning that the validation processes of the anthropological discipline occur primarily within the anthropological disciplinary field—Gordon terms this *disciplinary decadence* (Gordon 2006b). An example of this is Danish anthropologist Kirsten Hastrup's paper, 'Getting It Right: Knowledge and Evidence in Anthropology', where she examines a conception of evidence that respects the anthropological discipline itself, and is not rooted in positivist conceptions about the nature of evidence (Hastrup 2004, 458–59). Her central argument is that, from anthropology, we cannot talk about evidence outside the field of interaction within which anthropological knowledge is constructed. This is because anthropological knowledge 'emerges in a dialogical field', which makes it something relational that can, however, be objectified through processes of 'classification and articulation' (Ibid., 456). According to Hastrup, this change in the conception of knowledge implies that what is considered to be evidence emerges in relation to an object of study that has no fixed ontological status (Ibid., 458). How, she asks, can we speak of evidence if we accept that the facts—from which evidence necessarily emerges—are never neutral but embedded in fields of values? Her paper states:

> In anthropology, the instances to be generalized about consist in once-occurring acts
> (including speech-acts), emergent meanings, and unique events (in contrast to earlier

positivist claims about empirically identifiable structures), and it is difficult to see how social facts of this kind can be transformed into positive evidence. The actions and events are real enough, of course, but as 'instances' they simply do not add up to evidence for the anthropological understanding of their implications—past, present and future. 'Adding up' does not explain how or why particular acts were undertaken, let alone why they possibly made sense both to the agent and to his or her surroundings. (Hastrup 2004, 459–60)

On the basis of these considerations, Hastrup's idea is that in anthropology, evidence is built on the premise of a transparency that reveals the processes by which anthropologists arrive at their conclusions, through highlighting the ways in which links are made between one thing and another to support an argument or conclusion. This is because evidence in anthropology is determined by the contingency of events and the fragmented nature of the world (Ibid., 460) in specific situations of interaction (Hastrup 2004, 465).

Hastrup founds her ideas on reflections largely embedded in the practice of fieldwork. In this regard, she argues, regardless of whether fieldwork takes place at home or abroad, one of its central elements—arguably a central method—is the '*deliberate alienation* [of the anthropologist] from the world under study in order to understand it as it cannot understand itself' (Ibid., 468, italics added). In addition, she writes,

Practicing anthropology implies a 'using' of other people's understanding to further an anthropological understanding that is narratively mediated. In writing, anthropologists make connections and sort out hierarchies of significance that cannot bypass local social knowledge even while transcending it. The ethical demand is to 'get it right', not in any ontological sense, but in being true to the world under study and to the epistemological premises of anthropology. Rightness itself is a value, an ethical imperative imposed upon the narrative imagination of social and historical relations —including causal relations. . . . 'Getting it right' is backed by anthropologists being *in touch* with reality—not by standing outside it looking for evidence—and it is further sustained by a narrative imagination that figures out how parts and wholes are constructed and how individual acts and communal images are both mutual preconditions and challenges. 'Figuring it out' is to configure what at base is defiant of configuration and to do so respectfully is to acknowledge the mutual implication of epistemology and ethics. (Hastrup 2004, 469–70, italics retained)

Hastrup is part of a trend that attempts to overcome problems of cultural relativism and ethnographic authority through a phenomenological existentialism that focuses on narrative. The work of the New Zealand anthropologist Michael D. Jackson, in the Department of Anthropology at the University of Copenhagen (between 1999 and 2005), contributed to this focus on narrative. It also played an important role in my training as Jackson assessed my Master of Arts thesis, a dissertation that focused on narrativity and political violence in Colombia. Jackson's *narrative imperative* implies that narrative plays a crucial role in our lives inasmuch as it provides the means through which we get a sense of control *of* the world and *in* the world (Jackson 2002, 15). Hastrup further elaborates this concept arguing, as the above quotation demonstrates, that the narrative imperative of anthropology is an ethical imperative that involves 'to alert the world to the force of the everyday, to show the historical surplus of the moment, and point to sites of resistance in the given' (Hastrup 2004, 469). To a certain extent, this approach recognizes difference not only in ways of knowing, but also with regard to lived experience. Additionally, it is constructive because it acknowledges the nuances of reality—it permits, for example, an accounting that those who we consider to be victims *use* narratives about their status as victims existentially and politically, and when so doing, they are acting against their situation, transgressing the very label of victim (Jackson 2002).

Similarities exist between Hastrup's viewpoint and Santos's idea of expanding the present (Santos 2014), or Gordon's Africana existential phenomenological thought. However, in contrast to the latter two, upon further scrutiny, the value and contributions of Hastrup's perspective occurs predominantly *within* the master's house. It is necessary to revise her approach also from an *other* side in order to make visible the colonial politics of being implicit in Hastrup's presentation of a specifically anthropological knowledge, and in the possible answers that her text provides in relation to the problem of ethnographic authority.

According to Hastrup, the discussions in anthropology about the nature of knowledge and the nature of belief 'point to a still valid recognition of the fact that in human life, there is always both something that we *know* and something that we simply *sense* or feel' (Hastrup 2004, 457, italics retained). This may be true. Nonetheless, questions of ethnographic authority remain unanswered. For instance, who determines, then, what is experience and what is knowledge? What are the criteria of differentiation between sense and knowledge, from where are they issued, and what interests do they obey? What is the ontological status of that which 'we know' in relation to that which we 'sense or feel'? Are feelings and senses irrelevant to knowledge construction? By leaving these questions unanswered, Hastrup's text separates academics from the *other*, justifying a need for the anthropologist to maintain a critical distance. This critical distance—implicit in the 'deliberate alienation [of the anthropologist] from the world under study in order to understand it as it cannot understand itself' (Ibid., 468)—is guaranteed by the *theoretical integrity* of the anthropologist. In turn, the theoretical integrity emerges within anthropology itself, in implicit juxtaposition with a non-anthropologist *other*. As such, it incurs in disciplinary decadence, and constitutes an identification process clearly grounded within anthropology.

The idea of a deliberate alienation is an instance of border patrolling. Additionally, the argument that asserts the difference between *knowing* and *sensing* is an exercise of epistemic violence and ontological neglect because the criteria of differentiation between that which is to know and that which is 'simply sensed' stem *from* anthropology and respond to its interest. Indeed, this is also a Cartesian premise that separates knowledge from somatic experience, including the experience of sensing and of feeling—and this Cartesian proposition is not necessarily valid among the people whom the anthropologist studies. It is, significantly, an idea that collides with the Mamos' knowledge, and it allows the questions and concerns raised by colonized subjects to be sectioned off as emotional outbursts. By choosing this perspective, Hastrup also decontextualizes herself from the world, arguing instead on the basis of its contingency and fragmentation and by delimiting anthropological knowledge to something that arises in a given field of interaction. Indeed, anthropological knowledge arises within a field of interaction. The problem is where does one draw the boundaries that define the field of interaction, distinguishing relevant from irrelevant in scientific research? Of course, the problem is also concerned with issues of agency: who does what? Additionally, Hastrup does not discuss that her accentuation of the contingent and fragmented implies attenuation of continuity and of the whole, and that this choice inherently constitutes an ethical stance framed within a specific ontology of politics. My intent here is not to negate the contingent and fragmented aspects of the everyday. However, Hastrup's perspective is problematic in that the contingent and fragmented is *a priori* framed within the rationality of the master's house. Among other things, this position invisibilizes the aspects of the everyday by which mechanisms of oppression and exclusion operate.

Anthropology has been unable to address the crisis of representation that haunted it as a discipline from the 1960s to 1980s. Hastrup's disciplining of the discipline is a renewed contract to represent others in the image of the discipline. The dangers implicit in this practice connect to its open acknowledgement of the colonial problems of anthropology and representations of itself as having surpassed them. It is an example of an active covering over in bad faith, in the zone of being. To return to Lorde's metaphor of the master's house, anthropology uses a window in the house to see outside. From inside the house, one sees what is outside through one's own reflection. Very few, however, break the window glass and step outside. Hastrup's position amounts to approaching the glass and looking outside through a self-reflection, but her position retains the glass, and thereby the house, and actually defends its *raison d'être*. This stance amounts to a defense of the mechanisms of oppression. When Mamo Saúl Martínez ironically comments, when referring to monographs, 'anthropologists produce monologues', he is launching a critique that is similar to that expressed by Luis Guillermo Vasco. In his critique of North American postmodernists, Vasco argues that their approach does not solve the problem of ethnographic authority, because this decentring 'takes place only in the text and not in reality, only here [at home/ on campus] and not there where those to whom such knowledge relates live, [the decentering of authority takes place] by gracious concession of the author and not by a real change in social relations. To that extent, things are not fundamentally, really changed' (Vasco 2002, *Vivir y escribir en antropología*, translated from Spanish).

As an international or transnational academic discipline, anthropology cannot be separated from the world in which it operates and from which it continually emerges. That is, a world that not only consists of the specific places where fieldwork is carried out, but also a world where, indeed, anthropology remains in the zone of being. Many scholars have demonstrated the negative aspects of methodologies in the social sciences and the humanities in relation to critical thinking and transformative action (D'Amico-Samuels 1997; Fals Borda 1981; Fanon 1967; Gordon 2006a or b; Rivera Cusicanqui 2010; Sandoval 2000; Tuhiwai-Smith 1999; Vasco 2002). Positions that focus on the contingent and the fragmented often permit invisibilizing global and local mechanisms of oppression and exclusion because the one to decide what is the contingent and fragmented is the one who conducts the research, in the zone of being. That which to her might be contingent might very well be the basis of structural oppression for those in the zone of nonbeing, so blurring the recognition that coloniality and the death project are real can be studied and be transformed. Comparably, some social constructionist approaches make the mistake of treating social constructions as unreal. For example, indigenous peoples have been criticized for calling themselves indigenous, on the grounds that this category is a social construction of the colonial powers. It is; but this, however, does not mean the category is less real for being a creation of the zone of being. As an identity in the zone of nonbeing, being indigenous implies the possibilities of both negation, transformation, and rebellion. Social facts are social constructions that, as Gordon maintains, nevertheless remain real (Gordon 2006a, 46). While it is true that we cannot expect the social and human sciences to produce the same type of evidence as the hard sciences, Hastrup's leap to the contingency and fragmentation is, as suggested earlier, still framed within rationality. According to Gordon,

in the social sciences and the humanities, identification of phenomena requires working by rules whose subject matter always asserts an exception. The error is to make the exception the rule and the rule the exception. There are, as a matter of empirical fact, many aspects of social life over which we make fairly accurate predictions and assessments but it would be irresponsible to claim that we make foolproof claims. Those general moments are not of collapsing into essential*ism* but simply descriptions that are communicable because thematic. (Gordon 2006a, 17, emphasis retained)

Among the descriptions of the world that are communicable because thematic are those that speak to racism, coloniality, and the death project. When I simultaneously address the working of the world, and the ways the social sciences and humanities speak to and conceptualize that world, I imply that to *solely* attend to the ways the social sciences and the humanities conceptualize the world is, in the end, to pretend to detach these sciences from it. This is, for instance, one of the predicaments that attach to the problem of representation and ethnographic authority. By highlighting the death project, I not only present an analysis of the global configurations of power, I also sketch the context within which I work, which is crucial for the methods I employ. By highlighting the colonial politics of being, I address the existential and ontological dimensions of the global configurations of power.

SCIENTIFIC VALIDITY

When I stated in the introduction that while I work with the Mamos of the Sierra Nevada de Santa Marta, I also emphasized that I work *with* them, but not only to *study* them. My writing entails shifting the geography and temporality of reason, and so is guided by the opposition to the different aspects of knowledge production that sustain the death project. The theoretical support for this analysis is, *inter alia*, on the assessment of experts, the Mamos, who do not belong to the global elites, and on scholars and thinkers from the global south. Juan José Bautista's following formulation allows substantiating the significance of the Mamos' assessment:

If we conceive nature as Pachamama (Mother Life), that is, as a subject, we cannot relate to her as when we relate to an object, that is, we cannot relate to her as if she did not have voice and life. If we affirm that nature has life, but no voice, then she does not appear as subject, as Pachamama, but continues to appear as mere nature, as the modern romantics and now the ecologists speak about her, in the best of cases. If we, in turn, affirm that nature is a subject, that is Pachamama, then we are not only affirming that she has life but that she is also a subject, as humanity is, and if this is so, then we cannot avoid asking or consulting or talking with her of that which we want or can do with her in community. That is, it is not enough to care for her as one cares for a precious object; we need to respect her as we respect humanity as a subject. This is what our aboriginal peoples have done and do and it is perfectly rational, coherent with a rationality in which nature is not only the source of life but also subject of life. If this is so, then we have to go to her interpreters in order to relate to her, and they are not in the first world countries, they are not at any European or North American institution, they are among the peoples that this modernity has always wanted to negate. . . . The labels and sobriquets such as sorcerers, diviners, soothsayers, etc., with which the knowledge of modernity has named them has not done other things than to cover over the millennial wisdom with which we can now reclaim not only nature as Pachamama, but one of the fundamental sources from which it is possible to produce and reproduce life in general. (Bautista 2012, 92–93)

These experts, in this case the Mamos, offer a vital perspective with which to understand and interpret globalized power and its attending knowledge production and practices, so allowing for the transformation of such power, knowledge production, and practices. Their expertise is essential in the search for alternatives to human rights and development. To speak of the death project and to take the knowledge of the Mamos into account implies discussing a global society in crisis. According to Fals Borda, the role of sociology—and I add the social sciences and humanities—in times of crisis must be linked to the recognition that 'the events [Spanish: hechos] will determine whether the interpretations and assumptions about the crisis are correct or not, . . . sociology in times of crisis would only be justified [when] revealing the mechanisms that sharpen or mediate the crisis' (Fals Borda 1981, 34, translated from Spanish).

The scientific validation criteria here differ radically from Hastrup's. When Fals Borda speaks of *events* determining whether the interpretations and assumptions about the crisis are correct or not, I read him in this way—that is, only by doing, at the same time keeping continued attention to our embeddedness in the hierarchies of power, can we, as Mestizos, constantly assess whether our assumptions were correct, and whether our work serves the ends of liberation, or whether we are rather inhabiting and defending whiteness. However, when working with experts who commune with the Mother, their assessment is also crucial in relation to the validity of the research. This is why continued discussion with the Mamos has been pivotal in regard to this book. The criteria established by Fals Borda, when surveying his work of collaboration with several other Latin American sociologists, are linked to the recognition that the social and human sciences are not value-neutral. They are, instead, inherently political since they operate in wider a context than the ones normally taken into account. Because they are not value-neutral, and because they operate in wider contexts, according to Fals Borda, we cannot pretend that there is a difference between sociological (or anthropological) and political essays (Fals Borda 1981, 54). Fals Borda continues his summary:

> Consequently, the alternative presented to sociologists today is whether they will continue to prefer following the frameworks of structural balance and factual accumulation of routine, with its tendency to deal with inconsequential issues and known political implications, or those of imbalance and conflict, which would seem to be more in tune with our times of crisis, and of whose application one could also expect the effects to be, as before, both in the political realm and in the enrichment of science. (Fals Borda 1981, 54–55, translated from Spanish)

To use Santos's words, either we, as people in positions of relative power, ask weak questions, or we ask strong questions. Strong questions involve abandoning 'the reason that thinks, constructs and legitimises that which is criticisable' (Santos 2003, 30). This includes abandoning the idea that we can detach from the processes of colonization by critically addressing them.

Another facet to the dominant idea of methodologies and fieldwork connects to a crucial part of the academic writing process—and of scientific practice in general—being the continuous discussion with colleagues and other experts at conferences, seminars, and the like. In many instances, these discussions inform the academic's work as much as the issue, problem, or solution that academic is investigating. Often they influence our performances more notably than the subjects we study. However, in many methodological presentations, giving priority to what has happened in the field obscures this practice. The priority given to the description of the interrelationships in the field returns to the writer, placed in the academic realm, the power to define—she is not expected to continue discussions with the subjects of study after finishing the period of fieldwork. Rather, she returns home with some material on which she is expected to state something *scientifically* valid. The dividing line between knowledges that create the zone of nonbeing, the line that Hastrup also affirms, implies that research is usually divided between the anthropological knowledge and the knowledge of the investigated *others*. Therefore, fieldwork refers to a specific period or periods of research where the researcher is immersed in the *other's* world (D'Amico-Samuels 1997, 68–69).

When discussing the criteria of scientific validity that can be used against the death project, I emphasize the principles recollected by Fals Borda because they continue to echo in more contemporary decolonizing or liberation methodologies such as Vasco's. Although I present them separately below, these three criteria are to be applied concurrently to remain meaningful. The first criterion refers to the *type of commitment* (in the sense of the French term *engagement*) that the researcher has and has had with different groups in society; Fals Borda asks, 'Whom has she or he served, consciously or unconsciously, so far? How are the class, economic, political or religious interests of the groups to which she/he has belonged reflected in her work?' (Fals Borda 1981, 59). It is worth adding that it is also necessary to investigate in the interests of, at least, gender and race as reflected in a person's work, and that the question of who we have served needs to address us as communities, not as individuals. It must, thus, also include our ancestors. To this I would make explicit another criterion closely connected to this one: the criterion of *proximity*, which translates into ensuring our careful assessment of the type of questions we ask, and for whom these questions are relevant. The second criterion concerns the *objectivity*—here resignified in a way that leaves the logic of positivism aside—the logic from which Hastrup and Gordon also diverge. According to Fals Borda's presentation, a central measure of objectivity is connected to answering questions like, 'What are the groups that would not fear that one made a realistic estimate of the state of society and that, therefore, would provide support for the objectivity of science?' (Ibid., 59). As Malcolm X has put it: truth is on the side of the oppressed. A last criterion is the *ideal of service*: 'What are the groups, movements or political parties who seek to truly serve the whole society, not thinking about themselves but in the real benefit of the marginalized people that have hitherto been victims of history and institutions? What are the groups that, in turn, benefit from the ruling contradictions, inconsistencies and absurdities?' (Ibid., 59).

Obviously, the ideal of service is a hypothetical optimum. The total absence of exclusions therefore functions as a permanent ethical criterion (Dussel 1996) connected to the political concerns of liberation and to serving the benefit of all. The ideal of service as Fals Borda presents it resembles the Gramscian conception of the organic intellectual, as does Vasco's description of his methodologies of work. While these practices are important, they must be followed by the recognition of, and active engagement against, the privileges that are offered to the researcher if she commits to the colonial politics of being and defends the master's house. Paying attention to these privileges amounts to disclosing the everyday aspects and contingency of social life in a very different way than that conceptualized by Hastrup.

KNOWLEDGE AND PRIVILEGE

Although the white body is regarded as Presence, it lives the mode of Absence, and it offers, instead, its perspective as Presence. In other words, the white body is expected to be seen by others without seeing itself being seen. Its presence is therefore its perspectivity. Its mode of being, being self-justified, is never superfluous. (Gordon 1999, 103)

Lewis Gordon eloquently describes white privilege and the logic that grounds the colonial politics of being. The white perspectivity is what we are taught in university, itself a privilege that does not present itself as privilege, but rather as a self-justified scientific practice. To display the elements that allow for this perspectivity to uphold itself as self-justified scientific practice is a necessary step in the direction of decolonization (Biermann 2011, 394–95). The privileges offered by colonial rationality are teleological, epistemic, ontological, and methodological, and they offer important existential and material benefit to the ones who commit to them. I have, thus far in my elaborations, located three primary privileges and seven derivative, but no less important, ones.[2] The primary privileges are the teleological privilege, the privilege of epistemic perspective, and the privilege of ontology, respectively. These grant another set of privileges to the researcher, mainly through methodological and conceptual tools. In my elaborations concerning Gordon's distinction between reason and rationality, I used the metaphor of the master's house, and noted how the house defines itself as the other's future. This is what I mean by *teleological privilege*, inasmuch as it implies that those who defend and inhabit the master's house are those who determine the projects for the future of all. As I have already underlined, this is politically important inasmuch as the teleological privilege implies producing alternative political projects as impossible. In addressing the *privilege of epistemic perspective* I point to a problem that might be likened to that faced by white feminists, who addressed the tendency to 'add women' to traditional analyses (Harding 1987, 3) without abandoning the patriarchal frameworks of thought. In the case of epistemic racism, the problem involves the addition of some selected *other* scholars into the canon of Eurocentric knowledge construction without engaging with their conceptualizations and critique (Gordon 2006a, b). This addition not only leaves the master's house unchallenged, it also protects it. By stating this, my argument is that many of the streams of work in contemporary critical scientific practices are as colonial as the approaches they seek to criticize. This problem relates to many scholars who pretend to have transcended the problems of racism and coloniality in their scientific practices continue to enjoy and defend the privilege of epistemic perspective.

The privilege of epistemic perspective is inseparable from another privilege regarding *ontology*. By this I mean the privilege to define what is and what remains unsaid on the basis of ideas about validity, scientificity, and methodology. The privilege of ontology implies, for example, conducting scientific research about what *others* regard as the essence of being without reflecting upon whether indeed ontology is situational, or speaking about what *others* regard as the essence of being without conceptualizing the ontology whereby one puts oneself in the position of legitimately undertaking scientific work about ontology. Speaking about *other* ontologies cannot additionally be practiced without addressing the ways in which these specific academic streams, especially in ethnographic and anthropological studies, involve the scholar's meticulous self-representation and self-promotion as expert.

The privileges of teleology, epistemic perspective, and ontology carry with them other privileges that come along in dominant academic knowledge construction as naturalized, scientific principles. These are *not* scientific principles. Rather, they are requirements to incarnate and commit to the colonial politics of being—they are perspective as presence. The first methodological privilege is that of *choosing research subjects*. Any academic enquiry implies an *a priori* selection and prioritization concerning the subjects with whom one studies. Scholars and students alike like to choose subjects of research, and this choice is expected to be respected by the subjects themselves—the expected order of things is that one chooses and the subjects provide empirical material. Renouncing this privilege implies applying for the acceptance of one's research among the subjects of study, and this again implies waiving the privilege of defining the relevance of research foci, themes, or problems. The *privilege to define relevance* of research foci, themes, or problems connects to the words and tools that have been developed within the academic world to conceptualize the world—the master's house, or rationality. These words and tools provide legitimacy to research themes and to the focus of research.

The various disciplines operate with categories which ontologize the world—so that, for example, if we are to work with migrants, we can only do so legitimately if we inscribe ourselves within the large industry of migration studies—meaning that we are required to mold new bricks to add to the walls edified by that industry. In any case, the disciplines define that which is studied, and they very often work to reinforce dominant racist imaginaries about self, other, and belonging (Suárez-Krabbe 2014b). With this, they particularize, localize, and delegitimize as theoretically relevant the analyses made by those who are categorized as *other* and who critically engage in processes against these racist logics. The privilege to define relevance is accompanied by the *privilege to define context*. As we saw in the example of Hastrup, in dominant academic scholarship the researcher sets the boundaries that define the field of interaction, distinguishing relevant from irrelevant in scientific research. For example, when scholars set out to do 'thick description' of 'other ontologies', they are at the same time enacting the privilege that allows them to define that these are relevant, and to select what aspects of these ontologies are relevant (without discussing the 'relevant for whom', 'to what', and 'what for' questions). Is the description and analysis of shamanistic ontology relevant for the shaman, or is it more relevant for the scholar who is career building? The fourth privilege concerns *proximity (solidarity, sympathy) or distance* to research subjects. Even though many scholars work on the basis of a sense of solidarity with the *other*, they cover over the fact that solidarity enacted in this way is also a privilege. By this I mean that, like the sympathism of the Creoles presented in chapter 3, solidarity is embedded in the coloniality of power and often enacts the colonial politics of being. As French activist Houria Bouteldja has noted, the privilege of solidarity is exemplified by the ways in which it is seen as natural for Scandinavian women to share solidarity with Muslim women (implying that these last are oppressed), but Muslim women cannot share solidarity with Scandinavian women (implying that these last are free from oppression).[3] Research conducted on the basis of solidarity values the researcher's proximity to the researched, while at the same time advocating for different degrees of theoretical distance from them. Hence, many debates about fieldwork revolve around the dilemma concerned with nearness versus distance to the subjects of research. My point here is this is a false dilemma that covers over the real concern, which is the political and existential commitment of the researcher (Fals Bordas's *engagement*). In other words, by posing the problem as a methodological one concerning closeness or distance, scholars effectively enact the colonial politics of being by invisibilizing that both proximity and distance are complicit with the master's house when they require of the researcher that she depoliticize her work and ignore the existence of the master's house.

The privilege of proximity, solidarity, and distance is often enacted through another privilege, which is the *privilege to include other perspectives* into a seminar or research, defining the terms of inclusion on the basis of choice of research subject, of definition of context and of relevance. Indeed, contemporary academic knowledge construction includes long lines of people who are eager to give voice to the excluded other. For example, scholars interview immigrants, conduct workshops with sans-papiers, listen to people in indigenous movements, and carry out focus-group interviews with Muslim women. We strongly oppose oppression, we are against racism and intoler-ance, and defend qualitative and participatory methodologies to work with people. Again, the privilege lies precisely in our engagement, as participants, in these practices. This privilege speaks about racial hierarchies within the university, where it is per definition easier and more acceptable for a white-skinned person to speak about or from other perspectives than it is for a Per-son of Color. Lastly, the *privilege of the last word* speaks to the limits of inclusion and of solidarity. Indeed, many of the scholars who work with 'oth-ers' follow an ethical code that requires informed consent, and people's knowledge about the basic interest of the research. They, however, suspend this ethical code as soon as the information has been gathered, and so, despite their preoccupations concerning oppression and racism, they at the same time vigorously defend their privilege of having the last word, through which they are the masters of knowledge—the ultimate authorities to carry out the analy-ses and formulate conclusions. This privilege allows them to become the authority expert on people; the immigrant, the indigenous, the sans-papiers, the Muslim women, allowing them to be hailed as authentic, engaged, and committed within the academic realm.

ANDANDO

The methodology employed in the research process that informed the writing of this book was guided by my attempt to work against these privileges. It also used the criteria of scientific validity outlined earlier, and Vasco's *andar*. According to Vasco, in Colombia the questions about the role of the anthro-pologist and, more specifically, about how to study reality in order to trans-form it emerged in anthropology in the early 1970s with the rise and advancement of the indigenous organization and struggle (2002, *Replantea-miento del trabajo de campo*). This means that there is a direct correlation between the indigenous struggles of the country and the redefinition of anthropology: 'And these relationships of solidarity were the basis for creat-ing new ways of working, of research, since it was *necessary to know* in order to make effective the efforts of our solidarity' (*Descolonización y etnografía*, translated from Spanish, emphasis retained). The restatement of ethnographic work does not arise in writing but in the field. This is the reverse of many of the trends in dominant anthropology since James Clifford (1983) and his questioning of ethnographic authority to Hastrup (2004) with her concerns about evidence. This restatement also meant that the practice of publishing for the sake of academic publication lost its centrality. Publishing emerged more as a need to meet some of the purposes of struggle (Vasco 2002,

Replanteamiento de la relación con los indios). According to this perspective, writing is meaningless unless transformative processes validate it. Additionally, an important part of Vasco's discussions about methodology, and anthropological practice in general, is synthesized in his recognition of the need to *know*, highlighted above. To know, in Vasco's sense, implies the idea of 'unlearning to relearn' (Hernando-Llorens, Lorenso, and Pierce 2009; Walsh and García 2002; Santos 2005). That is, it highlights a need to unlearn our own notions of what science is and what is scientifically sound in order to generate—along the way—different notions with the subjects with whom we work. It also involves re*cognizing* the theories and stances of the people with whom we work, and adapting these theories and stances to scientific work and vice versa.

The methodology I defend is marked by the aim to contribute to decolonization and working against that, of producing a monograph. Herein lies the core of the distinction employed by Saúl Martínez between the mono-logic monographs of anthropologists and dialogue. It is, however, counterproductive to formulate an *a priori* determined method of research. This idea is not too removed from some of the approaches in anthropological methodology, such as in collaborative ethnography (Lassiter 2005). There are many approaches to methodology that speak of the large element of improvisation involved not only in the field, but also in the generation of theories, and of the way the researcher must be flexible to changes that the stay in the field itself may involve (Crandall 2008; Grasseni 2008; Halstead 2008; Retsikas 2008). However, in the dominant streams of anthropology, these approaches are often defended in a framework similar to the one used by Hastrup, where the concern with critical distance and the theoretical integrity of the researcher is connected to a notion of science as a separate sphere. While anthropology, the social sciences, and the humanities are immersed in the world and act in it, it is necessary to take into account that the contemporary world crises occur in different ways in different places, and that indeed, crisis is the norm in most places—not the exception. This complexity requires a methodological flexibility that follows not specific guidelines of action but a *commitment against the death project*. Nelson Maldonado-Torres has called *epistemic coyotismo* the practice of introducing 'theories and ideas that are banned or excluded from the halls of academia in the universities and formal centers of learning' (Maldonado-Torres 2006, 16). Disregarding our very different geo-body-politics, epistemic coyotes are often members of the global elites. We can find ourselves in marginal or even precarious positions within the university, and most of us, probably, practice an incorporated dissent, which is tolerated as long as it is not perceived as a threat. Nevertheless, we are (often a peripheral) part of the global elites. This means that we have some room to maneuver. As Santiago Castro-Gómez (2007, 80) has argued,

> [E]ven within the University new paradigms of thought and organization are being incorporated, [paradigms] that could help break the trap of [the] modern/colonial triangle, though still very precariously. I refer specifically to transdisciplinarity and complex thought as emerging models from which we could begin to build bridges towards a transcultural dialogue of knowledges. (Translated from Spanish)

Whichever strategy one follows to counter coloniality, the task of decolonization remains immense. Such enormous undertakings of collaboration can only reasonably happen by finding the way while walking—*andando*, as Vasco (2002) puts it. Finding the way while walking (*andar*) involves asking questions, discussing, learning while walking and changing accordingly.

Saúl Martínez has been my main guide in my process of andar with the Mamos. The majority of the discussions I had with the Mamos have occurred through him, and he has continued them with other Mamos and with me as often as we had the chance to do so. In practice, this was whenever we visited other Mamos' sites, or when they came to visit Martínez. I have worked with Saúl Martínez since the end of 2005. An important clarification concerning my work with the Mamos relates to my not having worked with their female counterparts—the Sagas. According to their philosophy, the Mamos need to conduct their work in complementarity with the Sagas, who are often their wives. However, for example, Mamo Martínez, a widower, does not work together with a Saga. As Martínez's protégé, I remained mostly in his sacred site and had very little interaction with the Sagas working with other Mamos. I did, however, learn how to weave with the Sagas that work with another important assessor, Mamo Juan, and weaving is a central step in the context of understanding the thought and work of the Sagas. At some point in our collaboration, when I asked Martínez whether I was speaking with him, with the Mother, or with all the Mamos when discussing things with him, he answered it was each, one and all. As we will see in the next chapter, this question is relevant because it takes into account the nature of communication that the Mamos have among themselves and with the Mother. When I say that my work is with the Mamos, this is done on the basis of my discussions with them, but also because they and the Mother have verified my work. Specifically, I have worked with the Mamos who are organized in the Council of Mamos. The Council of Mamos is an indispensable link to the Mother, as it consists of the experts who know what S/he says, dictates, and wants. In the Council of Mamos sit those people who are the interpreters and representatives of the Mother.[4] I have delivered versions of chapters to them in many different forms—either on paper or through spiritual means that I cannot make explicit here, but which have been carried out upon request of the Mamos as part of the process of verification and approval. Ironically, my way of working with the Mamos resembles the way that some scholars work when they study private companies—more specifically in the confidentiality agreements with these companies. As this book attests, my way of working with the Mamos breaks with the idea of the native informant. One can argue that I am in some ways their informant, and an informer on their behalf. In many ways my relationship to the Mamos has been similar to my ways of relating with my academic peers in which they have counseled me, we have had discussions, and I have learnt from them—crucially, the historization, theorization, and conceptualization have been undertaken from within the frameworks of the teaching of the Mamos, including the considerations about how academic scholarship is part of their context as well, among other localized globalisms. Working with the Mamos and from their theories does not mean that I agree with them on everything. Despite these differences, of which they are aware, the contents of the book are endorsed by the Mamos. Of course, responsibility for any errors is mine.

NOTES

1. See also Fotopoulos (2002).

2. I initially listed these privileges of research in the context of my work of collaboration with several of the movements involved in the Decoloniality Europe network between 2012 and 2014. These where disseminated informally in a document entitled "Charter of Decolonial Research Ethics."

3. http://www.decolonialtranslation.com/english/white-women-and-the-priviledge -of-solidarity.html.

4. See Bautista (2012, 94–95) on the 'Amautian Council'. *Amauta* is a Quechua word that corresponds to that of *Mamo* in Sierra Nevada.

Chapter Six

Common-Unity

As indigenous peoples, we are speaking from the spirit of thought, or from the dream of thought.

—Mamo Saúl Martínez

In September 2005, after the Mamos had approved our collaboration, I carried out one of the two formal interviews, which I did as part of our work. In this interview, I told Mamo Saúl Martínez that I wanted to discuss the epistemologies and ontologies of human rights with him, and suggested to him the concept of freedom as a point of inception. The starting point of the following pages is this, that when speaking about epistemologies and ontologies, as Mamo Martínez said, it is difficult to speak of *human rights* without speaking of *development* as well. As we have seen in previous chapters, the bond between human rights and development lies in the idea of race, which also organizes the dualisms that provide the rationale for these practices. The idea of race is tied to a specific long trajectory of practices of oppression, and human rights and development have consequently been formed as technologies of the implementation of the death project. Although the Mamos do not use the concept of the death project, it is clear that the conditions that they and their peoples have faced in the course of the last five hundred years have produced death and destruction in various ways. We saw the general outlines of this in chapter 2. But when Mamo Saúl Martínez states that one needs to analyze human rights and development as connected practices, he is not only criticizing their western hegemonic sense. He is also initiating a work of translation regarding Mamosean conceptions that in some ways may be likened to those of human rights and development. This chapter revolves around these ideas, and broaches some principles that provide an in-depth understanding of the *alternatives* to human rights and development from this particular locality in the global south. The notions presented, that is, the translation I do, has been approved by the Mamos. At the very least, this means that I have been able to understand the core grammar by which they live in the world and relate to the Mother.

FREEDOM

In the interview, Mamo Martínez explained that not only are people deemed free, other living beings, be they trees and stones, also have to be framed within the context of freedom. In addition, to be free is 'to respect the spaces of all existing elements in order to feel *compenetrados*', a term that I translate into English as *common-unity*.[1] Indeed, this quoted sentence is highly complex and conceptually dense. Freedom is a means to achieve the state of common-unity, or perhaps more accurately, freedom is what common-unity looks like in the material realm. Life does not include the connotation to individuality it often does when we employ the term as westernized subjects. Instead, life needs to be understood as the perpetual common-unity of the elements, be they human, fungus, wind, or fire. In a simplified way, becoming is a process not of this tree or that baby; it is, if you will, a complete package where everything within and in between the tree and the baby also becomes, and where the tree and the baby interact. The tree and the baby are, but only in common-unity. It might be useful to think metaphorically of common-unity as fire. Fire is the common-unity of air and matter, and is neither gas nor physical substance; it is itself, that is, it is flame. At the same time, fire is the process of becoming ash, which again marries earth to become the tree that can be part of fire—which the infant may have lighted. Fire *is*, and it is also *in* and *in between* air, matter and soot; and air, matter and ash are also in and in between flame. So are the tree and the infant.

The idea of common-unity is informed in this way by a metaphysical—at the same time material—emphasis on the interrelationships between living agents, including human beings. Common-unity also refers to *being* the whole. Common-unity is a vital state, especially for a Mamo whose work depends on unbroken communion with all other beings in order to assess the state of equilibrium or disequilibrium of life. Through these assessments of equilibrium or disequilibrium, the debts to the Mother are identified, and the appropriateness and subsequent price of any action settled. The system of payment to the Mother, the Mamos explain, is simple: in 'civilization' we pay taxes, we pay for the sewage system, etc.—everything costs. In a similar way, the Mother has to receive offerings—*pagamentos*. Additionally, every action must be committed only with her permission. While the Mamos translate this

aspect of the relationship to the Mother using the logic of the current capitalist system, the practice that they defend is corrosive to that capitalist structure. The Mother is a subject who is central in our activities, and when
everything we do passes through her and is reigned by a logic of reciprocity
where we pay for what S/he allows us creating and doing, the logic is no
longer that of accumulation. We can no longer exploit fellow human beings,
we can no longer practice the extensive extraction of natural resources without provision for their renewal, and we definitely have to abandon the pace
and the time-space of capitalism. In this sense, to continue offering payment
to the Mother is part of the offensive struggles; it is an act of rebellion.

We also need to note that common-unity does not suggest that there are no
differences among living agents. From this perspective, difference and diversity are prerequisites of life. To expand on this idea, just because a stone differs from a human being it does not mean that the stone and the human being
are not equally important. Each plays a different role in the world, and the
role played by each is essential to the world. Additionally, thinking through
common-unity shows how concepts like society and agency, central to the
social sciences and the humanities, are inherently political. They authorize
some political projects, and deauthorize others. Indeed, to conceive of the
social as only human-human dependent is an extremely limited way to think.
This is one of the ideas behind Actor-Network Theory (Yehia 2007; Latour
1993), as well as some of the Deleuzian-inspired approaches to reality such
as Tim Ingold's (2005, 2006, 2007). Juan José Bautista has also indicated this
problem, and criticized it on the grounds that the conceptualization of *social*
movements is a sweeping and generalizing way to address struggles that
might differ radically from one another (Bautista 2012, 109–16, ff 11, 13).
Some struggles, for instance, rest upon the ontological separation of the
human with nature and the other colonial dualisms; they rely upon the negation of the Mother, and center only in the social understood in this anthropocentric way. Other struggles reside in communitarism (Bautista) or in
common-unity with the Mother. This criticism of the social as an anthropocentric category implies considering how, for example, the problems of climate change, and not only its effects, are social—they connect to our
relationships with one another as human beings, as well as our relationships
to other beings. In a sense, climate change is the result of the lack of freedom,
that is, it is the result of our failure as human beings to act in common-unity:

[Freedom does not pertain only to] humans or animals, rather, freedom corresponds
to all—that which inhabits, and that which exists; freedom is of existence. For example, we do not have a law that says that one cannot mistreat animals nor corral and
control the waters because these are to us fundamental and probably basic

principles—every being needs to have its right to existence and life and permanence. (Mamo Saúl Martínez, Bogotá, February 2006)

The peoples of the Sierra Nevada do not have laws that prohibit actions that restrain the freedom of existence. But as we have seen, they have the Law of Origin. As we enhance our understanding of how the alternatives to human rights and development from the global south are configured, we need to return once again to the Law of Origin and common-unity, taking into consideration *relinking* and the realm of *aluna*.

RELINKING

To the Mamos from the Sierra Nevada, dialogue and interaction do not only occur between human beings but include speaking and listening to the mountains, the elements, and so on. The Mamos are trained to conduct this form of communication, and it is through this communication that the Law of Origin is *read*. This, to our perceptions, extended form of communication is central inasmuch as it challenges not only the conception of the social, but also the idea of culture as something limited to the human social realm. In this context it is important to address some issues regarding translation. Translation implies the possibility of mutual intelligibility. In our work, the Mamos and I have focused on discussing the ideas and practices of human rights and development, and the alternative conceptions than Mamosean thought provides. Human rights and development constitute a 'contact zone' (Santos 2009, 45–46), or a sort of *lingua franca*. In other words, they function as common frames of reference which both the Mamos and I have knowledge about. But more than translation, our work has been of *interlocution*, that is, a speaking between, as addressed by Mamo Martínez when three Colombian documentary filmmakers asked him about what the Law of Origin is:

> I would like to speak to the younger sibling some issues in which we might be able to have some inter-locution at this point. . . . To us the law is order. I know what law means in my language. Among other things, it is translated as an order, and orders are to be complied with. The Law of Origin is a word that we have found to be able to understand each other, [a word that] facilitates inter-locution with the younger sibling using the same word: law. Of course, to say, 'of origin', is to speak of an infinite principle that transcends human thought. As indigenous peoples, we are talking from the spirit of thought, or from the dream of thought, so to speak. Before the [moment] in which the sensation of having a question in our minds was formed, from behind there, from the spirit of thought, orders were given—I don't know whether to say orders; for who gave them?—[orders] of our tradition, our beliefs that beyond being beliefs are our fundamental criteria as indigenous [people].[2]

Mamo Martínez points to the concept of the Law of Origin being in itself an act of translation, an attempt to explain to the younger siblings what is at stake in order to have interlocution. Inasmuch as the younger siblings are, theoretically at least, respectful of laws, the word *law* is used to emphasize the necessity to comply with the guidelines and principles of the Mother. *Origin* is, in turn, used with *law* to give it the necessary weight and transcendence as something primordial, that is, as something permanent and fundamental. *Belief* is used to highlight the notion's limited usefulness to explain how the spiritual realm is just as real as the material; how sociality includes all beings, and how 'law' emerges in the interaction with all the beings. Additionally, when Martínez speaks about 'the spirit of thought' and 'the dream of thought', he is translating *aluna*. When I use common-unity, I am engaging in a doubled translation; common-unity is itself a translation of a complex condition, and I am translating in into a form by which I might enter into interlocution with dominant knowledge construction. Similarly, to continue this possible interlocution, *aluna* has to be taken into account when speaking and writing about culture, society, and identity, and these notions need to be changed in order to be able to capture some aspects of the reality of the Mamos and the peoples of Sierra Nevada. We will return to these aspects of reality in the next chapter. Understanding culture, society, and identity, taking into account common-unity and *aluna* additionally, allows us to grasp how precisely it is that the Mamos' knowledge and practice is *religious*.

For the concept of culture to be meaningful in discussions with the Mamos, it must at least be defined in terms that do not rely solely on human-to-human interaction. The dominant ideas of culture and society rely on the separation between that which is thought of as human and that which is considered as being nature. Indeed, an oft-neglected political characteristic of these terms becomes clear, in which there is a tendency to ignore the participation of the Mother in the making of the world and life. In this regard, an understanding of culture partly inspired by Enrique Dussel is useful. In similar ways to Antonio Gramsci, Dussel conceives of culture as a system of types of labor, where the physical outcomes of work (the material) and the symbolic creations are cultural productions. *Production* here refers to the etymological sense of bringing forth. This means that the ways in which we produce what we need *is* what constitutes us as subjects. Subjectivity is corporeal and lived, and the intersubjective (and hence also the cultural) is made as much of the embodied and material as of the symbolic. Considering the Mamosean knowledge requires us to extend the Dusselian conception of culture to include the Mother and all of her beings as much as the human—we all engage in processes of *bringing forth* (production). This extension of the Dusselian understanding of culture privileges processes of becoming. In

Mamosean thought, all beings are involved in cultural processes dictated by the Mother. While the processes of becoming are universal, in the sense that all that exists is engaged in them, the cultural processes dictated by this universal are partial and situational—to the Mamos culture implies a constant *relinking* in the world. Martínez has told me that only if religion is understood as relinking can we speak of the knowledge of the peoples of Sierra Nevada as being religious.

This realization adds another level of understanding to Mamo Martínez's observation that the peoples of Sierra Nevada have been colonized and conquered but never *dis-covered*. As we have seen, this statement points to the indigenous peoples having been *covered over*; they have never been taken as *who* and *what* they are. Who and what they are revolves around Martínez's distinction between the concepts of culture and identity. Remembering when Martínez uses these concepts, he is using them as concepts by which he is kept in the zone of nonbeing, and in his conceptual distinction, he reframes them in a way that opens a space for *being*. To Martínez culture changes but identity remains stable. Culture is to be thought of as customs, habits, ways of dressing, eating, and *relinking* (*re-ligar*) in the world. In a way, Martínez is speaking of culture in the colloquial sense of the term. For example, if he were to come to Denmark, he would of course adapt: he would dress differently because of the climate; he would eat food other than that he is used to; he would go about in the world in a radically different way than how he does in Sierra Nevada. In short, he would relink.

Relinking, as Martínez uses the expression, refers to the etymological meaning of *religion*—*re-ligare* as reconnection (that might imply a reconnection to the divine), and *re-legere* as rereading (the Law of Origin) in opposition to *nec-legere*, to disregard. However, Martínez's point is that while he would relink culturally, he would always be Kankuamo. So, he will change culturally, however, he will not alter in terms of his identity. To dis-cover the meaning of relinking is crucial in this concern. Relinking implies reestablishing a relationship in the world, that is, *relating* to it taking into account the actors present, as part of the practice of freedom. However, this would not change the circumstances of the one who is relinking—she continues to be *what* she is. Martínez is using culture to refer to the changing conditions of human interaction with one another and with our surroundings—to the changing conditions humans face in the world. In this sense, he is referring to a conception of culture that relates more to customs than to the conditions by which these customs—and identities—become meaningful. He does not call this condition culture; he calls it common-unity with the Mother. As we have seen, the Mother is the one who has given life and allows for the perpetuation of life; S/he is both *she* and *he*. S/he is intelligence and a universal will to live. Mainly, but not exclusively, S/he is in *aluna*. *Aluna* bears a striking resemblance to Wilson Harris's 'conception of the unconscious existence of consciousness' (Henry 2000, 95). Writing on Harris, Paget Henry notes the similarity between the unconscious existence of consciousness, Hegel's *spirit*, and the African idea of *axè* (Ibid., 94). Similarly, Bautista relies to some extent on a Hegelian notion of spirit to explain pivotal aspects related to the decolonization processes today (Bautista 2012). As we know, the notion of axè is commonly found in African diasporic societies as those in the Caribbean. According to Henry, the major difference between unconscious existence of consciousness and axè 'is that Harris' spirituality is radically immanent and does not have the permanent externalized and projected features of African spirituality' (Henry 2000, 94). This is precisely where Harris's spirituality is similar to the one of the Mamos—*aluna* is, beyond doubt, radically immanent. Additionally, Harris's consciousness is similar to the Mother, who most often—but not exclusively—communicates and interacts in the realm of *aluna*.

Both Martínez's interpretation of Mamosean thought and Harris's phenomenology offer important reflections on the ways in which some (of us) human beings forget or deny *aluna* and are thereby unable to acknowledge the Mother/consciousness. While it is beyond the scope of this examination to enter into a detailed discussion of the Mamos' conception of *aluna* and the denial of it in relation to Harris's self-enclosure of the ego, nonetheless, what some humans do in relation to the Mother, according to the Mamos, is a form of bad faith. Harris's self-enclosure of the ego is a form of self-enclosure that leaves the ego in a void from consciousness (Henry 2000, 97–104). Similarly, we ignore the existence of the Mother in our world when we are part of her in common-unity. By enclosing ourselves in ego-centred identities we live a lie—we affirm the Emperor is wearing beautiful attire—relegating the Mother to the realm of nonbeing. This happens, for example, when we rely only on five senses to grasp reality. In advantaging specific sensory perception, most notably sight, we simultaneously weaken the other senses through which the Mother can be felt, those senses that, among other things, connect us in *aluna*. Not using these other senses is like not using specific muscles of the body: the ones used the most prove the strongest; the others are weakened but not dead. This means that we do still sense the Mother, we just relegate these experiences to the realm of the unreal. Among the experiences we have in *aluna* are dreams, visions, and presentiments. In this regard, Harris's thought is also aligned with the Mamos—to him, consciousness 'breaks through the walls of the ego' precisely through dreams, visions, and so forth (Henry 2000, 99–100).

To be in common-unity implies being interconnected in the realm of *aluna* as well as in the material realm. In *aluna,* identity is sociogenic, so to speak, but sociogenic in an *extended* sense where the social also is composed of the interaction between humans, animals, the elements, the weather, spirits, plants, and so on. It is this interaction in the extended social realm that allows us to distinguish between humans and other beings. In *aluna,* all beings are ever-changing, but remain the same because they fulfill specific purposes in the processes of life and becoming. To be a Kankuamo, to Saúl Martínez, is then to be *human* as it is configured in the extended social realm, where *aluna* and the material world intersect. This intersection comprises the Law of Origin. This means, among other things, that what each human is relates to the Law of Origin. Additionally, if one cannot act according to the specific purposes in the processes of life and becoming in common-unity, one's freedom is restricted and one is unable to act according to one's responsibilities. According to Mamo Martínez,

> And those trees, braided into one another; each one of them is fulfilling their job in their freedom . . . of being an orange tree. No matter if it is embraced with an avocado tree, the orange will have oranges, and the avocado will have avocados, each one fulfills their function. Because there one understands freedom, freedom is to feel useful in the middle of the contexts in which one is, but respecting that the other, that the product of the other, is as useful as mine, and that we both can be useful to the rest. (Atánquez, July 2009)

This explanation is not to be read as a metaphor and legitimation of racial, social, and economic inequalities between people. It is to be understood literally; in that it speaks to interaction in situations, where the point of departure is that all are equal but different, such as the idea promoted by other indigenous groups and movements. Thus, to the Mamos, only humans living in an anthropocentric world can have different identities, or indeed change one identity for another. But human beings living in common-unity cannot do so—their role here is tied to larger processes, which, in this sense, make their identity essentially situated.

Mamo Martínez's distinction between culture and identity is neither colloquial nor essentialist. It entails a differentiation between the questions of the difference between being a human being *anthropocentrically,* and being a human being *biologically.* That is, in relation to other beings where what westerners call biologically and physically dependent features (such as having the ability to communicate through language) is privileged over more anthropocentrically understood features (such as making social constructions through language) (Wiredu 1996). Additionally, Mamo Martínez's distinction between culture and identity is also concerned with the consequences that these ways of being have in terms of our being in the world. Thus, humans remain humans in terms of biological uniqueness as human. In this regard, there are parallels to the discussions on species boundaries and phylogenetics (e.g., Wheeler and Meier 2000), and those of eco-criticism (e.g., Huggan and Tiffin 2010). Among other things, these discussions are about the distinction of, for example, a human from a monkey, being a human-made distinction that not only privileges the gaze of the human over that of the monkey, but that advantages the gaze of a specific human (in the biological sciences, the western man) over that of other humans (Schiebinger 1993). I have not discussed the taxonomy of species with the Mamos, however, what we might call the biologically dependent uniqueness with which they operate—for example, our ability to have complex communication—is universal for humans. Disregarding that in the anthropocentric social realm we are all different from one another, I purposely read the biological into Martínez's distinction between culture and identity, to interpose a crucial element. That element being, while the Mamos recognize a distinction between humans and other beings (that we conflate into *nature*), they, as mentioned, emphasize our community with these other beings through common-unity. It is through common-unity that *what* we are and *who* we are becomes meaningful. The Mamos define their identity, for example, as Kankuamo, not only on their differences to other people in an anthropocentric social realm. They also do so on the recognition of the community with the other beings, which in *aluna* is also decisive for the role that a Kankuamo, and every other human community, must play in the world—including our anthropocentric world. The role that different groups of humans can play in relation to the Mother might differ according to situation; all roles are, however, equally important, especially when played out in respect of the Law of Origin.

LAW, AUTHORITY, AND MANAGEMENT

The Mamos' purpose is to collaborate, in common-unity, with the Mother, who in turn *is* life and becoming. This is the essence of Mamo identity, and the necessary role of human beings is, according to the Mamos' expertise, to act in accordance with the Law of Origin. The Mother and *aluna* are constitutive parts of reality, where human beings cohabit with all other beings in common-unity. As we will see in the next chapter, the processes of identity reconstruction in which Saúl Martínez is engaged as a Mamo belonging to the Kankuamo people of the Sierra imply not only an affirmation of existence and a negation of the zone of nonbeing in the realm of human beings. Significantly, the processes of identity reconstruction also involve a defense of the processes of life and becoming, of the Mother. To understand these processes in terms of an anthropocentric notion of reconstruction of identity is a limiting way to approach the problems that the Mamos face. In the same way that reconstruction of identity, as conceptualized in the academic realm, does not allow an understanding of what is at stake in the work of the Mamos, the ideas of power and authority need to be redefined. Anthropocentric ideas of power make limited sense in the Mamos' philosophy. Instead, power needs to be conceptualized taking into account common-unity. The following summarizes these ideas:

> In the Law of Sé [Law of Origin] is order, harmony, in Serankwa is authority, organisation; in Seynekun is management, practice, and use of our territory; the three together sum up our vision of life, our system of territorial organisation [legal system].[3]

The Law of Origin contains order and harmony. Harmony understood within the idea of complementarity includes both the positive and the negative aspects of life. This means that harmony encompasses the balanced interaction between life and death, and the continuous processes of becoming that are regulated by the Mother. Dry periods with scarcity of food can, for example, be necessary for the general balance of the Mother and, despite indicating less food for the humans and animals, they are also balanced—for instance, as a consequence fewer children are born.

Gender, if such category is meaningful at all in this context, is organized loosely according to Serankwa and Seynekun. But my understanding is that more than speaking to gender roles, Serankwa and Seynekun are principles that allow comprehending some of the methods by which the Mother works in order to bring about and maintain the processes of life and becoming. They are also principles that allow meaningful organization in relation to the Mother. *Serankwa's* role in the material human world is attached to men and relates to authority and organization. *Seynekun*—whose role in the human material world is attached to women—is practice, management, and use of the territory. The use of the territory, as well as the social organization in relation to it, is connected to the Law of Origin. This is why the conjunction of the Law of Origin, Serankwa and Seynekun, is often explained as a legal system. It relates to norms concerning what can be done in the territory and how it can be done, which determine the ways in which authority and organization can be practiced. Consequently, these elements cannot be meaningfully understood by and in themselves.

Authority and power are, rather, the three together: *Sé, Serankwa,* and *Seynekun.* Only by suspending anthropocentric notions of gender, authority, and power is it possible to understand the ways in which they are practiced in common-unity—these are principles in *aluna* that are nevertheless also principles in the material world. The inseparability of *aluna* and the material world, which is also a dimension of common-unity, would then, in the perspective of the Mamos, correspond to the public realm of the political community—again keeping in mind the *other* subjectivities. To illustrate this, it is important to return to the metaphor of fire as common-unity. Indeed, when thought of that way, then questions arise: Who is the actor? Where does the field of force start, and where does it end? Who has the authority or power to light the fire? An obvious and humorous answer would be that the actor is the fire lighter; that is, the infant. This is of course anthropocentrically true. However, seen from the perspective of common-unity, this only confirms the rule: if it indeed were a person that lit the fire, she would *be* part of the possibility of fire in that specific *situation*, that is, she would be part of fire in *aluna*.

The Mamos are organized in the Council of Mamos, which communicates internally not only through reunions at different places of the Sierra, but also in *aluna*. The Mamos are their peoples' highest authorities in the sense that they are the mediums through which communion with the Mother takes place, and in the sense of Serankwa explained above. Consulting with the Mother is essential in the context of ensuring that every action abides with life and becoming, at an anthropocentric level, as at the level of common-unity. Their work is always concerted, and one Mamos' reading of the Law of Origin is done in consultation with the other Mamos in order to ensure accuracy. If a Mamo reads the Law of Origin without conferring with the other Mamos in matters that pertain to one or all the four groups—that is, if he gives counsel without the corroboration of his peers—he is excluded or suspended from the Council, exactly because the Council's role is to ensure precision. Consultation within the Mamo Council is the most important validation mechanism for the readings of the law. Of course, authority lies also in interpretation, and despite the processes of validation and control of the Mamo Council, the Mamos remain *interpreters*, they are not the law. One of the important roles of the Council of Mamos is to avoid single Mamos' abuse of their position of authority as interpreters of the law.

The Mamos do not command; they guide according to the law. People themselves decide whether they follow the guidelines; for the Mamos' role is to counsel. According to the Mamos, we can all communicate in *aluna* and do so constantly. By this, we too have access to the law. That the Mamos are the experienced readers of the Law of Origin does not change this fact, when carrying out their interpretations, they must take into account what other people—non-Mamos, so to speak—experience and sense in *aluna*. At

times, these other experiences and sensory perceptions require that the
Mamos reassess their interpretation of the law; the Law of Origin is never
absolute or abstract. It is highly complex. It is also conditional on circumstances and, as such, cannot be detached from the people and other beings
that comprise a given situation. In the realm of the humans, the Mamos'
authority—and by extension the wellbeing of the Mother—depends upon
their peoples' ability to take into account the Mother and what S/he communicates to them (the non-Mamos) in *aluna*. When their people live in bad faith
and relegate the Mother to the zone of nonbeing, the authority of the Mamos
is crushed, and their work to preserve life is being weakened. As we will
see in the next chapter, because their peoples themselves suffer the effects of
coloniality and live themselves in the zone of nonbeing, the processes of identity (re)construction are vital *both* in the anthropocentric realm of relations
and in the larger context of common-unity.

LIBERATION AND THE FUTURE

To the Mamos, freedom is within situations, and in the construction of the
future all beings participate: stones, trees, animals, the elements, spirits, and
humans. First, common-unity challenges the limitations of the anthropocentric premise regarding humans, as self-enclosed beings that are, at the same
time, isolated from one another and who, only through aggregation, conform
a *community*. Secondly, it disputes this anthropocentric premise's inability to
recognize the interconnectedness between the human and the nonhuman, the
common-unity. Thirdly, common-unity tests the death project's rejection of
those parts of humanity who see this relationship as essential to their existence. Finally, it leads to the negation of the hierarchical concepts implicit in
the death project; for example, a human being is considered, by definition,
more valuable than a stone and so has rights that a stone does not have. As
such, the notion of freedom attached to common-unity may be usefully likened to Cornel West's notion of justice as the public expression of love. To
the Mamos,

> freedom thinking is complex to the extent that to take a stone from one place to the
> other, one must already have thought that that hole that remains in the earth, in the
> Mother, must be replaced by other means. . . . To be free is also to respect the spaces
> of all existing elements in order to feel in common-unity. (Mamo Saúl Martínez,
> Bogotá, February 2006)

In these terms, Mamo Martínez expresses three crucial, interconnected issues
in Mamo knowledge, whereby freedom and justice are interdependent: the

first refers to the *situational legitimacy* of being/acting, the second to the *other, extended, subjectivities*, and the third as the *relationship between situations and responsibility*.

Against this backdrop, it is important to analyze the word 'situation' contextually; a situation is where time and place prove inseparable. Situation is, additionally, a relational concept; a situation can only be located in the interrelationship between the elements that compose it. To speak of something as being *situational*—a necessary redundancy—then refers to that which is governed by the circumstances that comprise a situation, considering also the realm of *aluna*. Everything is *in situation* as it were, but no situation is ever the same; this is why the Mamos' work is indispensable and permanent, and why the Law of Origin is necessarily dynamic. The language of colonial rationality implies, for instance, a centre *in* each individual. Framed in this language, freedom in common-unity means that my liberties stop where my respect and love for the other starts, that is, situational legitimacy. Freedom in common-unity also means actions are only legitimate to the extent to which they neither delink from the situation, nor universalize my own position, so that my ego becomes the only circumstance taken into account, thus invisibilizing any other. In Mamo Martínez's words:

> We need to understand that the bird, the ant, the snake, the scorpion, the tiger, the elephant and any other animal . . . they all have the same right of life in the universe as the *maloca* [house], the herbs; the same with the waters' [right] to run freely. We cannot inhibit the freedom of the animals, of people, but neither can we inhibit the freedom of nature, of the greenness, of biodiversity—as we can neither inhibit the freedom of a river. [The rivers] have the right to run freely, and keep the equilibrium between sea and land. Of not being interrupted in their courses.[4]

The problems of human rights and development include climate change issues. To the Mamos, the problems of violations of human rights, the degradation of nature, and illness all are an outcome of the inability or unwillingness to reimburse the Mother. They are the effects of a fundamental disequilibrium in terms of reciprocity regarding the Mother and all *other* subjectivities, which is caused by the universalization of some peoples' situation as being everyone's situation. Violence occurs when one is able to objectify *the other* to such an extent that their life and being no longer is relevant to one's own, and so not at issue. However, the objectification of the *other* is a choice, and as such, it can be *unchosen*. One has the freedom to choose or unchoose this attitude, which, in the context of the ideas of the Mamos, is an attitude complicit with the death project.

If I universalize my situation, the world inevitably revolves around myself, only and consequently, whoever (whatever) does not fit into this scheme is relegated as *other* to the zone of nonbeing. This applies both to people as to those beings that, in the dominant rationality, belong to the realm of nature, spirituality and materiality. This is why the problems of climate change also need to be viewed within this framing device. The situational legitimacy of being/acting implies that freedom has clear limits, and that these limits are dictated by the expression of the recognition of common-unity. The limits to freedom cannot be settled as an abstract universal principle; nor can they be dictated *a priori*. They can only be practically experienced (as situations, as responsibility, and as justice), and in this again it is imperative that we remember that humans are not the only ones who experience them. Freedom in common-unity then can only exist as an incorporated, coopted, principle—as the principle of consumption as freedom is an incorporated part of western-based notions and practices (Sen 1999, 14). According to Mamo Martínez,

> To us, to *be in freedom* does not mean that I have to use things at my command—but in *their* moment; even to take a plant that is sacred to us, in medicine, that has its *time*, its *way*, and its *place*. To take a plant and use it for headache, fever, it is not only about detaching the branch off the tree. Rather, it has its way to be taken, its permission of how it is to be taken, because it is a tree that is growing, at its command, *in its* freedom. (Atánquez, February 2009; emphases added)

Additionally, then, freedom includes possibilities of life and of death. A stone might, for example, provide cover, protection, and humidity for the seed, which is only starting to root. Removing the stone disrupts, in this case, a process of becoming. Then before carrying out this action, one needs to pay consideration to whether it disrespects common-unity between the stone, the tree-in-becoming and other beings, such as the weather, in which the tree can grow, or whether one's action may become part of a process of becoming in common-unity. Consequently, freedom is practiced in spatial and temporal contexts as well; that is, situationally. In the example I use, taking the stone is an action that may have direct consequences in present time, to the future, and in the landscape. Common-unity implies that beings constantly respond to each other, and that humans are embedded in these chains of interaction and responses as much as any other being—as much as the stone. To remove the stone is, then, not an insignificant action; it is interaction. Taking the stone away must be situationally legitimate, by this I mean a legitimacy developed through the relationship between situations, responsibility, and justice. My comprehension of responsibility in this instance is in the Dusselian sense (1996, 49), and is required and necessary to consciously be undertaken, as a prerequisite to situational legitimacy. In Sierra Nevada de Santa Marta, this legitimacy is established through the Mamos' consultations of the Law of Origin.

The death project refers to the practices of massive exploitation, murder, and displacement of the majority of the earth's population, and the massive exploitation, displacement, and annihilation of the natural world. Perceived through common-unity, the notion of freedom in dominant human rights is some humans' freedom *for* death, as in the freedom to manage nature at our command. Through situational legitimacy of being/acting, other subjectivities, and the relationship between situations and responsibility, freedom becomes freedom *for* life and *in* life. Freedom then requires respect, which in turn may be that which guarantees that freedom is just. In Mamo Martínez's words:

> If it is not associated with respect, it is not freedom. In a general context, freedom is nothing but a dictate. It is a formula. But it does not have a practical component—in order to have that, freedom has to depart from the principle of respect. Respect of the other's right to conviviality. I cannot use freedom in order to favor myself and invalidate the other. That is what happens. There is my freedom, but it is a freedom that only some can practice, and whose space only some can enjoy. Others cannot. There is no equilibrium. If there is no equilibrium, there is no profound reason [to ground freedom]. In Indigenous thought freedom must be of the integrity. And when there is freedom, there cannot be any situation of power [abuse].
> (Atánquez, February 2009)

An important consequence of considering the problems of human rights, development, and climate change through common-unity concerns disequilibrium. Disequilibrium in this context is synonymous with that which impedes freedom and justice, and more precisely the situations of power abuse mentioned by Mamo Martínez above. According to Tim Ingold, a shortcoming of his own elaborations of political ecology inspired by the challenge of the human-nature dualism relates to how to 'understand the dynamics of power in human environmental relationships' (Ingold 2005, 503–4). The Mamosean perspective on common-unity, while being important in grounding human rights and development in a nonracist and *ecological* ethics, seems to share some of the same problems. However, the understanding of culture as relinking does take into account that, among humans, the role that humans play towards each other—and towards the Mother and other subjects—varies. In this context, the discussion on freedom *for* death and freedom *for* life is important. The *for* in both freedoms point to the centrality of power. History, agency, and society are political concepts precisely because of their instrumentality in power relations both among humans and between humans and nature.

The vast majority of the difficulties relating to human rights, development, and climate change are human-made. More precisely, as detailed in part one of this book, these problems emerge in the context of coloniality as effects of the actions of the white, Christian, European man. Freedom as a means to achieve common-unity diverges from dominant human rights and development because it does not delink. Freedom is practical, situational, material, spiritual, corporeal, and contextual. The example of the stone and the seed proves salient, whereby landscape and time cannot be separated; time would be *in* the landscape as much as *of* it and vice versa. It entails also that the construction of the future is not only a matter of human beings; stones, seeds, and trees are also active actors in the construction of the future. Furthermore, the future is not only a matter of a horizon (or utopia) imagined by human beings, it involves as much the present actions and its contexts, including the acts of stones and trees. So, in the same way as freedom is not abstract, neither is the future.

In part one of the book we saw how coloniality also serves to negate the possibility of worlds and knowledges otherwise, that is, of different futures, different horizons, and different perspectives. To the Mamos, western modes of life and views on development do not constitute projects in which they wish to participate. This does not mean that they want to return to the past; their notion of time is different from the linear conception of time. Without the ancestral knowledge, the future simply does not make sense and indications of how to act in it are lost. The Mamos' view of the future is founded on common-unity and must accordingly respect the Law of Origin. The future is present in the sense that situational legitimacy forms part of it. It is concerned with the relationship between situations, responsibility, and freedom as explained previously. This can only be practiced *slowly* in order to feel the moment's constitutive-ness of the future in the terms of common-unity.

RUPTURE

I have suggested that Serankwa and Seynekun may be understood as methods by which the Mother works in her bringing about and perpetuating being, and that they, at the same time, are guiding principles of organization in common-unity with the Mother. In this second understanding, the principle of Serankwa dictates guidelines for authority and organization, while the principle of Seynekun pertains to the management and use of the territory. Serankwa's role seems to be more attached to the social relations in play in common-unity, while Seynekun's role appears to connect *aluna* and the material realm, making those social relations possible. In chapter 2, I mentioned that to the Mamos, Seynekun encompasses the vision of development of the four peoples, that is, Seynekun provides the guidelines for the material possibilities of reproduction of the Kankuamo, Arhuaco, Kogi, and Wiwa. This understanding of development (Seynekun) is closely linked to the Law of Origin and Serankwa. In the words available for translating these notions, then, one can say that development/management, authority/organization, and law are inseparable, and constitute the legal system of the four peoples. The Law of Origin is accessible through common-unity. Inasmuch as any human being has access to *aluna*, she has also access to the law. However, that access is not synonymous with the ability to comprehend. The Mamos are trained in reading the Law of Origin, and in consultation with one another and with the experiences in *aluna* of non-Mamos, they ascertain the interpretation of the law. This is a profoundly democratic procedure that occurs among living beings, led by those among us who have the necessary expertise to facilitate these processes. Herein lies another facet of the understanding of authority/ Serankwa. In this manner, we now also dis-cover the links between law, development, and democracy in Mamosean knowledge.

The Law of Origin is an alternative to human rights and development. It involves freedom as practice of common-unity in the material realm, and this practice requires respect and love; that is, the practice of freedom requires justice. The Law of Origin requires a way of being in time, as well as a way of thinking together in common-unity. This is impossible to achieve if we solely rely on the frameworks of thinking intrinsic to hegemonic human rights and development. Within these dominant frameworks, the tools available for change are limiting; they incarcerate the future. For instance, one of the tools we have to transcend unjust social conditions is *transitional justice*.

The idea of transitional justice is being debated in Colombia in the context of the current peace negotiations between the government and the FARC. This notion functions on a series of interdependent assumptions. First, transition implies a teleological movement from an aberrant social condition to its normalization, which presupposes a sort of social healing that puts an end to the aberration that gave way to war or violence. Second, the telos that underpins the previously referred to normalization is shaped by a notion of justice understood as the absence of the aberrant violence. Third, the aberration, as well as that which is or is not violence, that which is or is not relevant in the transitional process, is defined from within the dominant epistemic and ontological frameworks, that is, the aberration is defined in relation to the dominant normativity and it is understood as being external to it. Fourth, justice is linked to the international and state institutions that monopolize its definitions and delimit how it is to be exercised. Fifth, the transition implies the activation of those international and state institutions so that they fulfill their function—that of guaranteeing and defending justice. Finally the idea of transitional justice implies restricted notions about what we understand as the material, the historical, the symbolic, the religious, and the psychosocial.

When I refer to the offensive struggles, I also imply that the alternatives we have do exist and indeed abound, and that they demand revolution. The offensive struggles require rupture, not transition. Indeed, if freedom is the practice of common-unity in the material realm, that which inhibits freedom has to die. Likewise, if justice is what love looks like in public, that which inhibits love has to die. The impediment to the alternatives to human rights and development such as the Law of Origin cannot be overcome by a process of transition operating from within the six presuppositions mentioned above, which materialize and are executed through the international and state institutions of justice. For this reason, these presuppositions, and the institutions, have to die. That process is, then, a necessary rupture—not a transition but the very condition of being.

NOTES

1. After hearing my presentation of a paper based on these ideas at the *Global Dialogue* conference in Aarhus, Denmark, in November 2009, Professor Fred Dallmayr brought to my attention that the notion of compenetración shares similarities with the Buddhist concept *pratītya samutpāda*. It is beyond the scope of this book to discuss the similarities and differences between Mamo thought and Buddhist thought, as well as Dallmayr's translation of pratītya samutpāda as coexisting coarising. My choice of common-unity to translate the Mamo conception of compenetración is inspired by Ati Quigua, who has used the term *común-unidad*. See, for instance, http://www.atiquigua.co/index.php/todos-atierra.html. Accessed August 2015.

2. Interview by Frank Chávez, Juan David Cañas, and Felipe Donoso in Atánquez, July 2009.

3. Consejo Territorial de Cabildos (CTC), draft, *Lineamientos para la coordinación institucional*, March 2003.

4. Interview, cf. footnote 2.

Chapter Seven

Identity and the Preservation of Being

Identity is also to wish to preserve the foundation of the word.

—Mamo Saúl Martínez

The Mamos' work involves a continuous effort to preserve their own and their peoples' identity. However, these efforts to sustain identity inherently relate to a larger venture—the conservation of life and being of all existence. The preservation of Mamosean selfhood cannot be understood without taking into consideration this larger project, implying that identity can be conceptualized on two interdependent levels: a metaphysical level (aluna) and a social and physical level. Although from the Mamos' perspective the one cannot be understood without the other, in the dominant society they are disconnected. To grasp the complexity of the problems that arise in this context, Enrique Dussel's covering over, Frantz Fanon's zone of nonbeing, W. E. B. DuBois's double consciousness, and Lewis Gordon's bad faith prove important ideas. The problems themselves relate to the colonial relations in the dominant society that validate a specific mode of being, which does not include the sphere of aluna in which all beings are interconnected with the Mother. To the Mamos, the negation of the Mother and of the realm of aluna is a form of bad faith. The Mamos and all other beings are relegated to the zone of nonbeing. In the sphere of the humans, the authority of the Mamos depends upon their peoples' ability consider the Mother and what She communicates to them in *aluna*. When their people live in bad faith and relegate the Mother to the zone of nonbeing, the authority of the Mamos is crushed, and their work to preserve life and being is weakened. Because their peoples themselves suffer from bad faith and live themselves in the zone of nonbeing, the processes of identity (re)construction are vital *both* in the anthropocentric realm of relations *and* in the broader context of life. Some fractions among the four peoples of the Sierra engage in projects where identity is utilized for ends that work against the principles of the preservation of life and being—that is, the Law of Origin.

Despite its many undemocratic processes, Colombia has a rich tradition in legal pluralism. The Constitution of 1991 recognized the country as 'multi-cultural and pluriethnic', and established the right to an indigenous citizen-ship that includes self-determination and self-government. Accompanying the new constitution was the ratification of Convention 169 of the International Labour Organisation concerning the rights of indigenous peoples. These changes implied that the frames within which indigenous peoples could con-duct their struggles were improved, and that some of the problems that they had previously faced in the Colombian society were being recognized. These changes were primarily a product of the struggles of the Colombian social and ethnic movements, which in the 1960s and 1970s started to emerge as powerful national organizations. In various ways, the indigenous and black movements in Colombia have stressed their identities as indigenous and as black in these struggles. However, one should be careful to characterize these affirmations of belonging only as identity politics. This focus is problematic because it can direct attention away from what people are actually saying. What is more, as Gordon contends in the context of Africans and the African diaspora,

> Identity politics and the politics of difference that locate Africans and the African diaspora on the 'margins' find themselves at the outset situated by the confines of white normativity. By 'white normativity' I mean the centering of whiteness as the perspective on and of reality. In an African-centred world, the question of African marginality would make no sense, it would mean, literally, for the African to look at the African self wholly from the perspective of the non-African. (Gordon 2006b, 64)

In the example of the Mamos, such focus on identity politics would not allow us to understand that to them, identity is metaphysical, which goes against the grain of many discussions of identity politics in North American and European scholarship.

In relation to the larger Colombian society—and to the legal frameworks that regulate indigenous action—the peoples of the Sierra recognize the Mamos' authority; indeed, they consistently appeal to them. Undeniably, the Mamos are respected and many people abide by their counsel. However, their authority is repeatedly attacked. In the next two sections, I analyse two such cases to illustrate how the zone of nonbeing, double consciousness, and bad faith work from the Mamos' perspective. The first concerns the conflict that emerged among the Kankuamos concerning the implementation of the Makú Jogúki, an educational model that, coherently with the recent developments in Colombian legislation concerning indigenous self-determination and self-rule, is to obey the principles and philosophy of the peoples of the Sierra Nevada. The second scrutinizes another conflict—one between the Council of Mamos and the more politically oriented base organizations, the *cabildos*, in the context of the ritual held in the Sierra for Juan Manuel Santos, Colombian president between 2010 and 2014, and recently reelected for yet another four years (2014–2018). These examples illustrate a central point concerning the necessity to discern between identity as *affirmation* of existence, and identity as *negation* or *disregard* of existence. They also elucidate the problems of double consciousness, nonbeing, and bad faith as mechanisms which reinforce the death project. These misadventures raise crucial issues regarding the ways in which the Colombian national legal frames regulate indigenous action and being.

MAKÚ JOGÚKI

It is still happening . . . now they say brother Kankuamo, little brother Kankuamo what is happening? . . . and they say they are settlers . . . they are not settlers, they are Indian, just Indians . . . in the Sierra Nevada, [we] were four [peoples], and imagine, the *godo* [conservative][1] has deceived them. . . . [The *godo*] said, 'No, these savages, we have to take their language away from them, they are not speaking anything there.' (Mamo José Gabriel Alimato, cited in Laurent 2005, 26)

Remember the Mother gave the Kankuamo, Kogi, Wiwa, and Arhuaco each specific parts of the territory of Sierra Nevada de Santa Marta into their care. The Kankuamo territories include the lower southeast-facing parts. Due to their location, these territories have been relatively easy for the colonizing powers to access. Although one should not underestimate the impact that the colonizing endeavor has had upon all four peoples, the Kankuamos have been more exposed to the colonizing enterprise than the other peoples and were actually considered extinct in the nineteenth century (Reichel-Dolmatoff 1961). Mamo José Gabriel Alimako addresses some problems regarding colonization in the above quotation.

The Kankuamos were not allowed to speak their language. They were evangelized. They were scattered by force, among other devices, through the *encomienda* system and forced placement of children in *orphanages*. They were killed—the Mamos were prioritized targets of this latter exercise of violence. The quote from Mamo Alimako also refers directly to bad faith; many indigenous people have been deceived, and believe that they are what they can never be, that is, white. The combination of nationalism and citizenship appeals to some indigenous people in the Kankuamo territory. Both nationalism and citizenship are figured as a horizontal relation whereby nationality guarantees equal citizenship, and they are presented as if a person either is, or is not, a Colombian citizen. The appeal of this idea relates to an imaginary of a nonexistent equality—as in, for example, the expression: 'all are equal before the law'—where no one can be more, or less, than others. However, when the social-historical realities materialize the actualities for indigenous people are very different. In spite of these problems, the Kankuamo have survived. They are, as Mamo Martínez says, weakened, but they continue *to be*. Indeed, in the 1970s and 1980s, confronted by these problems, the Kankuamos started a process of 'cultural recontextualization' (OIK 2006, 2), as they themselves have characterized it. Contrary to the idea of reconstruction, recontextualization is coherent with the logic of relinking and entails the relationship with the Mother in common-unity.

In 1993, the Organización Indígena Kankuama (OIK) was established, and ten years later, in 2003, the Kankuamos were acknowledged as an indigenous people by the Colombian state. The Mamos, organized within the Council of Mamos, have supported the processes of the Kankuamos because the survival of the Mother depends upon the four peoples together. To recollect the metaphor of the table presented in chapter 2—each of the peoples correspond to one leg of the table, the table being the Sierra. If one leg is weakened or absent, the table will lose stability and possibly fall. This is why the four peoples work together and are interdependent. In 2006, the OIK started an important process in the context of the cultural recontextualization—the elaboration of an educational model that was to counter the effects of the attempts at epistemicide waged against them:

> Since the First Congress of the Kankuamo Indigenous People, we define the education imposed by the dominant society for over 500 years as 'the most refined instrument of ethnocide, the spearhead of our acculturation', an education that has expanded and consolidated the enforcement of another way of thinking, beyond that which was facilitated by the conqueror's sword and the crucifix of the evangelist. . . . Education plays a fundamental role and, as an ideological element, it must be transformed and evaluated in accordance with the spiritual and cultural principles of the Kankuamo Indigenous People. (OIK 2008, 19)

The educational model was made possible because of over five hundred years of resistance of the four peoples and, more recently, because of the educational reform in Colombia implemented in 1994 in extension of the new Constitution of 1991.

However, when the Makú Jogúki entered the phase of implementation in 2009, there was considerable political agitation in the Kankuamo territory. The organization Atánquez Libre emerged as the response of a small number among the Christian groups in Kankuamo territory to the ways in which the OIK practiced government. They strongly opposed the Makú Jogúki, their main critique being that the Makú Jogúki is outdated and will negatively affect their children's access to higher education and employment in wider Colombian society. In the context of this conflict, the struggle of Atánquez Libre is a defense of colonial and neo-liberal society in accordance with the national governmental discourse and politics. They believe that they have the same possibilities in Colombian society as any other Colombian, ignoring that they are racialized and 'classed' subjects as are the vast majority of Colombians. Once more, we find the appeal to the supposed egalitarian conceptualization of national identity (people) and citizenship (the subject under the state), both of them constituted on the idea of sameness.

Two major issues are at play in the critiques launched by Atánquez Libre. These issues show how bad faith is expressed. The first is concerned with religion as a school subject, which has been suppressed in the Máku Jogúki, which instead is grounded in the Law of Origin. To the members of Atánquez Libre, the subject religion is understood as education in dominant Christianity. A non-Christian logic and a non-Christian worldview as the point of departure of education is, to them, seriously problematic. In effect, the Makú Jogúki shifts the geography of reason as the most important measure to counter epistemicide. The second significant matter is concerned with a—completely understandable—double play that Atánquez Libre conducts concerning their identity. On the one hand, they adopt the indigenous identity as outlined by the Colombian state when it comes to the increased access to rights that indigenous populations have achieved since the 1991 Constitution. On the other hand, when the base organizations start implementing initiatives according to indigenous principles, as understood from within the Law of Origin, they feel left out. The colonial rationality where there is only *one* way of being dominates, and *other* forms of being are labeled unrealistic or, even, corrosive/separatist.

This points to a major flaw in the 1991 Constitution, which has been raised by several Colombian scholars and addressed by peasant movements. The problem is that the constitution has granted rights to ethnic groups but in the process, it has left behind other groups that would not necessarily have labeled themselves *indigenous*, had they had the chance to achieve access to the same rights with a different label like, for instance, that of *peasant*.

Significantly, many peasants who do not live in indigenous territories continue suffering an acute lack of access to rights. By this, I am of course implying that the people from Atánquez Libre have the right to access a Christian-based school. This, however, does not mean that the Kankuamos must relinquish their decolonization projects.

Atánquez Libre opposed the realization of the Makú Jogúki with such force that the process of implementation was arrested for some time. The OIK was the main target of criticism by Atánquez Libre, and in the wake of the initial phases of implementation of the Makú Jogúki, both parties started to visit Mamo Saúl Martínez's sacred site regularly as one of the strategies to seek a solution to the conflict. It might seem a strange strategy that Atánquez Libre, whose rejection of Kankuamo spirituality is explicit, has gone to a Mamo in their quest for justice in the case of the implementation of the Makú Jogúki. However, this maneuver is key to understanding the whole conflict: Mamo Martínez, a powerful Mamo who belongs to the Council of Mamos, had *not* been involved in the process of the Makú Jogúki. The Council of Mamos had not been consulted in the process carried out by the OIK. Instead, the OIK worked with two Mamos who, according to Martínez, do not form part of the Council of Mamos because of their disregard of the Law of Origin and their rejection of the processes of validation of the reading of the law. Additionally, the OIK has tirelessly promoted the Makú Jogúki as conforming to the *national* political community (winning the Ministry of Education's price for best ethno-educational model in December 2009), but has done little to debate and advocate it with the people in the Kankuamo territory.

Indeed, the OIK was criticized by many other people in Kankuamo territory for not being democratic according to the Kankuamo principles. Some of the people of the OIK, at least those working in the higher echelons of the organization, demonstrated another form of bad faith: they have lived *indigenousness* as the dominant Colombian society defines it. Hence, the OIK did not act in accordance with the principles of self-determination and self-government of their people where all processes, large or small, are to be carried out in consultation with the Mother. According to the Mamo Council this means that, although the *contents* of the Makú Jogúki are a small step in the right direction, the *path* it took was troublesome from start. This is why it faced so many difficulties. Indeed, to the Mamos of the Council, who found themselves undertaking damage control, these problems could have been avoided by following the Law of Origin.

The case of the Makú Jogúki illustrates how the legal frameworks in Colombia, in the wake of the 1991 Constitution, are important measures for the indigenous peoples because they allow them to work more consistently in the affirmation of being. However, it also elucidates that the legal frameworks are not only used in the context of strengthening the offensive struggles. They can be employed against these if the transformations sought continue to follow the logic of the defensive struggles. Identity politics are, in the context of powerful sectors of the OIK, performed *utilizing* the ideas of the Law of Origin without changing the terms and contents of their struggle accordingly. In other words, they continue to be undertaken in bad faith. From this standpoint, the OIK still needs to work in the context of *intraculturality*, affirming their identity not in the terms that identity is understood in the larger Colombian society, but in the terms laid out in the Law of Origin.

SUPPORTING THE DEATH PROJECT?

Multicultural constitutions like the Colombian one have a darker side. This darker side connects to the defensive struggles that, of course, continue to take place. While largely arising out of the offensive struggles led by Colombian racialized subjects to open alternative spaces of *being*, the 1991 Constitution currently risks formally legalizing the existence of the spaces of *nonbeing*. In other words, it can be used to underscore segregation and strengthen the death project, rather than to transform the state. Many offensive struggles aim at significantly changing the state and its institutions, including altering education and the university, in their effort to negate the zone of nonbeing. In Colombia, these processes for transformation have still a long way to progress to effect meaningful change. As sustained in the previous chapter, transformation may be problematic without rupture. Within Colombia, the concept 'multicultural' is officially understood in the terms of neo-liberal logic. This means that the existence of different cultures is recognized, and their specificities tolerated. However, neither recognition nor tolerance in this logic allows for changing the fundamentals of the Colombian state.[2] In the worst of possible circumstances, this can lead to a Bantustanization in Colombia.

The idea of the ecological native (Ulloa 2004) is, in many ways, compelling in this regard. As an actualized version of the notion of the *noble savage*, it provides a powerful image that is used by the global elites to justify and legitimate their political projects. In this context, the elites are helped by racialized subjects, who find themselves striving to live up to the idea of the ecological native, that is, the elite definition of what it is to be an indigenous person or group. Bad faith is not only a lie to the self; it is also, and most importantly, an evasion of freedom—in the case of the indigenous groups of the Sierra, of freedom *for life*. A telling example of the ways in which some indigenous—and other racialized—peoples have sold their freedom for a place in the zone of being concerns the ways in which they have directed attacks at their own people in collaboration with the elites. In Colombia, evidence indicates the elites undertaking a clear strategy of dividing in order to rule by assisting indigenous people to found organizations that parallel traditional ones in exchange for their support.[3] Supposedly, in this way, both parties are happy. The elites, because they can display support from the indigenous organizations—which, of course, are homogenized in the public discourse that is managed through the mass media that, unsurprisingly, belongs to the elites—and the indigenous ecological natives because they, at least theoretically, gain a space in the zone of being. To extrapolate on Malcolm X's metaphors of the house Negro and the field Negro; these last become a kind of house Indians. Considering the cases discussed here, in Sierra Nevada, these elite strategies have functioned as political attacks on the authority of the Mamos, and must be seen contextually in relation to efforts at epistemicide of the peoples of Sierra Nevada.

In 2010, the people who work in the CTC participated in the political propaganda program of newly elected Colombian president Juan Manuel Santos. The CTC is the organization that unites the civic organizations of the four peoples. As any other organization of the Sierra, it was to follow the Law of Origin from its inception, whereas Juan Manuel Santos's standing is at odds with the Law of Origin. He won the elections as the heir of former president Álvaro Uribe Vélez, whose fundamentalist politics of Democratic Security in many ways preceded the current global antiterror politics. Despite the customary methods used during the presidential campaign and, in the context of the elections and vote-counting—methods that include buying votes or exchanging them for presents, the use of threats, falsification or modification of votes, media propaganda, and a massive military presence—Juan Manuel Santos's victory has not been questioned by the national or international society at large. However, Juan Manuel Santos's complicity with the death project is undeniable. As Minister of Defense from 2006 to 2009 under the Uribe administration, he was in a significant position of responsibility under diverse critical scandals concerning the administration's Democratic Security policies, most notably the problem of the *false positives*, civilians murdered by the armed forces and then presented in the media as guerrilla members killed in battle. The tragedy of the false positives was an effect of the requirement that Uribe's government made to the Armed Forces to show results, and of the monetary incentives attached to this requirement offering approximately 2,000 USD for each dead person.[4] In his time of government between 2010 and 2014, Santos distanced himself politically from the Democratic Security line of Uribe, and indeed brought about the rage and opposition of the *uribistas*, many of whom had voted for him in the elections. Santos also initiated the current peace negotiations with the guerrillas of the FARC. Santos was reelected for presidency in 2014, and in this occasion his strongest opponent was one of ex-president Uribe's close allies. As such, the elections were, in the alternative media, cast as a choice between the possibility of some peace (as in the continuation of the peace negotiations) and war (as in the return of the Democratic Security policies).

The CTC engaged in an act that favored the president in several ways. Following the events in Colombia through the national news, I read in the only newspaper with national coverage—owned in part by the Santos family—that the authorities of Sierra Nevada were performing a ritual in the context of Juan Manuel Santos's inauguration as the president of the country. In order to allow for a thorough understanding of the depth of the corrosive effects that this ritual can have, I quote the newspaper article at length. It begins with the headline 'Juan Manuel Santos will begin his inauguration with ritual in Sierra Nevada de Santa Marta' and continues:

> He will be accompanied by his family, the Minister of the Environment, Sandra Bessudo, and some advisors.
>
> Spiritual authorities and councils [*cabildos*] of the Kogi, Arhuaco, Kankuamo and Wiwa peoples, settled there, will give him symbols of authority and of values [related to] balance with nature.
>
> The president-elect, Juan Manuel Santos, will attend two inaugurations this Saturday [7th of August, 2010]: one symbolic and one formal. The first, no less important than the second, will take place early in the morning, in the Sierra Nevada de Santa Marta.
>
> Before the spiritual authorities and the cabildos of the four peoples settled in that territory (Kogi, Arhuaco, Kankuamo and Wiwa), Santos will receive a baton and a number of sacred stones "called Tumas" that represent values of balance with nature.
>
> María Clemencia Rodríguez de Santos, who from tomorrow will be the first lady, will receive a spindle of the indigenous women, used to make cotton thread and which symbolizes the way life should be knitted.
>
> "Never [before] had any president begun the day of his inauguration in an act of such characteristics," said Juan Mayr, former environment minister, who will accompany them.
>
> The sacred objects that he will receive during the event have an enormous significance for the Indians. The baton symbolizes government: both the Mamos, "spiritual leaders of the communities" and the commissioners hold one. The one that Santos will receive is the most representative and is made of Macana palm wood, black and very delicate.
>
> Mayr explained that each of the Tumas that the new president will receive have different values: "The quartz represents the clouds and water, the jade represents the

forests and nature, the carnelian represents blood, and the black tuma represents fertile earth."

Between 300 and 400 Indians will attend the ceremony. Several presidents have visited the Indians of the Sierra, but Santos is the first one to inaugurate before them.[5]

Reading this news nine thousand kilometres away from Sierra Nevada, I was completely stunned. I could not believe that the Mamos were carrying out a symbolic act of inauguration of Santos. Because if indeed the Mamos cannot reject anyone in the same way that the sun cannot be selective either, my position was that this radical principle of nonexclusion in this case had devastating political effects. It gave the impression that the indigenous peoples of the Sierra politically supported the executioner. In effect, in my view the radical principle of nonexclusion ended up bolstering exclusion, violence, and death. And in this manner, I did not understand how it could take place because according to the Mamos, as to many others, life is sacred. I was in such an outrage that I considered terminating my work of collaboration with the Mamos. Instead, I decided to call Mamo Martínez and presented to him the above-mentioned criticism. He was in a meeting with several other Mamos of the Council of Mamos, who participated in our conversation. They agreed with me: carrying out the ritual in the context of the presidential inauguration affirmed exclusion, violence, and death. Martínez also informed me the event had been organized by the cabildos without consultation with the Council of Mamos. Rather, they brought with them what Martínez called 'pocket-Mamos'. The ritual was, rather, part of the political management of the cabildos.

This experience provides a window to how bad faith works in complicity with the defensive struggles' appropriation of indigenousness. Such complex issues can easily divert attention, and suggest that the intricacy of a case like this is due to the fragmented and contingent nature of social life. However, such perspective would, wittingly or unwittingly, work against the struggles of transformation and in complicity with the struggles of appropriation. This strategy of appropriation is neither novel nor unexpected; it is an ancient practice connected to elitist power. In chapter 4, we saw how the indigenous was appropriated by the Creole elites in Latin America in the context of the legitimation of independence movements and republican governments. The recent concern of the global institutions of power (such as the World Bank, the IMF, and the UN) with regard to indigenous knowledges, and the patenting of life, are examples of this practice in the global realm.

In general terms, the practice consists in proving that one matters with the support of the excluded, of those from below and, supposedly, takes their viewpoints into account in projects whose ends follow the interests of the death project. That is, they work for the legitimation of the death project. The collaboration of representatives of the indigenous groups is central to these practices. Bad faith and double consciousness operate in these circumstances, and persons who identify themselves as indigenous believe that they are working according to their peoples' interests while serving the appropriator's interests. Juan Manuel Santos could legitimize his regime, through a ritual with the indigenous authorities, and thus counterpoise—by turning it upside down—the corresponding ritual that took place among the political and spiritual indigenous authorities in the inauguration of Bolivian president Evo Morales in Bolivia (Burman 2009). Ironically, Juan Manuel Santos was able to stage a ritual because of the strength of the offensive struggles, and also because of images of the ecological native in which the indigenous peoples concerned garnered ostensibly international support and sympathism.

THE RIGHTS OF NATURE AND THE ECOLOGICAL NATIVE

Without disregarding the importance of the offensive struggles in opening up spaces, such as those achieved through the 1991 Constitution, the case of the ritual conducted on Juan Manuel Santos's behalf, illustrates how multiculturalism can function for the convenience of the Colombian elites. The example of the ritual demonstrates the 'pocket Mauros's authorization of Santos, and reminds of the Bantustans's convenience for the apartheid regime in South Africa.[6] For this reason, it is essential to take into account the conditions upon which a given action is conducted under the banner of multiculturalism or interculturality. There is a significant difference in the terms by which the position of Evo Morales has been endorsed by the Aymara indigenous authorities,[7] and the terms upon which the ritual for Juan Manuel Santos was carried out in the Sierra. While the former indicated decolonization, the latter seems to indicate recolonization. While the former was an affirmation of being, the latter seems to be its negation.

In the examples that I discuss here, the OIK, the CTC, and the Atánquez Libre have, in different degrees, practiced an interculturality of segregation. These groups have worked in harmony with the logic that relegates them to the zone of nonbeing. In diverse ways, they strive to be the negation of themselves, that is, they attempt to be indigenous as the elites continuously define them. Among other things, the image of the ecological native homogenizes indigenous peoples; they all fit into this category and, when they do not, they are labeled as terrorist or as being manipulated by so-called terrorist groups.

Perceived through the category of the ecological native, the indigenous people are apolitical. And indeed, many indigenous peoples reject party politics
not because they are apolitical, but precisely because party politics are constituted upon terms that do not cohere with their worldviews and political projects. Rather, indigenous peoples engaged in processes of decolonization often
regard party politics as being complicit with colonialist practices. Thus, as
many indigenous peoples, the Mamos prefer to frame their struggles in different terms, such as the ones I mentioned here, as struggles *for* life and being
or as struggles *against* the death project.

The homogenization of the indigenous peoples in the image of the ecological native is an element characteristic to the appropriation of the indigenous
by the defensive struggles. According to several indigenous philosophies,
homogeneity is impossible—in the case of the Mamos, as we have seen, identity does not change but each being is assigned different roles, and is in this
sense unique. Consequently, the Mamos do not presuppose that every individual is identical. However, they do expect every individual to be faithful to
who she or he *is* according to the Law of Origin. The notion of the ecological
native is, in this context, a form of bad faith that affects the authority of the
Mamos negatively. As we have also seen, this authority is central to the negation of the zone of nonbeing, and to the larger efforts at preserving life and
being.

Common-unity encourages a complex understanding of what the ideas of
the rights of nature, or the Mother, imply. These ideas attempt to address the
obstacles that emerge in the context of colonial rationality and, among other
things, they balance the negative effects of the separation of the human and
the natural world as a universalized principle as significant as the Cartesian
divide. The inseparability of the Mother and the Law of Origin suggests that
to the Mamos it does not make sense to speak of the rights of the Mother.
Rather, S/he is the source of rights. However, inasmuch as S/he has been subjected to increasing violence, Her ability to work for the perpetuation of life
is reduced. Thus, the ideas of the rights of nature are, similar to the ideas of,
for example, racial equality, elaborated in their absence. As with the latter,
the need to struggle for the rights of nature is a necessity derived from the
capitalist and colonial logic, not an element inherent to indigenous peoples'
thought, as many people mistakenly believe. The indigenous peoples in struggles for the defense of the Mother also translate vital elements that transform
society and secure the Mother's future.

The terms of the struggles for the defense of the Rights of the Mother are
the fruit of these acts of translation, and result in an *ecology of knowledges*
(Santos 2014). As Santos has also noted, the idea of the rights of nature
requires of the indigenous peoples to follow a logic that, in their philosophy,

is absurd—that of an idea of secularized rights—and it requires of westerners to follow a logic equally absurd to them—that of the Mother. Nonetheless, it is, in this context, necessary to recollect that, in part, because the survival of elements of European *other* knowledges, the sensitivity to nature inherent in the idea of the rights of the Mother is not absurd to many Europeans either. Indeed, in the moments of the globalization of localisms, *other* European knowledges became *other*, subalternized, localized and folklorized (Guardiola-Rivera 2010). The witch hunts, the conquest of Al-Andalus, the persecution of the Roma populations, and the Holocaust were also key historical events aimed to eradicate *other* knowledges and ways of life inside the European geographical space.

Among the *otherized* European knowledges to which I refer here is, for example, the works of English Romantic movement (1798–1830) indebted to German philosophy of the late 1800s to early 1900s and have been read both as a reaction against the Enlightenment, and a reembracing of what many referred to as the natural world. Arguably, these ideas re-emerged in the North American *flower power* movement of the 1960s and 1970s. Additionally, currently, this sensitivity is produced in the fields of biology, geography, and ecology (Grove and Damodaran 2009), and in the ecological movements that engage in working with indigenous peoples around the world. What we could describe as a sensitivity towards the Mother is also to be found among some of Europe's peasantry and some of Europe's Muslim, Buddhist, Jewish, Christian, Pagan, Afro, Roma, and other populations. This suggests that similar ideas are dis-coverable among the indigenous knowledges and European *other* knowledges.

However, there is an intrinsic danger in presupposing that these knowledges are *the same*. Pluriversality is there, but diverse groups do not share the same position in the global hierarchies of power, and all have played different roles in this context. Decolonial historical realism is key to displaying these differences. For example, the English Romantic movement and the flower power movement are positioned radically different than the Roma peoples. Additionally, the concern with *covering over*, emancipation, and the subsuming of emancipation by hegemonic powers reemerges, as well as the recurrent element in the whitewashing of *other* knowledges: they are taken as exotic alternatives, and to become exotic their criticism of coloniality is left out. As already mentioned, over the last decades, nonindigenous people have tended to associate indigenous knowledge with ecology and harmony with nature. In effect, they have regarded indigenous people as being part of 'Mother Nature' and their ideas as being consistent with their own notions of sustainable development. These notions constitute the new guises of old colonial discourses on the *other*, relegating them to nature and sustaining their absence in the social spheres.

The idea of the ecological native is an interpretation of indigenous world-views and practices from a mono-logic viewpoint. Such a narrow perspective means, among other things, that indigenous knowledges are stripped of their historical, political, spiritual, and environmental context, and so recreated through distillation into another abstract set of principles that deal with the interrelationship between humans and nature and with ideas concerning sustainable development as they are understood from within the colonial rationality. This abstraction also gives room for the colorblindness within the environmental movements. In these conceptions, 'Mother Nature' is understood largely in terms that are coherent with the Christian idea of the Garden of Eden. The idea of the ecological native has been elaborated mainly through 'transnational indigenist environmental movements' and NGOs, and their interrelations with indigenous peoples. This means, according to Astrid Ulloa, that the idea of the ecological native has been incorporated into indigenous peoples' identity, sometimes in order to obtain funding, and at other times as a political strategy—that is, as identity politics or strategic essentialisms.

The Mamos of Sierra Nevada, however, do not refer to the ideas that circumscribe the image of the ecological native when they speak; nor do they essentialize identity. When the Mamos of Sierra Nevada present themselves in terms that we name 'ecological', when they struggle for the respect of their territory as sacred, and when they underscore the radical difference between their own practices and western practices, they are doing so because their territories *are* sacred, their practices *are* radically different from western practices, and because 'ecological' is one of the western concepts that may allow inter-locution.[8] While some indigenous people intend to live up to the image of the ecological native, others use the term in attempts to translate their knowledge. In the case of the Mamos, beyond the act of translation are substantive preoccupations with disseminating some of their knowledge to the rest of the world because upon this depends the restoration of the world's equilibrium.

NOTES

1. In Colombia, *godo* is used to refer to conservatives. In the wars of independence, *godo* was used by the Creole elites to refer to those who were against independence (Spanish and Creole). The term also has some connotations of authoritarianism.

2. See Walsh (2008) for a compelling discussion of the different ways in which multiculturality, interculturality, pluriculturality, and plurinationality can be understood and used.

3. Similar problems are found among the indigenous peoples of the Cauca region in Colombia. Here, the government created a parallel indigenous organization, the OPIC, which supports the government.

4. Concerning Santos's complicity with the death project, see the Special Report of the CINEP (2010), a recognized human rights organization in Colombia on the 'Legacy of Uribe's Policies: Challenges for the Santos Administration'. The report account has one major deficiency, which is that it does not make explicit, nor does it include in its analysis, the tragedy of the false positives. Some of the proofs concerning the generalized state of crisis in Colombia were concerned with the DAS' (Departamento Administrativo de Seguridad-the National Security Agency) systematic persecution of any kind of dissent.

5. http://www.eltiempo.com/colombia/politica/la-posesion-de-juan-manuel-santos -en-la-sierra-nevada_7845644-1. Translated from Spanish.

6. On the convenience of the Bantustans for the apartheid regime in South Africa, see Mamdani (1996).

7. For a thorough presentation of the conditions that led to Morales's presidency, see Burman (2009).

8. Personal communication with Mamo Saúl Martínez (Kankuamo), Mamo Ramón Gil (Wiwa), and Mamo Juan Vicente (Kogi).

Chapter Eight

Pluriversality

Pluriversality entails examining how different sociohistorical and economic-political experiences in the global articulations of power produce diverse realities and life—or death—projects. It also involves paying attention to the different knowledges that constitute our worlds. But pluriversality also implies acting in and with the pluriverse, and not simply observing or standing apart as those who are the legitimate conceptualizers of what it means or how it is to be done. My efforts in this book are but one approach among many, and are influenced by my position as a Danish-Colombian Mestiza, and by my commitment to working against coloniality and the death project. The decolonial historical realism employed in this book is a necessary step to take in a Mestiza offensive struggle.

I have opposed the antiessentialist attitude in the social sciences and the humanities when it covers over the other and simultaneously conceals the process of identification of those who pinpoint and critique essentialisms. Antiessentialism is often an enactment of the colonial politics of being. We need to reject antiessentialist practice that is based on a homogenizing idea of essentialism grounded on coloniality. At best, antiessentialism works as an attempt to warn the other of the dangers of essentialism in terms of its effects in the nonpresent future. It tends to presume that identity is constructed and understood in the same way everywhere, and that social constructions are not real. It ignores the centrality of identity in the struggles that happen in a near future that resides right here, and their effects in opposition to the death project. It disregards that, in many cases, to affirm identity is to deny the zone of nonbeing, and it is to articulate the conditions that make us who and what we are. In the case of the Mamos, it is also to protect life—being and becoming. In the academic environment, 'essentialism' is not only a term referring to the past errors of the industry of knowledge construction and its attachment to the colonial endeavor. It is also a pejorative term, containing connotations that the ones accused of essentialism are dangerously uninformed and in that sense underdeveloped.

To classify these struggles as essentialist is to speak from a position that has a desire to define how these struggles must or should be formed, and to design the future that they need to construct. Ultimately, because not acknowledging the realities that which is classified as essentialism describes, the desired future for the radical antiessentialist is a white future. There is no room for pluriversality in radical antiessentialism. Consequently, the antiessentialist attitude often functions in a similar way as the humanist idea that Frantz Fanon criticized. In their present dominant expressions, antiessentialism and humanism are ideas and practices that conceal the *other* and produce the zone of nonbeing. Significantly, the antiessentialist practice is one of the reasons why colonial subjects increasingly reject working with white academics. White or westernized academics often regard their diagnosis of the dangers of the essentialism of the other as justified—but are blind to the ways in which this classification is part of their own subjectivity and complicity with power. Their subject position closes dialogue and inhibits transformation. Additionally, antiessentialism is often framed from within the Creole sympathism, or a similar version of it, white sympathism/solidarity. As a Mestiza, I have touched some hurtful aspects of the legacy of my people. This has been done as an act of freedom, with respect and love, as a means to achieve pluriversality. However, whether or not I break with Creole sympathism is not my own judgment—nor my peoples'—to make.

As a human being, whose skills at communicating with beings other than human are limited, my perspective continues to be anthropocentric, for example, I privilege the gaze of the human over the gaze of the animal, and privilege interhuman relationships over the tree's relationship to the lizard. Nevertheless, this anthropocentric situated-ness of knowledge must not obscure that in the process of the making of our cultural productions, we interact intersubjectively with matter, the dead, the weather, and the like. In this context, it is important to highlight once more that the theories of the Mamos are collective knowledge. Collective knowledge both in the sense that it is achieved on the basis of their interaction with the Mother, spirits, and so on, and in the sense that the Mamos reassess their analyses by peer review, by taking into account other peoples' experiences in *aluna*, and through continuous rereadings (as *re-legere*) of the Law of Origin.

I am convinced, as the Mamos, that the offensives against the death project necessarily must pass much more through consultation and engagement with those who are experts in communicating with Her, and less in discussions with those academic authorities (such as Hegel, Marx, Foucault) with whom many scholars continue to debate. By this I am not dismissing such referencing, nor defending the position that the anthropocentric perspective must be abandoned altogether. To do so would be foolish. It would be a form of bad faith that would argue that denying the anthropocentric perspective will ensure its disappearance, or solve the problems of coloniality. We would have to deny historical fact, and with it coloniality. Coloniality and the death project continue shaping our lives and the horizons of possibility that we have, and solid analyses of these processes are imperative. But it is equally important to break with its time-space paradigm and its framework of thinking. These are structures that must be destroyed.

From this perspective, it remains relevant to speak of culture and cultural interaction. When referring to intercultural interaction or even to dialogues between peoples, the asymmetries between anthropocentrically defined cultures remain as important as the symmetries. With Mamo Martínez, I argue that analytically, as well as ethically, cultures are distinct from each other because there are significant differences in the ways cultural productions come into being. These differences connect to the diverse and unequal sociohistorical and economic-political conditions (and possibilities) that people experience in order to produce what they need. Approaches such as world-system analysis and the decolonial perspective have theorized on the ways we are united in a global web of unequal power relationships. In the approach I have defended here, cultures must be seen as distinct from each without negating interaction and codependence, and highlighting the importance of *situations* and the *situatedness* of all cultural encounters.

Situatedness allows us to consider that cultural differences are also colonial differences. In other words, colonial differences are an integral and decisive dimension to both the conceptualization and the reality of cultural differences, at least since Columbus. This implies that the last few decades' cultural encounters, which we tend to label as part of the process of globalization, are interwoven with this history, and not in that historical sense *post*colonial. Therefore, I have defended that the conceptualization of current conditions within the frameworks of dominant globalization theories effectively cover over colonization.

Precisely because of coloniality, interculturality requires *intra*culturality (Walsh 2008). Intraculturality has different meanings depending on the place that a person or group occupies in the world; that is, depending on her place in the global hierarchies constituted through coloniality. In broad terms, the meanings of intraculturality depend on whether one's position in the world lies in the zone of being, or whether it lies in the zone of nonbeing. For the position in the zone of being, including that of the person belonging to the global elites, intraculturality requires that he is willing to question his (held in bad faith) convictions and is prepared to self-destruct. Allowing one's fundamental perspectives to be challenged and consequently to change entails more than a mere recognition of the other's viewpoint and a then-continued existence as if nothing had happened. To continue to live as if nothing happened would amount to a recognition of the *other* common to neoliberal society's use of the idea of multiculturality; it would be peering outside the master's house but leaving the house intact.

For the Mestizos, intraculturality must necessarily pass through the acknowledgment of our own heritages, and careful consideration of how the colonial politics of being are in play in our lives. Above all, intraculturality for us needs to pass through attentiveness to the fact that taking a stance against the death project does not exonerate us from being part of it, nor does it delete the global structures of power by which we—to greater or lesser extent—continue being privileged. Due to the colonial politics of being, intraculturality entails working towards a new humanity, as Fanon put it, not in the comfortable new-age self-change-and-the-world-will-change way, but perhaps, above all, by learning to be led, and unlearning to lead—and, in this process, to learn to become ancestors worthy of the generations to come. To merge with the *other* or pretend that we are the *other* is equally aggressive an act to the *other*—it is a form of subjugation and control and lacks respect for otherness. Such merging with the other fails to recognize the unequal power relations shaped through coloniality, including those shaped under the liberal notion of tolerance of difference as long as this difference does not change the unequal ordering of the world.

For the person or group that is relegated to the zone of nonbeing, intraculturality implies locating and affirming an identity which has been denied, made absent, and used by the powerful in order to oppress. This is highlighted among several indigenous peoples throughout Latin America, who find intraculturality a first step towards interculturality. This is the case of the *katarista* movement in Bolivia (Burman 2009), as well as that of the *Nasa* in the Cauca region in Colombia (Rappaport 2005). As we have seen, in the case of the Mamos from Sierra Nevada, affirming identity is inextricably connected to the preservation of being. Only through intraculturality can absence be negated, existence affirmed, and only through the affirmation of existence is interculturality possible.

I have already mentioned that a recurring concern in discussions on identity politics relates to the danger of reifying and essentializing culture. These discussions often forget to question who names essentialism, who uses it, and to what purpose it is named and used. It is important to distinguish between the essentialism named and pinpointed by the academic world on the one hand, and the affirmations of existence and identity that are linked with offensive struggles on the other. In accord with the idea of *andar,* and as demonstrated by various movements in Latin America, I view interculturality as a permanent process of relating to and negotiating with others. Interculturality is a way to pay respect to, and hopefully enlarge, pluriverse. In this sense, interculturality can also be seen as a practice of freedom. Pluriverse, in turn, needs to be regarded as a process—not the end of a process—because when we think of things as complete, we have already killed the possibility of ways of becoming, and of radical change. We have also abandoned our role as part of the Mother, as always in the making, and we have relinquished politics in favor of totalitarianisms.

HUMAN RIGHTS AND DEVELOPMENT

Common-unity raises a crucial feature concerning human rights and development thinking, which is worth exploring. Those in the zone of being are used to thinking of the globalized localisms of human rights and development, as ideas by which they are protected. However, they then do not see those aspects by which these ideas are constitutive of the problems they seek to protect humanity from and their complicity in problems they regard as belonging to different realms entirely, such as the problems of climate change. Here is yet another aspect of the cover story of human rights. Additionally, as globalized localisms, human rights and development 'are driven by the desire for homogeneity and the implicit need of hegemony' (Mignolo 2000, 310). While processes to recover dignity might go through strategic uses of human rights and development as globalized localisms, human rights and development ideas and practices do not suffice. The globalized localisms of human rights and development are technologies of implementation of the death project. The violence and racism that started to be configured as global designs with the six processes of extermination detailed in chapter 3—and which continue to exist—initiated the conceptualization of human rights and development.

From a Mamosean perspective, human rights and development specifically, and western ways of knowing generally, are inherently violent ideas and practices. They are an *unethical choice*. They are *unethical* in the sense that the subjectivity of many crucial actors is ignored. In this sense, overlooking the subjectivity of all those human and nonhuman beings that are relegated to the realm of nature and superstition, or seen as objects, is acting in bad faith. The problems of climate change are the effects of violations of the rights of *others*, which are the rights of all. Human rights and development are a *choice* because other possibilities of relating to these *other* subjectivities exist; possibilities grounded in *other* knowledges.

This criticism entails consideration of the racist aspects of the problems of climate change as well. While all suffer from the consequences of the problems of climate change, these consequences are worse for those humans who are relegated to the zone of nonbeing, and who live the effects of the globalized localisms of, for example, the war on drugs (in terms of fumigation, violence, and persecution, for instance). Additionally, common-unity necessarily implies considering the environment as another crucial actor in the processes of becoming. Mamo Martínez explained to me that freedom is also the water's freedom. Using the example of a project to build a dam in Sierra Nevada, he illustrated how not only the freedom of the water is violated, but also that of the river and the beings and environment of, in, and near the river when the environment is abruptly flooded and the beings in the flooded area are abruptly killed:

> From our viewpoint, freedom is also the wind's . . . freedom is also the water's. This is why our view does not contemplate water dams . . . that amounts to not letting the water run, to make a dam so that same water drowns its surroundings . . . it is removing the right of growth to that, which is on the riverbanks, and removing the liberty of the waters to run in their beds. To make a dam is like putting a man between four walls, or behind bars. This is why the western world and *developmentalism* do not understand why we sometimes keep silence or oppose when things cannot wend their way [*andar*] freely, when birds cannot fly, when water cannot follow its trail . . . when fruits cannot come out in their time but are manipulated with many things so that they come out prematurely. That is also to inhibit freedom. (Saúl Martínez, personal communication, Atánquez 2006)

In this sense, freedom is of the movements and the temporalities of a vast diversity of processes of life and becoming. This is the logic that is found at the core of many indigenous peoples' resistance to development projects that inhibit movement—for example, river dams.

Human rights and development are interrelated. These globalized localisms are constantly readapted in processes of absorption and adulteration of *other* knowledges into their hegemonic logic, thereby invisibilizing *otherness*. Although it is not possible to speak of human rights and development as such before they are named, formulated and institutionalized as such, that is, before the post–Second World War period, it is possible to trace the history of the globalization of the localisms that support them. Researching the history of human rights and development as intertwined ideas and practices contributes to a nuanced understanding of the conjunction between the ontological, the epistemological, the political, the economic, the ethical, the cultural, the material and the existential in these globalized localisms. The dominant historical accounts are partial, and they are immersed in the global articulations of power. History reflects temporal ideas, which again are embedded in specific values. Within this framework, the history of the peoples of Sierra Nevada illustrates how human rights and development have worked as localized globalisms through history. It also permits us to sense how the places of enunciation of the Mamos have been shaped, and the different strategies of resistance waged.

The globalized localisms of human rights and development are not universal. Nonetheless, there are social groups who are interested in globalizing them hegemonically. To characterize the globalized localisms of human rights and development as being universal is connected to a general tendency to confuse internationalization with universality (Hastrup 2001, 3) or, more precisely, to mistake the ideas and practices of the global elites as universality and ethics. Kirsten Hastrup, whose approach concerning anthropological evidence I discussed in chapter 5, has stressed the importance of discussing 'in what sense human rights are universal' (Ibid., 1), and argued that the starting point for the quest of universality might be, for instance, equal worth (2). Implicit in Hastrup's suggestion is a recognition that the universal, at least when attached to human rights, is not value-neutral. Accordingly, her idea of equal worth could be enriched through discussions with indigenous peoples who defend the principle of equality in difference. Yet, notions of *human* universality or equal worth, when delinked, seem a limited way to think of universals. The Mamosean notion of relinking, instead, contributes to the process of pluriversality. Indeed, we have seen that the universalized idea of the human is a description of the white, European man, a covering over of his conquering subjectivity sustained upon the doubt concerning the humanity of the *other*. It is also an idea that places the general characterizing condition of the human being as *inherent* and *internal* to it.

In the Mamos' philosophy, the human being is defined in terms that take into account interrelationships with all other beings and our different roles in relation to the processes of life and becoming. The values attached to this definition are related to the situational responsible aspects in these interrelationships. In Mamosean thought, then, the idea of equal worth among humans is implicit because we are all the offspring of the Mother. But we are different, not only because we live in different places and have our realities shaped from within different sociohistorical and economic-political experiences and so relink differently, but also because we all have different roles to play in common-unity.

These ways of understanding the connections between human rights and development provide alternatives to them beyond the current hegemonic link between them constituted by race. The recognition of how human rights and development are joined through race makes obsolete questions concerning their universality, displaying instead their coloniality. Even though the trans-formations of these ideas by the offensive struggles are important, human rights and development, nonetheless, remain the master's tools. If we only think change through human rights and development, we are operating within the dominant rationality and allowing it to define the possibilities and the frameworks for transformation.

BEING ANCESTORS

The shift in the temporality of reason is key to thinking through the thought of the Mamos. From the thought of the Mamos, there in turn emerges yet another rhythm, which brings into the present the role of the spirits, of matter, of plants, humans, animals, and elements, and it places the future within our physical reach by carefully taking the basic condition of these elements into account: their interrelationships, codependence, and becoming. The pace of the Mamos illustrates the close relationship between human values, notions of time, human practice, inclusion and exclusion, life, and the Mother, and points to new directions in regard to what we might call time-spaces of dignity.

The current is a historical moment in which the weakening of colonial power is perhaps reflected the most in the spaces of political feeling-thinking-action of those groups of people who struggle against the death project. Aca-demics that in different ways align with these struggles also reflect these processes of change. We find examples of thinking that move beyond the descriptive and ontological frameworks of colonial rationality and, although they are relatively few, they are no less significant: they contribute to expand-ing the present, contracting the future, and opening up time-spaces of dignity from within academia as well. The time-spaces of dignity are those places of thinking-acting-feeling where radical alternatives against the death project are being enacted.

The challenge that the struggles against the death project pose to intellectu-als is significant—it is of translation aimed to contribute to widen the impact (the power, in Gordon's understanding) of the offensive struggles in which we take part. This translation is not easy, first because it breaks with the dom-inant frameworks of thinking. Second, because we cannot leave aside consid-erations about our role as intellectuals in that endeavor, of our position of power in the global hierarchies, and we cannot underestimate the power of assimilation and neutralization of those who defend the death project, both within and outside academia. Finally, it is not an easy task simply because there are things that cannot be translated yet, perhaps they can never be translated—as the Mamos teach us, everything has its time and its moment.

The mountains, the ancestors, and so on are also part of the political field; they participate in the construction of the future. The time-spaces of dignity to which I refer here are those that necessarily constitute through an exercise of dignity that is not only limited to the space of interaction among human beings. Rather, it expands the present by taking into account the respect towards, the love for, and the dignity of these other actors and the Mother. In the dominant understandings, however, these *other* political projects are unthinkable precisely because the dominant rationality itself delimits the horizon of possibilities and, as such, produces political inertia. This inertia also sustains the persistence of injustice, exploitation, and extractivism on the entire planet.

To contribute to open time-spaces of dignity inside academia also implies working for the liberation of the future, so to speak. In addition to the considerations presented throughout the book concerning dialogue, translation, and interlocution, it is important to highlight that this work concerns the notion of, and self-identification as, experts addressed, among others, in my discussion on the colonial politics of being in chapter 5. In this context, it is also important to recall Juan José Bautista's point concerning Pachamama as a subject and Her interpreters and interlocutors as being important to the processes of decolonization (Bautista 2012, 92–93). For those of us who work closely with these experts, our work is, in many senses, that of dis-covering that which has been concealed. Dis-covery, however, needs to be carried out as dictated by those whose knowledge has been covered over.

The knowledges and ways of being in the world are there precisely because people live differently, walk differently, socialize differently, and among whom the social realm is not only composed of a community, but of a common-unity with life, Mother World. In this sense, I suggest that common-unity might very well be the condition that makes pluriversality possible, that is, there can be no pluriversality without common-unity. This because common-unity requires that we think our place in it, and this feeling-thinking-being our place in common-unity is necessarily situational. If common-unity is a fundamental condition for pluriversality, then we, as scholars and intellectuals, are compelled to think through where our place is in common-unity as part of the pluriverse, and what aspects of the place we inhabit in the pluriverse may be corrosive to common-unity.

The discussions with those who are experts in communicating with the Mother has led me to speak from the Mestiza situation from within the pluriverse, and forced me to think, and to be, beyond the epistemological and ontological frameworks of the death project. That positioning is fundamental if we are to avoid falling into the conventional trap of social sciences and humanities, which, when all is said and done, raise themselves as privileged sites of enunciation from which one can speak about everyone else without situating oneself in the world or the worlds from—or about—which one speaks. This requirement is, in the end, a political imperative that emerges from the projects in which we participate. It demands that, beyond explaining, translating, and describing epistemologies and ontologies, we decide which path we want to walk, and recognize, in a profound and consequential way, the quality of experts of those who were engendered and trained to commune with those other-than-human subjects.

The above considerations about our sites of enunciation call on us to consider who we are, what we are, what is our role in the world, and how we are going to work to become worthy ancestors of future generations. As a Mestiza, this question connects also to the very ways in which mestizaje potentially plays the game of whiteness as much as it contributes to the struggles against it, and against the death project. It is important in this context to highlight that although the death project operates because (among other reasons) it naturalizes many of the lies that it cements with violence, an important part of working against it is to recognize bad faith. I have defended that, contrary to most tendencies, Gordon's bad faith emphasizes that we have the option of listening to the little inner voice that whispers in our ears, 'The Emperor is naked.' Because we have that option, we are also responsible for our actions—for choosing to listen and change accordingly, or to ignore conscience. If freedom is what common-unity looks like in the material realm, then rupture is what freedom looks like in relation to human rights and development.

Ancestry plays an important role in relation to choosing freedom at the expense of the privileges that are offered to us by coloniality and the death project if we defend them. Indeed, ancestry reintroduces spirituality and changes the ways in which we think of ourselves in time and space. Ancestry is central to time-spaces of dignity. First, the ancestors are in stones, in the elements, they are part of the Mother. By taking care of our ancestors we take care of the Mother. Second, although not all ancestors are worthy, we can learn important lessons from all of them—sometimes I recall my ancestors and the violence that some of them have committed. Third, although not all my ancestors are worthy, thinking with them is important in relation to answering questions about who we are, what we are, what reasons we are in the world, and how we can work to become worthy ancestors to those generations that are to come. Finally, to think of ourselves not only as heirs of our ancestors but as ancestors ourselves also means that we rebel against the nihilism of the death project that incarcerates the future by trying to convince us that we can do nothing.

Bibliography

Alimonda, Héctor, ed. 2011. *La naturaleza colonizada. Ecología política y minería en América Latina*. Buenos Aires: CLACSO.

Anderson, Benedict. 1991. *Imagined Communities: Reflections on the Origin and Spread of Nationalism*. London: Verso.

Anghie, Anthony. 1996. "Francisco de Vitoria and the Colonial Origins of International Law." *Social and Legal Studies* 5: 321–36.

———. 1999. "Finding the Peripheries: Sovereignty and Colonialism in Nineteenth-Century International Law." *Harvard International Law Journal* 40 (1): 1–71.

———. 2004. *Imperialism, Sovereignty and the Making of International Law*. New York: Cambridge University Press.

Arias, Arturo. 2008. "Anti-Colonial Struggle in Latin America from the Conquista to the Present." In *A Historical Companion to Postcolonial Literatures: Continental Europe and its Empires*, edited by Prem Poddar, Rajeev Patke, and Lars Jensen, 522–26. Edinburgh: Edinburgh University Press.

Avilés, William. 2005. "The Democratic-Peace Thesis and U.S. Relations with Colombia and Venezuela." *Latin American Perspectives* 32:33–59.

———. 2008. "US Intervention in Colombia: The Role of Transnational Relations." *Bulletin of Latin American Research* 27 (3): 410–29.

Balfour, Ian, and Eduardo Cadava. 2004. "The Claims of Human Rights: An Introduction." *The South Atlantic Quarterly* 103 (2/3): 277–96.

Barreto, José Manuel, ed. 2012. *Human Rights from a Third World Perspective: Critique, History and International Law*. Cambridge: Cambridge Scholars Publishing.

Battle, Michael. 2009. *Ubuntu: I in You and You in Me*. New York: Seabury Books.

Bautista, Juan José. 2012. *Hacia la Descolonización de la Ciencia Social Latinoamericana. Cuatro ensayos metodológicos y epistemológicos*. La Paz: Rincón Ediciones.

Blaser, M. 2009. "Political Ontology." *Cultural Studies* 23 (5): 873–96.

Beck, Ulrich. 2000. *What Is Globalization?* Oxford: Polity Press.

Ben-Ari, Eyal. 1999. "Colonialism, Anthropology and the Politics of Professionalisation." In *Anthropology and Colonialism in Asia and Oceania*, edited by Jan van Bremen and Akitoshi Shimizu, 382–409. Hong Kong: Curzon.

Beverley, John. 2008. "Spain, Modernity and Colonialism." In *A Historical Companion to Postcolonial Literatures: Continental Europe and its Empires*, edited by Prem Poddar, Rajeev Patke, and Lars Jensen, 599–601. Edinburgh: Edinburgh University Press.

Biermann, Soenke. 2011. "Knowledge, Power and Decolonization: Implication for Nonindigenous Scholars, Researchers and Educators." In *Indigenous Philosophies and Critical Education*, edited by George J. and Sefa Dei, chap. 24. New York: Peter Lang.

Bjork, Katharine. 1998. "The Link That Kept the Philippines Spanish: Mexican Merchant Interests and the Manila Trade: 1571–1815." *Journal of World History* 9 (1): 25–50.

Bocarejo Suescún, Diana. 2002. "Indigenizando 'lo blanco': conversaciones con arhuacos y koguis de la Sierra Nevada de Santa Marta." *Revista de Antropología y Arqueología* 13:3–44.

Bogues, Anthony. 2012. "The Dual Haitian Revolution and the Making of Freedom in Modernity." In *Human Rights from a Third World Perspective: Critique, History and International Law*, edited by José Manuel Barreto, 208–36. Cambridge: Cambridge Scholars Publishing.

Bongmba, Elias. 2006. *The Dialectics of Transformation in Africa*. New York: Palgrave.

Borch, Merete Falck. 2004. *Conciliation—Compulsion—Conversion: British Attitudes Towards Indigenous Peoples, 1763–1814*. Amsterdam: Rodopi.

Buck-Morss, Susan. 2000. "Hegel and Haiti." *Critical Inquiry* 26 (4): 821–65.

Burman, Anders. 2009. *As Though We Had No Spirit: Ritual, Politics and Existence in the Aymara Quest for Decolonization*. PhD diss. University of Gothenburg.

Carozza, Paolo G. 2003. "From Conquest to Constitutions: Retrieving a Latin American Tradition of the Idea of Human Rights." *Human Rights Quarterly* 25:282–313.

Castillo, Luis Carlos. 2007. *Etnicidad y nación. El desafío de la diversidad en Colombia*. Cali: Universidad del Valle.

Castro, Daniel. 2007. *Another Face of Empire: Bartolomé de Las Casas, Indigenous Rights, and Ecclesiastical Imperialism*. Durham, NC: Duke University Press.

Castro-Gómez, Santiago. 2000. "Ciencias sociales, violencia epistémica y el problema de la 'invención del otro.' In *La colonialidad del saber. Eurocentrismo y ciencias sociales. Perspectivas Latinoamericanas*, edited by Edgardo Lander. Buenos Aires: CLACSO.

———. 2005a. *La Hybris del Punto Cero. Ciencia, raza e ilustración en la Nueva Granada (1750–1816)*. Bogotá: Editorial Pontificia Universidad Javeriana–Instituto Pensar.

———. 2005b. *La poscolonialidad explicada a los niños*. Popayán, Bogotá: Universidad del Cauca–Pensar.

———. 2007. "Decolonizar la universidad. La hybris del punto cero y el diálogo de saberes." In *Educación superior, interculturalidad y descolonización*, edited by Ramón Grosfoguel and Santiago Castro-Gómez, 79–91. La Paz: PIEB.

Castro-Gómez, Santiago, Freya Schiwy, and Catherine Walsh. 2002. "Introducción." In *Indisciplinar las ciencias sociales. Geopolíticas del conocimiento y colonialidad del poder. Perspectivas desde lo andino*, edited by Santiago Castro-Gómez, Freya Schiwy, and Catherine Walsh, 7–16. Quito: Abya Yala y Universidad Andina Simón Bolívar.

CDP (Comunidad de paz de San José de Apartadó). 2004. *Un proyecto de caminar comunitario*. www.cdpsanjose.org. Accessed December 2004.

Césaire, Aimé. 2000. *Discourse on Colonialism*. Translated by Joan Pinkham. New York: Monthly Review Press.

CINEP. 2010. *El legado de las políticas de Uribe: retos para la administración de Santos.* http://www.cinep.org.co/node/1083. Accessed November 2010.

Clifford, James. 1983. "On Ethnographic Authority." *Representations* 2: 118–146

Cmiel, Kenneth. 2004. "The Recent History of Human Rights." *American Historical Review* 109 (1): 117–35.

CONAIE, Acción Ecológica, Instituto de Estudios Ecologistas del Tercer Mundo and Oilwatch n.d. *Somos hijos del sol y de la tierra. Derecho mayor de los pueblos indígenas de la Cuenca amazónica.* Manthra Editores.

Crandall, David. 2008. "The Transformation of Indigenous Knowledge into Anthropological Knowledge: Whose Knowledge Is It?" In *Knowing How to Know: Fieldwork and the Ethnographic Present*, edited by Narmala Halstead, Eric Hisch, and Judith Okely, 38–54. Berghahn: London.

Crehan, Kate. 2002. *Gramsci, Culture and Anthropology.* London: Pluto Press.

Cromwell Cox, Oliver. 1959. *Caste, Class and Race. A Study in Social Dynamics.* New York: Monthly Review Press.

Cuatro Etnias (Sierra Nevada de Santa Marta). 1999. *Declaración conjunta de las cuatro organizaciones indígenas de la Sierra Nevada de Santa Marta para la interlocución con el estado y la sociedad nacional.* http://www.unimag.edu.co/antropologia/SIERRA%20NEVADA.htm. Accessed January 2006.

D'Amico-Samuels, Deborah. 1997. "Undoing Fieldwork: Personal, Political, Theoretical and Methodological Implications." In *Decolonizing Anthropology: Moving Further toward an Anthropology for Liberation*, edited by Faye Harrison, 68–87. Arlington, VA: Association of Black Anthropologists—American Anthropological Association.

Dainotto, Roberto M. 2007. *Europe (in Theory).* Durham, NC and London: Duke University Press.

Dalby, Simon. 1998. "Globalisation or Global Apartheid? Boundaries and Knowledge in Postmodern Times." *Geopolitics* 3 (1): 132–50.

Dávalos, Pablo. 2008. "El 'Sumak Kawsay' ('Buen vivir') y las cesuras del desarrollo." *América Latina en Movimiento.* Agencia Latinoamericana de Información. http://alai net.org/active/23920. Accessed December 2008.

Davis, Angela. 2012. *The Meaning of Freedom and Other Difficult Dialogues.* San Francisco: City Lights Books.

Daza, Vladimir. 2006. *Los orfelinatos de dios y la cultura wayúu.* Popayán: ICANH/ Universidad del Cauca.

De Francisco Olmos, José María. n.d. "La evolución de la tipología monetaria en Castilla y América durante el Siglo XVI." https://www.ucm.es/data/cont/docs/446-2013-08-22 -6%20evolucion.pdf. Accessed July 2015.

de la Cadena, Marisol. 1996. "The Political Tensions of Representations and Misrepresentations: Intellectuals and Mestizas in Cuzco (1919–1990)." *Journal of Latin American Anthropology* 2(1): 112–1

———. 2010. "Indigenous Cosmopolitics in the Andes: Conceptual Reflections Beyond 'Politics.'" *Cultural Anthropology* 25 (2): 334–70.

Douzinas, Costas. 2000. *The End of Human Rights: Critical Legal Thought at the Turn of the Century.* Oxford: Hart.

———. 2007. *Human Rights and Empire: The Political Philosophy of Cosmopolitanism.* New York: Routledge-Cavendish.

DuBois, W. E. B. 1903. *The Souls of Black Folk: Essays and Sketches*. Chicago: A. C. McClurg and Co.

Dudziak, Mary L. 2000. *Cold War Civil Rights: Race and the Image of American Democracy*. Princeton, NJ: Princeton University Press.

Dussel, Enrique. 1983. *Historia general de la Iglesia en América Latina. Tomo I/1: Introducción general a la historia de la Iglesia en América Latina: Primera Época*. Salamanca: Ediciones Sígueme.

———. 1995. *1492. El encubrimiento del Otro. Hacia el origen del mito de la modernidad*. La Paz: Biblioteca Indígena.

———. 1996. *Filosofía de la liberación*. Bogotá: Nueva América.

———. 2000. "Europa, modernidad y eurocentrismo." In *La colonialidad del saber. Eurocentrismo y ciencias sociales. Perspectivas Latinoamericanas*, edited by Edgardo Lander, 41–53. Buenos Aires: CLACSO.

———. 2004. "La China (1421–1800) (razones para cuestionar el eurocentrismo)," *Archipiélago. Revista cultural de nuestra América* 11 (44): 6–13.

———. 2007. *Política de la Liberación. Tomo I: Historia Mundial y Crítica*. Madrid: Trotta.

———. 2008. "Meditaciones anti-cartesianas: sobre el origen del anti-discurso filosófico de la Modernidad." *Tabula Rasa* 9:153–97.

Elias, Sean. 2009. "W. E. B. DuBois, Race and Human Rights." *Societies Without Borders* 4 (3): 273–94.

Ereira, Alan. 1990. *The Elder Brother's Warning*. London: Tairona Heritage Trust.

Escobar, Arturo. 1996. *La invención del Tercer Mundo. Construcción y deconstrucción del desarrollo*. Bogotá: Grupo editorial Norma.

———. 1998. "Whose Knowledge, Whose Nature? Biodiversity, Conservation, and the Political Ecology of Social Movements." *Journal of Political Ecology* 5:53–82.

———. 1999. "After Nature." *Current Anthropology* 40 (1): 1–16.

———. 2003. "Mundos y conocimientos de otro modo." El programa de investigación de modernidad/ colonialidad latinoamericano." *Tabula Rasa* 1:51–86.

———. 2010. *Territorios de diferencia. Lugar, movimientos, vida, redes*. Popayán: Envión Editores.

Espinosa, Mónica. 2007. "El que entiende esa palabra, ¿de qué manera aprendió?" *Nómadas* 26:138–53.

Eze, Chukwudi Emmanuel. 1998. "Modern Western Philosophy and African Colonialism." In *African Philosophy: An Anthology*, edited by Chukwudi Emmanuel Eze, 213–21. Oxford: Blackwell Publishers.

Fabian, Johannes. 1983. *Time and the Other: How Anthropology Makes Its Object*. New York: Columbia University Press.

Fals Borda, Orlando. 1979. *El problema de cómo investigar la realidad para transformarla por la praxis*. Bogotá: Ediciones Tercer Mundo.

———. 1981. *Ciencia propia y colonialismo intelectual*. Bogotá: Carlos Valencia Editores.

Fanon, Frantz. 1963. *The Wretched of the Earth*. New York: Grove.

———. 1967. *Black Skins White Masks*. Translated by Charles Lam Markman. London: Grove Press.

Faverón Patriau, Gustavo. 2006. *Rebeldes. Sublevaciones indígenas y naciones emergentes en Hispanoamérica en el siglo xviii*. Madrid: Tecnos.

Federici, Silvia. 2010. *Calibán y la bruja, Mujeres, cuerpo y acumulación originaria.* Translated by V. Hendel and L. S. Touza. Madrid: Traficantes de sueños.

Fernández Garcés, Helios, Nicola's Jime'nez Gonza'lez & Isaac Motos Pe'rez. (n.d). *Guía de recursos contra el antigitanismo.* Alicante: Federacio'n Autono'mica de Asociaciones Gitanas de la Comunidad Valenciana (FAGA).

Fernández Herrero, Beatriz. 1992. *La utopia de América. Teoría, Leyes, Experimentos.* Madrid: Anthropos.

Ferreira da Silva, Denise. 2014. "No-bodies: Law, Raciality and Violence." *Meritum— Belo Horizonte* 9 (1): 119–62.

Ferro, Marc. 2005. "Kolonialismen: koloniseringens bagside." I: *Kolonialismens sorte bog.* København: Høst og Søn. 17–50.

Figueroa Pérez, José Antonio. 2001. *Del nacionalismo al exilio interior. El contraste de la experiencia modernista en Cataluña y los Andes americanos.* Bogotá: Andrés Bello.

Fotopoulos, Takis. 2002. "The Global War of the Transnational Elite." *Democracy and Nature: The International Journal of Inclusive Democracy* 8 (2): 201–40.

Gargallo, Francesca. 2009. "Feminismo mestizo, epistemología racista." http://francesca gargallo.wordpress.com/ensayos/feminismo/no-occidental/feminismo-mestizo-episte mologia-racista/. Accessed June 2014.

———. 2012. *Feminismos desde Abya Yala. Ideas y proposiciones de las mujeres de 607 pueblos en nuestra America.* Bogotá: Ediciones desde abajo.

Giddens, Anthony. 1991. *Modernitet og selvidentitet. Selvet og samfundet under senmoderniteten.* København: Hans Reitzels Forlag.

Giddens, Anthony, and Christopher Pierson. 1998. *Conversations with Anthony Giddens: Making Sense of Modernity.* Stanford, CA: Stanford University Press.

Gilmore, Ruth Wilson. 2007. *Golden Gulag: Prisons, Surplus, Crisis, and Opposition in Globalizing California.* Berkeley and Los Angeles: University of California Press.

Giraldo Jaramillo, Natalia. 2010. "Camino en espiral. Territorio sagrado y autoridades tradicionales en la comunidad indígena iku de la Sierra Nevada de Santa Marta, Colombia." *Revista Pueblos y Fronteras Digital* 6 (9): 180–22.

Gledhill, John. 2000. "The Political Anthropology of Colonialism: A Study of Domination and Resistance." In *Power and Its Disguises: Anthropological Perspectives on Politics,* edited by John Gledhill, 67–91. London: Pluto Press.

Glendon, Mary Ann. 2003. "The Forgotten Crucible: The Latin American Influence on the Universal Human Rights Idea." *Harvard Human Rights Journal* 16:27–39.

Gómez, Diana. 2011. "Feminismo y modernidad/colonialidad: entre retos de mundosposibles y otras palabras. A propo'sito de efeme'rides y nuevos encuentros." *Revista en Otras Palabras.* (19): 43–67. Bogota': Universidad Nacional de Colombia.

Gómez Rivas, León. 2005. "Economía y Guerra. El pensamiento económico y jurídico desde Vitoria a Grotio (y después)." *Stud. his., H.a mod* 27:135–59.

González Casanova, Pablo. 1992. "Colonialismo interno. Una definición." In *América Latina. Historia y Destino. Homenaje a Leopoldo Zea,* 263–66. México: UNAM.

González Ferrín, Emilio. 2006. *Historia general de Al Ándalus. Europa entre oriente e occidente.* Córdoba: Editorial Almuzara.

Gordon, Lewis. 1995. *Fanon and the Crisis of European Man: An Essay on Philosophy and the Human Sciences.* London: Routledge.

———. 1999. *Bad Faith and Antiblack Racism.* New York: Humanity Books.

———. 2004. "Fanon and Development: A Philosophical Look." *Africa Development* 29 (1): 71–93.

———. 2006a. "African-American Philosophy, Race, and the Geography of Reason." In *Not Only the Master's Tools: African-American Studies in Theory and Practice*, edited by Lewis Gordon and Jane Anna Gordon, 3–50. Boulder, CO and London: Paradigm.

———. 2006b. *Disciplinary Decadence: Living Thought in Trying Times*. Boulder, CO and London: Paradigm.

———. 2009. "A través de la zona del no ser. Una lectura de Piel negra, máscaras blancas en la celebración del octogésimo aniversario del nacimiento de Fanon." In Franz Fanon, *Piel negra, máscaras blancas*, 217–60. Madrid: Akal.

———. 2011. "Shifting the Geography of Reason in an Age of Disciplinary Decadence". *Transmodernity* 1(2), 95–103.

Gordon, Lewis, and Jane Anna Gordon. 2010. *Of Divine Warning: Reading Disaster in the Modern Age*. Boulder, CO: Paradigm.

Grasseni, Cristina. 2008. "Learning to See: World-views, Skilled Visions, Skilled Practice." In *Knowing How to Know: Fieldwork and the Ethnographic Present*, edited by Narmala Halstead, Edith Hisch, and Judith Okely, 151–72. Berghahn: London.

Grosfoguel, Ramón. 2009. "Human Rights and Anti-Semitism after Gaza." *Human Architecture* 6 (2): 89–102.

———. 2013. "The Structure of Knowledge in Westernized Universities: Epistemic Racism/Sexism and the Four Genocides/Epistemicides of the Long 16th Century." *Human Architecture: Journal of the Sociology of Self-Knowledge* 11 (1): 73–90.

Grove, Richard, and Vinita Damodaran. 2009. "Imperialism, Intellectual Networks, and Environmental Change: Unearthing the Origins and Evolution of Global Environmental History." In *Nature's End: History and the Environment*, edited by Sorlin Sverker and Paul Warde, 23–49. London: Palgrave.

Grueso, Libia, Carlos Rosero, and Arturo Escobar. 1998. "The Process of Black Community Organising in the Southern Pacific Coast Region of Colombia." In *Cultures of Politics, Politics of Cultures: Re-visioning Latin American Social Movements*, edited by Sonia Alvarez, Evelina Dagnino, and Arturo Escobar, 196–219. Boulder, CO: Westview.

Guardiola-Rivera, Oscar. 2009. *Being Against the World: Rebellion and Constitution*. New York: Birkbeck Law Press.

———. 2010. *What if Latin America Ruled the World? How the South Will Take the North into the 22nd Century*. London: Bloomsbury.

Hale, Charles (1996) Mestizaje, Hybridity and the Cultural Politics of Difference. *Journal of Latin American Anthropology*. 2 (1): 34–61.

Halstead, Narmala. 2008. "Knowledge as Gifts of Self and Other." In *Knowing How to Know: Fieldwork and the Ethnographic Present*, edited by Narmala Halstead, Edith Hisch, and Judith Okely, 92–109. Berghahn: London.

Harding, Sandra. 1987. "Introduction: Is There a Feminist Method?" In *Feminism and Methodology*, edited by Sandra Harding, 1–14. Bloomington: Indiana University Press.

Harrison, Faye. 2002. "Global Apartheid, Social Policy and Human Rights." *Souls* 4 (3): 48–68.

Hastrup, Kirsten. 2001. "The Quest for Universality: An Introduction." In *Human Rights on Common Grounds: The Quest for Universality*, edited by Kirsten Hastrup, 1–24. The Hague: Kluwer Law International.

———. 2004. "Getting It Right: Knowledge and Evidence in Anthropology." *Anthropological Theory* 4:455–72.

Henry, Paget. 2000. *Caliban's Reason: Introducing Afro-Caribbean Philosophy*. New York: Routledge.

Hernández, Juan Antonio. 2008. "*Marronage* and Rebellion in the Hispano-American Caribbean." In *A Historical Companion to Postcolonial Literatures: Continental Europe and its Empires*, edited by Prem Poddar, Rajeev Patke, and Lars Jensen, 569–73. Edinburgh: Edinburgh University Press.

Hernando-Llorens, Belén, Sílvia Lorenso, and Joseph M. Pierce. 2009. "Entrevista a Boaventura de Sousa Santos." *Pterodáctilo* 6. http://pterodactilo.com/numero6/?p = 422. Accessed May 2010.

Herrera, Joaquín. 2005. *Los derechos humanos como productos culturales. Crítica del humanism abstracto*. Madrid: Catarata.

Huanacuni Mamani, Fernando. 2010. *Buen Vivir / Vivir Bien. Filosofía, políticas, estrategias y experiencias regionales andinas*. Lima: Coordinadora Andina de Organizaciones Indígenas–CAOI.

Huggan Graham, and Helen Tiffin. 2010. *Postcolonial Ecocriticism: Literature, Animals, Environment*. New York: Routledge.

Huinca Puitrín, Herson. 2013. "Los Mapuches del Jardín de Aclimatación de París en 1883: objetos de la ciencia colonial y políticas de investigación contemporáneas." In *Ta iñ fijke xipa rakizuameluwün. Historia, colonialismo y resistencia desde el país Mapuche*, edited by Comunidad de Historia Mapuche, 109–14. Temuco: Ediciones Comunidad de Historia Mapuche.

Ingold, Tim. 2005. "Epilogue: Towards a Politics of Dwelling." *Conservation and Society* 3 (2): 501–8.

———. 2006. "Rethinking the Animate, Re-Animating Thought." *Ethnos* 71 (1): 9–20.

———. 2007. "Materials Against Materiality." *Archaeological Dialogues* 14 (1): 1–16.

Ishay, Micheline R. 2004. *The History of Human Rights: From Ancient Times to the Globalization Era*. Berkeley: University of California Press.

Jackson, Michael. 2002. *The Politics of Storytelling: Violence, Transgression and Intersubjectivity*. University of Copenhagen: Museum Tusculanum Press.

———. 2005. "Whose Human Rights?" In *Existential Anthropology: Events, Exigencies and Effects*, edited by Michael Jackson. New York: Berghahn Books.

Jensen, Lars. 2012. *Danmark. Rigsfællesskab, tropekolonier og den postkoloniale arv*. Copenhagen: Hans Reizels.

Kohler, Gert. 1995. "The Three Meanings of Global Apartheid: Empirical, Normative, Existential." *Alternatives: Social Transformation and Humane Governance* 20 (3): 403–13.

König, Hans Joakim. 1998. "Introducción." In *El indio como sujeto y objeto de la historia latinoamericana. Pasado y presente*, edited by Hans Joakim König, 13–34. Madrid: Iberoamericana.

Koskenniemi, Martti. 2010. "Colonization of the 'Indies': The Origins of International Law?" In *La idea de América en el pensamiento ius internacionalista del siglo xxi*, edited by Gamarra Chopo, 43–64. Universidad de Zaragoza.

Kumar, Vidya S. A. 2003. "A Critical Methodology of Globalization: Politics of the 21st Century?" *Indiana Journal of Global Legal Studies* 10 (2): 87–111.

Lander, Edgardo, ed. 2000. *La colonialidad del saber. Eurocentrismo y ciencias sociales. Perspectivas Latinoamericanas.* Buenos Aires: CLACSO.

———. 2004. "La utopía del mercado total y el poder imperial." *Revista Tareas* 118:31–64.

———. 2008. "Eurocentrism, Modern Knowledges and the 'Natural' Order of Global Capital." *Kult* 6:39–64. http://www.postkolonial.dk/KULT_Publikationer#udgivelse4.

Langebæk, Carl. 2007. *Indios y españoles en la Antigua provincia de Santa Marta, Colombia. Documentos de los siglos XVI y XVII.* Bogotá: Centro de Estudios Socioculturales e Internacionales (CESO), Universidad de los Andes.

Las Casas, Bartolomé. n.d. [1552]. *Brevísima relación de la destrucción de las indias.* http://www.ciudadseva.com/textos/otros/brevisi.htm.

Lassiter, Luke Eric. 2005. *The Chicago Guide to Collaborative Ethnography.* Chicago: University of Chicago Press.

Lasso, Marixa. 2003. "Haiti como símbolo republicano popular en el Caribe colombiano: Provincia de Cartagena" (1811–1828)." *Historia Caribe* 3 (8): 5–18.

———. 2006. "Race, War and Nation in Caribbean Gran Colombia. Cartagena 1810–1832." *American Historical Review* (April): 336–61.

———. 2007. "Un mito republicano de armonía racial. Raza y patriotismo en Colombia 1810–1812." *Revista de Estudios Sociales* 27:32–45.

Latour, Bruno. 1993. *We Have Never Been Modern.* Cambridge, MA: Harvard University Press.

Laurent, Virginie. 2005. *Comunidades indígenas, espacios políticos y movilización electoral en Colombia, 1990–1998. Motivaciones, campos de acción e impactos.* Bogotá: Instituto Colombiano de Antropología e Historia (ICANH), Instituto Francés de Estudios Andinos (IFEA).

Leets Hansen, Nanna. 2011. *Når mænd er kønnets anden halvdel!—epistemologier om køn, mænd og udvikling.* Master's thesis. International Development Studies and Cultural Encounters. Roskilde University.

Liebler, Carolyn A., et al. 2014. *America's Churning Races: Race and Ethnic Response Changes between Census 2000 and the 2010 Census.* CARRA Working Paper Series Working Paper #2014-09. Center for Administrative Records Research and Applications. Washington, DC: US Census Bureau. http://www.census.gov/srd/carra/Ameri cas_Churning_Races.pdf. Accessed September 2012.

Linebaugh, Peter. 2008. *The Carta Magna Manifesto: Liberties and Commons for All.* Berkeley: University of California Press.

Loptson, Peter. 1998. *Readings on Human Nature.* Ontario: Broadview Press.

Losada Cubillos, Jhon Jairo. 2014. *Ontología y poder colonial: Claves analíticas a propósito de la Colonialidad del Ser.* Bogotá: Universidad de San Buenaventura.

Lugones, Maria. 2007. "Heterosexualism and the Colonial/Modern Gender System." *Hypatia* 22 (1): 186–209.

Luna, Lola G. 1991. "La nación chimila. Un caso de Resistencia indígena en la gobernación de Santa Marta." In *Conquista y resistencia en la historia de América*, edited by Pilar García Jordán and Miquel Izard, 123–38. Barcelona: Universitat de Barcelona.

Maestre Sánchez, Alfonso. 2004. "Todas las gentes del mundo son hombres. El gran debate entre Fray Bartolomé de las Casas (1474–1566) y Juan Ginés de Sepúlveda (1490–1573)." *Anales del Seminario de Historia de la Filosofía* 21:91–134.

Maldonado-Torres, Nelson. 2006. "Post-continental Philosophy: Its Definition, Contours, and Fundamental Sources." *Worlds and Knowledges Otherwise* 1 (3).

———. 2007. "On the Coloniality of Being: Contributions to the Development of a Concept." *Cultural Studies* 21 (2–3): 240–70.

———. 2008a. *Against War: Views from the Underside of Modernity.* Durham, NC and London: Duke University Press.

———. 2008b. "Descolonización y giro descolonial." *Tabula Rasa* 9:61–72.

Mallon, Florencia. 1996. "Constructing Mestizaje in Latin America: Authenticity, Marginality and Gender in the Claiming of Ethnic Identities." *Journal of Latin American Anthropology* 2 (1): 170–81.

Mamdani, Mahmood. 1996. *Citizen and Subject: Contemporary Africa and the Legacy of Late Colonialism.* Princeton, NJ: Princeton University Press.

Mamigonian, Beatriz, and Karen Racine. 2010. *The Human Tradition in the Black Atlantic, 1500–2000.* New York: Rowman and Littlefield.

Massé, F., and J. Camargo. 2012. *Actores Armados Ilegales y Sector Extractivo en Colombia,* CITpax-Observatorio Internacional sobre DDR y la Ley de Justicia y Paz. http://www.askonline.ch/fileadmin/user_upload/documents/Thema_Wirtschaft_und_Mens chenrechte/Bergbau_Rohstoff/Gold/Actores_armados_ilegales_sector_extractivo.pdf. Accessed March 2014.

Mbembe, Achile. 2003. "Necropolitics." *Public Culture* 15 (1): 11–40.

McCullagh, C. Behan. 1980. "Historical Realism." *Philosophy and Phenomenological Research* 40 (3): 420–25.

Mendoza, Breny. 2007. "Los fundamentos no democráticos de la democracia: un enunciado desde Latinoamérica posoccidental." *Encuentros, Revista Centroamericana de Ciencias Sociales* 6:85–93.

Mignolo, Walter D. 2000. *Local Histories/Global Designs. Coloniality, Subaltern Knowledges, and Border Thinking.* Princeton, NJ: Princeton University Press.

———. 2005. *The Idea of Latin America.* Oxford: Blackwell.

———. 2006. "Islamophobia/Hispanophobia: The (Re)Configuration of the Racial Imperial/Colonial Matrix." *Human Architecture: Journal of the Sociology of Self-Knowledge* 5 (1): 13–28.

———. 2009. "Who Speaks for the 'Human' in Human Rights?" *Hispanic Issues Online* 5 (1): 7–24.

Mikkelsen, Britta. 2005. *Methods for Development Work and Research: A New Guide for Practitioners.* London: Sage.

Mora, Luis Adrián. 2009. "Francisco de Vitoria y Bartolome de Las Casas desde la perspectiva del pensamiento decolonial: Encubrimiento o reconocimiento del Otro?" *Revista Ixchel* 1:30–43.

More, Mabogo P. 2002. "African Renaissance: The Politics of Return." *African Journal of Political Science* 7 (2): 61–80.

Moreno Figueroa, Mónica. 2010. "Distributed Intensities: Whiteness, Mestizaje and the Logics of Mexican Racism." *Ethnicities* 10 (3): 387–401.

Motos Pérez, Isaac. 2009. "Lo que no se olvida: 1499–1978." *Anales de Historia Contempora'nea* 25:57–74.

Mudimbe, Valentine. 1988. *The Invention of Africa: Gnosis, Philosophy, and the Order of Knowledge.* Bloomington and Indianapolis: Indiana University Press.

Ndlovu-Gatsheni, Sabelo J. 2013. *Coloniality of Power in Postcolonial Africa: Myths of Decolonization.* Dakar: CODESRIA.

Ochoa Muñoz, Karina. 2014. "El debate sobre las y los amerindios: entre el discurso de la bestialización, la feminización y la racialización." In *Tejiendo de otro modo: Feminismo, epistemología y apuestas descoloniales en Abya Yala*, edited by Yuderskys Espinosa Miñoso et al., 105–18. Popayán: Editorial Universidad del Cauca.

O'Gorman, Edmundo. 1991/1957. *La invención de América. Investigación acerca de la estructura histórica del nuevo mundo y del sentido de su devenir.* México: Fondo de Cultura Económica.

OIK (Organización Indígena Kankuama). 2006. *Documento de autoprotección colectiva del pueblo indígena kankuamo de la Sierra Nevada de Santa Marta-Colombia.* Unpublished document.

———. 2008. *Makú Jogúki. Ordenamiento educativo, pueblo indígena kankuamo.* Valledupar: Kampanäkê.

O'Manique, John. 1992. "Human Rights and Development." *Human Rights Quarterly* 14 (1): 78–103.

Olusoga, David and Casper W. Erichsen. 2010. *The Kaiser's Holocaust. Germany's Forgotten Genocide.* London: Faber & Faber.

Peñaranda, Jorge. 2005. "De Avingüe al Duklindúe: aspectos históricos locales, regionales y nacionales en la SNSM. Desde la historia de vida de Ramón Gil para la emergencia de nuevos Poblados wiwa." *Jangwa Pana* 4:70–89.

Pineda Camacho, Roberto. 2000. "Demonología y antropología en la Nueva Granada. Siglos XVI y XVII." In *Culturas científicas y saberes locales. Asimilación, hibridación, resistencia*, edited by Diana Obregón, 23–88. Bogotá: Universidad Nacional de Colombia.

Powell, Mike. 2006. "Which Knowledge, Whose Reality? An Overview of Knowledge Used in the Development Sector." *Development in Practice* 16 (6): 518–32.

Pumarejo, Adriana, and Patrick Morales. 2003. *Recuperación de la memoria histórica de los kankuamo: un llamado de los antiguos. Siglos XX–XVIII.* Bogotá: Universidad Nacional de Colombia.

Quijano, Aníbal. 1992. "'Raza,' 'etnia,' y 'nación': cuestiones abiertas." In *José Carlos Mariátegui y Europa: la otra cara del descubrimiento*, edited by Raúl Forgues. Lima: Amauta.

———. 2000a. "Coloniality of Power, Ethnocentrism, and Latin America." *Nepantla, Views from the South* 1 (3): 533–80.

———. 2000b. "Colonialidad del Poder y Clasificación Social." *Journal of World-Systems Research* 4 (2): 342–86.

———. 2009. "Diálogo sobre la crisis y las ciencias sociales en América Latina. Interview by Jaime Ríos." *Sociológica. Revista del Colegio de Sociólogos del Perú* 1 (1): 19–42.

Rappaport, Joanne. 2005. *Intercultural Utopias: Public Intellectuals, Cultural Experimentation and Ethnic Pluralism in Colombia.* Durham, NC: Duke University Press.

Reichel-Dolmatoff, Gerardo. 1951. *Datos histórico-culturales sobre las tribus de la antigua gobernación de Santa Marta.* Bogotá: Instituto Etnológico del Magdalena/Imprenta del Banco de la República.

Reichel-Dolmatoff, Gerardo, and Alicia Reichel-Dolmatoff. 1961. *The People of Aritama: The Cultural Personality of a Colombian Mestizo Village.* Chicago: University of Chicago Press.

Restrepo, Eduardo, and Arturo Escobar. 2005. "'Other Anthropologies and Anthropology Otherwise.' Steps to a World Anthropologies Framework." *Critique of Anthropology* 25 (2): 99–129.

Retsikas, Konstantinos. 2008. "Knowledge from the Body: Fieldwork, Power and the Acquisition of a New Self." In *Knowing How to Know: Fieldwork and the Ethnographic Present*, edited by Narmala Halstead, Eric Hisch, and Judith Okely, 110–29. Berghahn: London.

Ribeiro, Gustavo Lins, and Arturo Escobar. 2006. "Las antropologías del mundo. Transformaciones de la disciplina a través de los sistemas de poder." *Universitas Humanística* 61:15–49.

Rist, Gilbert. 1997. *The History of Development: From Western Origins to Global Faith.* London: Zed Books.

Rivera Cusicanqui, Silvia. 2010. *Ch'ixinakax utxiwa. Una reflexio'n sobre pra'cticas y discursos descolonizadores.* Buenos Aires: Tinta Limón.

———. 2012. "Ch'ixinakax utxiwa: A Reflection on the Practices and Discourses of Decolonization." *The South Atlantic Quarterly* 111 (1): 95–109.

Robinson, Cedric. 2000 [1983]. *Black Marxism.* Chapel Hill, NC: University of North Carolina Press.

Rodríguez, Gloria Amparo, and Kasokaku Mestre Busintana. 2007. "Concepción cultural y aplicación de la ley de origen del pueblo Iku (Arhuaco)." In *Somos hijos del sol y la tierra. Derecho mayor de los pueblos indígenas de la cuenca amazónica*, edited by CONAIE, 57–67.

Romero Jaramillo, Dolcey. 2003. "El fantasma de la revolucio'n haitiana. Esclavitud y libertad en Cartagena de Indias 1812–1815." *Historia Caribe* 3 (8): 19–33.

Rossiter, Ned. 2010. "The Informational University, the Uneven Distribution of Expertise and the Racialization of Labour." *Edu Factory Web Journal* 0 (January): 62–73.

Rubio Angulo, Jaime. 1979. *Historia de la filosofía latinoamericana, I.* Bogotá: Universidad Santo Tomás de Aquino.

Sánchez Mojica, Dairo Andrés. 2008. "Batallas por el corazón del mundo: La emergencia de 'Ciudad Perdida' y las luchas por el uso diferencial del territorio en la Sierra Nevada de Santa Marta." In *Genealogías de la colombianidad. Formaciones discursivas y tecnologías de gobierno en los siglos XIX y XX*, edited by Santiago Castro-Gómez and Eduardo Restrepo, 70–95. Bogotá: Universidad Javeriana.

———. 2009. "La instauración del cuerpo conquistador en los primeros años de la gobernación de Santa Marta." *Nómadas* 31:182–95.

Sandoval, Chela. 2000. *Methodology of the Oppressed.* Minneapolis: University of Minnesota Press.

Sanjinés, Javier. 2002. Mestizaje Upside Down. Subaltern Knowledges and the Known. *Nepantla: views from South* 3(1). 39–60.

Sano, Hans Otto. 2000. "Development and Human Rights: The Necessary, but Partial Integration of Human Rights and Development." *Human Rights Quarterly* 22:734–52.

Santiago-Valles, Kelvin. 2003. "'Race,' Labor, 'Women's Proper Place,' and the Birth of Nations: Notes on Historicizing the Coloniality of Power." *New Centennial Review* 3 (3) 47–68.

Santos, Boaventura de Sousa. 1995a. *Toward a New Common Sense: Law, Science and Politics in the Paradigmatic Transition.* London: Routledge.

———. 1995b. "Three Metaphors for a New Conception of Law: The Frontier, the Baroque, and the South." *Law and Society Review* 29 (4): 569–84.

———. 2000. "Toward a Muticultural Conception of Human Rights." In *Moral Imperialism: A Critical Anthology,* edited by Hernández-Truyol, 39–60. New York and London: New York University Press.

———. 2002a. "The Processes of Globalisation." *Revista Crítica de Ciências Sociais* and *Eurozine,* 1–48.

———. 2002b. "Between Prospero and Caliban: Colonialism, Postcolonialism, and Inter-Identity." *Luso-Brazilian Review* 39 (2): 9–43.

———. 2003. *Crítica de la razón indolente. Contra el desperdicio de la experiencia. Vol. 1.* Bilbao: Desclée.

———. 2004. "A Critique of Lazy Reason: Against the Waste of Experience." In *The Modern World-System in the Longue Durée,* edited by Immanuel Wallerstein, 157–97. London: Paradigm Publishers.

———. 2005. *El milenio huérfano. Ensayos para una nueva cultura política.* Madrid: Trotta.

———. 2007. "Beyond Abyssal Thinking: From Global Lines to Ecologies of Knowledges." *Revista Crítica de Ciências Sociais* and *Eurozine,* 1–35.

———. 2009. "A Non-Occidentalist West? Learned Ignorance and Ecology of Knowledge." *Theory Culture Society* 26:103–25.

———. 2014. *Epistemologies of the South: Justice Against Epistemicide.* London: Paradigm Publishers.

Schiebinger, Londa. 1993. "Why Mammals Are Called Mammals: Gender Politics in Eighteenth-Century Natural History." *The American Historical Review* 98 (2): 382–411.

Segato, Rita. 2010. Los cauces profundos de la raza latinoamericana: Una relectura del mestizaje. *Cri'tica y Emancipacio'n.* 2 (3): 11- 44.

Sepúlveda, Juan Ginés de. 1996 [approx 1550]. *Tratado sobre las justas causas de la guerra contra los indios.* México: FCE.

Sen, Amartya. 1999. *Development as Freedom.* Oxford: Oxford University Press.

Serje, Margarita. 2007. "Iron Maiden Landscapes: The Geopolitics of Colombia's Territorial Conquest." *South Central Review* 24 (1): 37–55.

Serrano Gassent, Paz. 2002. Introducción. *Vasco de Quiroga. La utopía en América.* Madrid: Promo Libro.

Silverblatt, Irene. 1987. *Moon, Sun, and Witches: Gender Ideologies and Class in Inca and Colonial Peru.* Princeton, NJ: Princeton University Press.

Steiner, Henry J & Philip Alston. 1996. *International Human Rights in Context. Law, Politics, Morals.* Oxford: Clarendon Press.

Stratton, John. 2003. "'It Almost Needn't Have Been the Germans': The State, Colonial Violence and the Holocaust." *European Journal of Cultural Studies* 6:507–27.

Suárez Salazar, Luis. 2007. "The New Pan-American Order: The Crisis and Reconstitution of the US System of Global Domination." *Latin American Perspectives* 34:102–11.

Suárez-Krabbe, Julia. 2008a. "Spanish Colonialism in a World Perspective." In *A Historical Companion to Postcolonial Literatures: Continental Europe and its Empires,* edited by Prem Poddar, Rajeev Patke, and Lars Jensen, 601–6. Edinburgh: Edinburgh University Press.

———. 2008b. "Postcoloniality and Alternative Histories: Latin America." In *A Historical Companion to Postcolonial Literatures: Continental Europe and its Empires*, edited by Prem Poddar, Rajeev Patke, and Lars Jensen, 584–89. Edinburgh: Edinburgh University Press.

———. 2013a. "Democratising Democracy, Humanising Human Rights: European Decolonial Movements and the 'Alternative Thinking of Alternatives.' *Migration Letters* 10 (3): 333–41.

———. 2013b. "Race, Social Struggles, and 'Human' Rights: Contributions from the Global South." *Journal of Critical Globalisation Studies* 6:78–102.

———. 2014a. "The Other Side of the Story: Human Rights, Race and Gender from a Historical Transatlantic Perspective." In *Decolonizing Enlightenment: Transnational Justice, Human Rights and Democracy in Postcolonial Worlds*, edited by Nikita Dhawan. Berlin: Barbara Budrich Publishers.

———. 2014b. "Pluriversalizing Europe: Challenging Belonging, Revisiting History, Disrupting Homogeneity." *Postcolonial Studies* 17 (2): 155–72

———. 2015. Decolonization, Africanization and Pluriversalization. Unpublished manuscript.

Truman, Harry S. 1949. *Inaugural Address. January 20, 1949*. Online by Gerhard Peters and John T. Woolley, The American Presidency Project. http://www.presidency.ucsb.edu/ws/?pid = 13282. Accessed August 2015.

Tuhiwai-Smith, Linda. 1999. *Decolonizing Methodologies: Research and Indigenous Peoples*. London: Zed Books.

Ulloa, Astrid. 2004. *La construcción del nativo ecológico. Complejidades, paradojas y dilemas de la relación entre los movimientos indígenas y el ambientalismo en Colombia*. Bogotá: Instituto Colombiano de Antropología e Historia–Colciencias.

———. 2010. "Reconfiguraciones conceptuales, políticas y territoriales en las demandas de autonomía de los pueblos indígenas en Colombia." *Tabula Rasa* 13:73–92.

Universities Denmark. 2009. *Building Stronger Universities in Developing Countries*. Universities Denmark. http://www.dkuni.dk/English/Test-page.

Uribe, Carlos Alberto. 2000. "La etnografía de la Sierra Nevada de Santa Marta y las tierras bajas adyacentes." In *Geografía Humana de Colombia. Nordeste Indígena* (Vol. 2). Bogotá: Instituto Colombiano de Cultura Hispanica.

Vasco, Luis Guillermo. 2002. *Entre selva y páramo. Viviendo y pensando la lucha india*. Bogotá: Instituto Colombiano de Antropología e Historia.

———. 2007. "Así es mi método en etnografía." *Tabula Rasa* 6:19–52.

Vitoria, Francisco de. 1981 [1539]. *Relecciones sobre los indios*. Bogotá: El Búho.

Walsh, Catherine. 2006. "Introducción: (Re)pensamiento critico y (de)colonialidad." *Pensamiento crítico y matriz (de)colonial (reflexiones latinoamericanas)*, edited by Catherine Walsh, 13–35. Quito: Universidad Andina Simón Bolívar and Ediciones Abya-Yala.

———. 2008. "The Plurinational and Intercultural State: Decolonization and State Refounding in Ecuador." *Kult* 6:39–64. http://postkolonial.dk/artikler/WALSH.pdf.

Walsh, Catherine, and Juan García. 2002. "El pensar del emergente movimiento afrocuatoriano. Reflexiones (des)de un proceso." In *Estudios y Otras Prácticas Intelectuales Latinoamericanas en Cultura y Poder*, edited by Daniel Mato, 317–26. Caracas:

Consejo Latinoamericano de Ciencias Sociales (CLACSO) y CEAP, FACES, Universidad Central de Venezuela.

Warren, Karen. 1999. "Care-sensitive Ethics and Situated Universalism." In *Global Ethics and Environment*, edited by Nicholas Low, 131–45. New York: Routledge.

Wheeler Quentin and Rudolf Meier (Eds.) 2000. *Species Concepts and Phylogenetic Theory* New York: Columbia University Press.

Wilson, Richard. 1997. "Human Rights, Culture and Context: An Introduction." In *Human Rights, Culture and Context: An Anthropological Perspective*, edited by Richard Wilson, 1–27. Chicago: Pluto Press.

Wiredu, Kwasi. 1996. *Cultural Universals and Particulars: An African Perspective.* Bloomington: Indiana University Press.

World Bank. 2005. "World Bank Group Historical Chronology." Produced by the World Bank Group Archives. http://web.worldbank.org.

Wright, Shelley. 2001. *International Human Rights, Decolonisation and Globalisation: Becoming Human.* London: Routledge.

Wynter, Sylvia. 2003. "Unsettling the Coloniality of Being/Power/Truth/Freedom Towards the Human, After Man, Its Overrepresentation—An Argument." *New Centennial Review* 3 (3): 257–337.

Yehia, Elena. 2007. Descolonización del conocimiento y la práctica: Un encuentro dialógico entre el programa de investigación Modernidad/ Colonialidad/ Decolonialidad Latinoamericanas y la Teoría Actor-Red. *Tábula Rasa* 6: 85–114.

Zambrano Pérez, Milton. 2007. Piratas, piratería y comercio ilícito en el Caribe: la visión del otro (1550–1650). *Historia Caribe* 12: 23–56

Index

193

and history of, 81–82; human beings lacking, 76–77; imperialism and humanity of, 116–17; negation of, 102; subhumanizing, 41; war civilizing, 63; zone of nonbeing for, 68–69
other worlds, 102
ownership, 74
OWYBT. *See* Organización Wiwa Yugumaiun Bunkwanarrwa Tayrona

Pachamama (Mother Life), 123, 177
pagamentos, 136
paramilitary forces, 44–45
paternalism, 64
patrolling, 110
people's interrelations, 140
Perdida, Ciudad, 30
Pérez, Isaac Motos, 56
Perijá, Serranía de, 42
phenomenological existentialism, 119
PIGS, 83, 105n3
piracy, 39, 50n6
Plan of Sustainable Development, 50n12
pluralism, legal, 154
plurality, 20
pluriversality, 18, 27, 49, 107, 169; common-unity needed for, 177; radical antiessentialism in, 170
political organizations, 45–48
politics, 164, 172
politics of being, 115–17, 169, 172
Poma, Guaman, 92
popular sovereignty, 94
poverty, 100–101, 105n10
power, 22, 144
power relationships, 30
pratītya samutpāda, 152n1
president, of Colombia, 155
president's inauguration ritual, 161–63
private property, 17, 62, 74
privilege: to define context, 129; of epistemic perspective, 127–28; to include other perspectives, 129; of last word, 130; teleological, 127; white, 16, 103, 127
process transparency, 119

production, 139
proximity, 126
public discourse, 1
public relations, 110
publishing, 131
Pufendorf, Samuel, 79n14
Puitrín, Herson Huinca, 59

Quijano, Aníbal, 16, 75

race, 51, 135–36, 175–76
racial equality, 77; in Colombia, 90–91; elite's fears of, 90; hierarchies in, 130; in Latin America, 89, 93; stereotypes in, 14
racialization, 3, 54, 66, 82
racism, 19, 55–56; coloniality and, 127–28; human beings hierarchization in, 73–74; offensive struggles and, 88; white feminism and, 96–97
rational capacity, 71
rationality, 114–15
reality, 143
realm of interaction, 33
reason, 114–15
rebellions, 89–90
reciprocity, 147
recolonization, 163
reflexive modernity, 22
religion, 139–40
relinking, 138–43, 149
Republic of Colombia, 43
research subjects, 128, 130
rights of nature, 163–66
Rights of People, 52
Roma population, 56
Roosevelt, Eleanor, 96
Roosevelt corollary, 92
Rousseau, Jean-Jacques, 84

sacred sites, 158
Sagas, 4–5
sameness, 32
Sánchez, Dairo Andrés, 30–31, 38
Santa Marta, 37, 40, 42
Santos, Boaventura de Sousa, 4, 22, 24, 26n7, 107, 120, 125